Praise for The Su
of Lifespan Integration

"I was totally absorbed reading this book. It is a fantastic contribution to Pace's work and a clear illustration of what most LI therapists are going through with their clients. I really appreciate the way Cathy Thorpe makes a very clear and simple distinction between working with LI protocols versus having a discussion with a patient. This work hits it right on the dot!"

Catherine Clement, MD;
Lifespan Integration Trainer in France

"Cathy Thorpe's way of describing stories and marvelling at the results of LI touches the child-heart in all of us. I totally agree with her: Lifespan Integration can be miraculous since it changes the very deep structure of a personality. With LI, someone can change from an insecure attachment style to a secure one, an outcome previously thought to be impossible. Now we can change people; deeply and profoundly heal them."

Élise Castonguay, M. Ps.;
Psychologist in Montreal, Canada

"As a surgeon, I'm trained to view new therapeutic approaches with skepticism. But when my son was diagnosed with PTSD after our house fire, I would have done anything to alleviate his suffering. We found our way to Cathy Thorpe. Cathy described her proposed treatment course, and I liked the idea of tapping into the brain's innate healing system. I suspended my surgeon's disbelief and sat in the sessions with my son. I witnessed a miracle. Then Cathy worked her wonders on me.

"Buy this book. Learn this therapeutic technique. It works."

Vicki Rackner MD;
President, Medical Bridges in Seattle, Washington

"I am a staunch witness to the truthful contents of Cathy Thorpe's book. In a half dozen sessions of Lifespan Integration, I experienced a therapeutic effect that I have not yet found in other therapies. I am fortunate to have benefitted from such an efficient therapy. After this therapy I have a better idea of myself, I have found more of an inner peace and I feel much stronger. I have also noticed the beneficial effects from LI for my clients.

"I am delighted to savor life today and I would like to show my enormous gratitude to Peggy Pace and Cathy Thorpe."

Docteur Michel Meignant, Psychotherapist
Président de la Fédération Française de
Psychothérapie et Psychanalyse

THE SUCCESS AND STRATEGIES OF

LIFESPAN INTEGRATION

An Overview and Client Stories

CATHERINE THORPE, M. A.

FOREWORD BY PEGGY PACE, M. A.

TimeLine Press, L.L.C.
P. O. Box 53473
Bellevue, WA 98015

ISBN-13 978-0-9819137-2-8
Library of Congress Control Number: 2012937802
Copyright information available upon request.

Cover Design: Copen Marketing & Design
Interior Art: © iStockPhoto.com/Kumarworks and HiDesignGraphics
Interior Design: J. L. Saloff
Typography: Bell MT

v. 1.0
First Edition, 2012
Printed on acid free paper.

To
Peggy Pace
who gave the world Lifespan Integration.

And

To the memory of my mother
Lee Barber
who encouraged me to be myself in the world.

Acknowledgments

When I reflect on my journey with Peggy Pace and Lifespan Integration (LI), I liken it to standing in the field where Clark Kent (alias Superman) first fell onto our planet. I am grateful I was in the right place when something revolutionary began. Lifespan Integration is a super therapy and Peggy is a super person. Peggy has sacrificially given of her time, energy, and effort to deliver LI to the world.

Thank you to my husband Craig, and our three children David, Tim, and Kelly. I love you all deeply. I know life changed dramatically when Mom went to graduate school and I appreciate all the ways you sacrificed and survived. To quote Polly Pig in a favorite bedtime story, "Thank you, thank you, thank you!" David also proofread the text and made important suggestions in this book.

Joelle North served as colleague, research assistant, and Editor Extraordinaire. She gave many hours to reviewing this text and also offered helpful comments and suggestions. I am grateful to share a psychotherapy practice with her. She is a rising star who contributes to my life in many ways.

I would like to acknowledge the support and encouragement of my extended family, friends, and consultation groups. Your input is helpful and appreciated.

Special thanks to my friend Corky Morse who has impacted my life in more positive ways than is possible to mention. Through her I have been nudged, healed, and guided on life's journey.

Once again, Jamie Saloff skillfully designed the book interior and kindly accommodated many rounds of edits and changes. Christy Bishop brought her gentleness and patience to the cover design and produced a beautiful piece of work. Creating a book is a team effort and these two women are amazing teammates.

Thanks to you all.

Love,

Cathy

Contents

Foreword

In *The Success and Strategies of Lifespan Integration: An Overview and Client Stories,* Cathy Thorpe has shared stories about how Lifespan Integration (LI) has transformed the lives of some of her clients. The case studies you are about to read represent a small fraction of the many lives which have been positively impacted by Lifespan Integration. It is Cathy's hope, and mine as well, that making these case studies available to psychotherapists and to the general public will help both mental health professionals and laypeople to become more aware of this new option for healing.

In 2002, I discovered a new technique which enabled my clients to heal deeply, quickly, and gently. When I began seeing consistent and profound changes in my clients, I wanted to let other therapists know about my discovery so that other people throughout the world could benefit. I had been developing what is now LI for about eight months when I asked Cathy if she would like to experience my new technique. She was willing and I guided her through a session of what is now LI. After her first session of LI, Cathy immediately understood how powerful this new, yet unnamed, method was and how different it was from any mental health treatment known to either of us.

Cathy was the first therapist to learn LI from me, and she was also the first person with whom I could share my excitement about the amazing changes I was seeing in almost all the people with whom I had tried my new method. Cathy came up with the fitting name "Lifespan Integration," or LI for short. She began using LI in her counseling practice and soon began seeing the same profound changes in her clients as I was seeing in mine. Later, as I began to train therapists to use Lifespan Integration, Cathy accompanied me and facilitated the workshops.

From the beginning, Cathy has dedicated herself to the tasks of informing other therapists and the public at large about the benefits and effectiveness of Lifespan Integration. In *The Success and Strategies of Lifespan Integration* Cathy has explained LI in easily understandable terms, and has written very readable case studies. These true life stories show some of the many ways in which Lifespan Integration therapy can improve a person's quality of life gently and quickly, and without cognitive behavioral therapy. I hope you will enjoy reading them as much as I did.

Peggy Pace
March 2012

Introduction

For more than a decade, I have been using a therapy which came to be known as Lifespan Integration (LI). Peggy Pace, a friend and colleague, developed LI and taught it to me not long after we entered the 21st century. At that time several shifts were occurring in the field of psychotherapy and brain science. Greater understanding was emerging regarding the physiology and changeable nature of the brain, and talk therapy was facing its limitations. The non-measurable forces of human connection—including attachment style—were being assessed as important components of mental health.

Into the midst of these shifts, Pace introduced a therapeutic method that synthesized the best of these emerging forces. Her method activates neural firing patterns associated with difficult memories and appears to alter these patterns throughout the mind-body system. Among other components, Pace's work stresses that a therapist with a calm and peaceful presence is part of the modality for change. She also developed protocols—as opposed to conversations—for helping clients lower their distress. With Lifespan Integration, the body and brain come to believe that hardship has passed, and the self-system reorganizes into a more adaptive, higher level of functioning.

Since using her therapy over many years, I have come to consistently observe the following three outcomes from Lifespan Integration therapy:

1) The distress of any remembered event can be resolved with repetitions of the timelines from LI.

2) Unconscious, body-based memories can be resolved with repetitions of the LI timeline.

3) Clients change the way they relate to others after they have experienced Lifespan Integration. We hypothesize that attachment style can be positively altered through LI.

In a recent training where I proposed theses outcomes, one participant raised her hand and said, "I'm sorry, but I am a skeptic. I find it very hard to believe that this can really be true." Her skepticism was based on the collective experience that therapy takes a lot of time and money in order to be effective. I responded by inviting this participant to keep an open mind and experience Lifespan Integration for herself.

Two occurrences followed the participant's skeptical remark. First, a psychiatrist sitting behind her immediately said, "Our current understanding of neuroscience supports the validity of these outcomes." Second, the skeptic was changed by LI in the workshop, as was each participant. More than one trainee said during the practice sessions, "The issue I chose to work on in the practice session is something I have talked about for years in therapy, yet it still brings up a lot of emotion today." After experiencing one session of LI, the participants reported a greater degree of resolution on the issues they had talked about in traditional therapy. Current findings in neuroscience support our hypothesis that a neurological shift occurred for these workshop participants when they experienced LI. We believe that LI targets the body-mind system, and impacts more than just a person's cognitive process.

This book introduces Lifespan Integration methods and

includes the cases of real people who have been changed by the therapy. All client examples are from my personal work with adults, children, and couples. This text could be called *Much of What I Know About Lifespan Integration.* It is not a training manual, nor a scientific document, even though basic tenets of neuroscience are presented here in order to underpin our hypothesis behind the success of LI. This text is a collection of client stories, nuances, and the strategies for success that I have learned over the years as I have employed Pace's method. For therapists, this piece can be a method for introducing LI to their clients and a reference to help them succeed with LI. For clients reading this book, I hope they will be encouraged that long-held traumas and sorrows can be healed. For the general public, I desire to put forward my belief, based on many of years of experience, that Posttraumatic Stress Disorder (PTSD) can be cured by Lifespan Integration. *Cured* is a strong word, but my clinical experience, and that of my colleagues, supports the proposition that LI can permanently eliminate the symptoms of PTSD.

New modalities based on current neuroscience are emerging in the field of psychotherapy. Lifespan Integration appears to be one such therapy. We now have research to support our clinical evidence that LI works.

Dr. Nuri Gene-Cos, MD, Senior Clinician at Maudsley Hospital in London, uses Lifespan Integration for PTSD patients who have been unresponsive to other therapies. She finds that LI eliminates the PTSD symptoms in patients with complex trauma. She said, "They send me patients who have failed the main therapies. People come after many other treatments and they respond to LI." Gene-Cos has been collecting pre- and post-session data for all treatments with LI and will be tabulating the results in the near future. Another clinician, Bethany Balkus, has completed her doctoral research using LI and found the measurable results to be clinically very significant (Balkus, 2012). Her work is summarized in Chapter Two: The Science Behind the Success.

As a Lifespan Integration enthusiast, I am pleased to highlight this new method available for healing trauma, anxiety, and emotional distress. Advanced LI techniques have been omitted from this book in service to the general introduction about Lifespan Integration and its applications. People in many parts of the world are now being trained in LI and are using it successfully. They are telling others about their success, just as I am personally sharing my success with LI through this collection of client stories.

Important Note: This book does not equip the reader to practice Lifespan Integration in the same way that watching a medical television show does not equip the viewer to practice medicine. LI is a very powerful tool. Although it is presented here in simple-to-understand concepts, the method itself is not simple and is to be practiced only by trained clinicians with advanced degrees.

Mandalas appear throughout the text. The Collins English Dictionary (2009) defines mandala as "...a symbol expressing a person's striving for unity of the self." Lifespan Integration is an integrating, unifying process in which individuals become more wholly themselves. Swiss Psychiatrist Carl Jung stated that a mandala's "...basic motif is the premonition of a centre of personality, a kind of central point within the psyche, to which everything is related, by which everything is arranged.... This centre is not felt or thought of as the ego but, if one may so express it, as the self." (Jung, 1950a, p. 73).

In another text, Jung (1950b) wrote, "Integration gathers many into one" (p. 69). Thus the mandalas used throughout this book symbolize the task of Lifespan Integration: increasing wholeness of self through integration.

Lifespan Integration sometimes feels miraculous, and I am so grateful for this tool. It works; it truly brings clients into much greater health and much better ability to be in relationship with others. I know of no other form of therapy more powerful.

Peggy Hurd, LI therapist

1. Lifespan Integration (LI)

 Why would a psychotherapist say Lifespan Integration can be miraculous? In the introduction I strongly endorsed Lifespan Integration, postulating that any remembered event can be resolved with LI, unconscious memories can be healed, and people positively alter the way they relate to others after they have experienced the therapy. This is a bold, yet realistic, proposal in my experience with Lifespan Integration.

Becky's Story

Becky was traumatized by an event known around the world. She also used the word "miraculous" when describing her healing through LI. Her story is typical of the outcomes we see with Lifespan Integration, and yet each person's healing is unique to them. Becky was a young professional woman who was going to work in New York City on September 11, 2001 when two airplanes hit the World Trade Center near the place where she worked. Lifespan Integration positively changed her life after she suffered from Posttraumatic Stress Disorder (PTSD) from the ordeal.

When Becky got off the subway at her usual stop underneath the World Trade Center, she met a panicked crowd of people running for their lives. Initially she thought a bomb had exploded in the building. Becky joined the running melee outside in time to witness a plane hit the second tower in the terrorist attack known as 9/11. Becky saw the building implode. *This is it,* she believed, *I'm going to die.*

After the 9/11 horror, Becky took a leave of absence from work because she was not able to function in her regular duties. As she described the experience to me, it was clear that Becky met the criteria for PTSD: She had witnessed a life-threatening event; she actively avoided reminders of the experience; her mental acuity was diminished; relationships changed; and she had difficult, recurring dreams. Visual reminders of the experience triggered terror in her body. Specifically, Becky's dating relationship of five years deteriorated and she withdrew from her coworkers. Eventually, Becky packed up her apartment and left the New York City life she loved. A few months later she tried to return and resume her professional life, but she was distracted, depressed, and unable to concentrate at work. As a last resort, Becky resigned from her job and moved in with her family across the continent.

Five years later when I met Becky she still suffered from PTSD. She had trouble sleeping, struggled to find a job, had difficulty forming close relationships, and was terrified to fly—all symptoms which were not present before 9/11. On the west coast where Becky relocated, the bus to work took her past an airport. "When I see airplanes in the sky I become frozen," she said. "I'm afraid they are going to hit a building. Last week I saw an airplane out of a window at work and I began to cry. People think I should be over 9/11 but I'm stuck."

Becky struggled with her symptoms until she experienced the PTSD protocol of Lifespan Integration in 2006. After three sessions of LI she said, "I feel like an ostrich raising my head out of the sand. Oh my, I've disconnected from my life and a lot of people!" After five sessions she remarked, "I've had a 50 percent improvement in my PTSD. When I see a plane in the sky I can keep looking at it." After the tenth session of LI, Becky visited the site of her trauma in New York City. "I walked around Ground Zero. The path of my trauma and the area seemed smaller and different. I stopped and looked around. Before, everything was frozen, but on this day I saw lots of movement; cars and people were moving on, living. I felt like I was done with that. I was aware of a significant shift, a sense that I was done. While I was walking I let my body absorb what was happening. Life was going on and I needed to be a part of that. My life really was like a movie that I had put on pause. After the work we did with LI, I hit the 'play' button." She continued, "For five years I had never told people that I was present at 9/11, but last week I told the whole story at a staff meeting. I was very calm about it. The PTSD from 9/11 opened the door for lots and lots of other healing, also."

On the tenth anniversary of 9/11, five years after our work together, I had the opportunity to speak with Becky about her healing. She said, "Lifespan Integration definitely healed me from my PTSD. It also unlocked and loosened other healing that I needed to do. I talk about 9/11 occasionally but I don't do it fearfully. I can talk about my experience matter-of-factly and I have compassion for the people who went through deaths and knew somebody who died."

"What happens when you see a plane in the sky now?" I asked.

"Rarely do I associate the plane with 9/11. It doesn't trigger the memory," Becky replied.

"Do you feel frozen or afraid?" I inquired.

"No, not at all. This healing has been very effective. And the biggest thing is that it led to other healing in my life. 9/11 was just the tip of an iceberg," she responded. Becky initially came to therapy to address some relationship issues and anxiety. Because the 9/11 trauma was still quite prominent five years after the event, we began LI focused on her trauma and moved onto other topics after her PTSD symptoms were cleared.

The Basics of LI

Lifespan Integration is a therapy well described by its name—one that enables clients to integrate difficult experiences into their lives through repetitions of a timeline comprised of real memories from their lifespans. As Becky's story portrays, after a difficult experience is integrated, it no longer controls a person's thoughts, feelings, or actions. Thus, outdated defense mechanisms drop away and clients respond differently to their current problems. Multiple sessions using Lifespan Integration will produce multiple changes.

Like most therapies, a typical LI counseling session begins with a client sharing how he or she is experiencing a certain problem. Early in the conversation, an LI therapist asks the client to focus on the emotional and physical feelings associated with the distress. This is the Standard Protocol of LI in which a therapist guides the client to remember a previous time when these same feelings were experienced in the body and emotions. The client is then guided to integrate the previous experience through repetitions of a timeline that is comprised of real memories from the client's life. Once the trauma is cleared and integrated, the client gets to experience the wondrous aftermath that follows LI. By integrating the real life memory, clients permanently heal their previous hurts and spontaneously think, feel, and act in healthier ways regarding their presenting problem. This may seem too good to be true, but Lifespan Integration therapists witness this process repeatedly.

Peggy Pace developed Lifespan Integration in 2002. Before becoming a psychotherapist, Pace was a chemist working in a research lab. Later she pursued a graduate degree in Systems Counseling Psychology. Her science degree and early therapeutic training laid the foundation for her development of Lifespan Integration. The year Pace developed LI, she read everything she could find concerning brain development and the latest brain research. In her book *Lifespan Integration* (2012), Pace describes the scientific brain research which supports her hypothesis that integration creates lasting emotional, mental, and sometimes physical health. Her book explains the supporting theory and techniques for using Lifespan Integration. Additional information about Peggy Pace is available at the end of this book and her website: www.lifespanintegration.com.

For the purpose of understanding the case studies in this book, I am presenting the following non-scientific description of Lifespan Integration: People, like trees, are cumulative. Trees develop a new ring for every year of life just as humans develop throughout the years by building upon every thought, feeling, and experience which they have stored in their minds and bodies. As we grow older, we do not stop being one age when we become the next age, nor do we lose the person we used to be when we become our newer, older selves. Brett (2010) accurately described the collective self when she stated:

> Somewhere inside us we are all the ages we have ever been. We're the 3-year-old who got bit by the dog. We're the 6-year-old our mother lost track of at the mall. We're the 10-year-old who got tickled till we wet our pants. We're the 13-year-old shy kid with zits. We're the 16-year-old no one asked to the prom, and so on. We walk around in the bodies of adults until someone presses the right button and summons up one of those kids. (p. 87)

In other words, we might feel like a functional adult in the morning and be catapulted into trauma in the afternoon by a comment or experience over which we had no control.

By looking at a cross-section of a tree, we can see every ring that comprises its lifetime. Some rings are darker or larger than others depending on the environment and circumstances surrounding the tree during each of its years. The center of the tree, like us, is quite small in the beginning. Throughout its lifetime, the tree builds upon its core. Like a tree, all the 'rings' of our lives comprise who we are today. The very energy that gives us life comes through them. Although we may not know it, the way we thought when our 'rings' developed still influences our thinking today. Our sense of self is informed by the way we interpreted our life experiences during the former years of life. Difficult years of life skew our values, beliefs, and behaviors in the present.

Humans are highly sophisticated data receivers. The data we receive over a lifetime develops into language, patterns of relating, and beliefs about the world. A child born in Japan learns to speak Japanese because he or she has soaked in the environment of the native language. Without willfully choosing it, a child's brain is influenced by the language, culture, mood, and behaviors of his or her environment. When and how do we change the patterns that become embedded in our brain circuitry? It can be assumed that the purpose of education and brain development is to increase adaptive skills as a child matures. But what if the environment in which a child developed his or her life skills and emotional language is dysfunctional, violent, and maladaptive? How do we unlearn what we absorbed by just living? Lifespan Integration appears to provide a way to help clients go back and impact brain circuitry that developed in earlier years of life. The hypothesis about this will be discussed further in Chapter Two.

Returning to the analogy of tree rings, it appears that LI integrates earlier 'rings,' which are sometimes called ego states, producing significant change in peoples' lives. The human self is comprised of many aspects, and we propose that disconnected or isolated aspects of the self can be connected to the whole self-system by repetitions of the LI timeline.

The more traumatic our life experiences are, the more it seems they are isolated inside our human 'tree.' When a foreign object is taken into a living organism, the body tries to heal itself and dispel the wounding agent. If unable to dislodge it, the body will encapsulate the foreign object so it does the least amount of damage to the rest of the body—our living tree. People seem to hold trauma and difficult experiences in a similar way. When first experienced, our bodies try to process distress through dreams, talking, or other emotional outlets. If unable to dispel the impact, the emotional self finds a way to isolate the memory or hurtful event in order to protect the rest of the mind-body system from its negative impact. When this happens, the symptoms of PTSD and dissociation follow.

Lifespan Integration goes back to the isolated ego state and shows it that the negative experience really has passed. The body and ego states are convinced the bad thing is over when they see a visual timeline of the client's life from the point of trauma to the present. It is hypothesized that repetitions of the timeline actually cause neural reconfiguration, which results in lasting emotional and behavioral change. The method has been quite successful and is used by therapists throughout the world. Bill Bedell, a clinician who uses Lifespan Integration regularly, said, "LI has been really successful in working with trauma as a way to help people begin to address their trauma without being re-traumatized. Before with talk therapy, people would get re-traumatized, re-triggered, and re-stuck. LI is a very effective tool." Pace's book further describes how integrating an unprocessed or traumatic state leads to healing.

Siegel (2003) made a powerful statement about integration in a workshop on attachment in which he stated his view that integration is the equivalent to mental health. He explained that complexity combined with integration achieves the highest level of functioning for an individual or system. He demonstrated his view though this example:

Siegel asked members of the audience who sang in choirs to come forward. Eighteen participants responded. Following his instructions to sing, each participant sang something on his or her own and the audience heard cacophony. Then Siegel instructed the participants to sing one song together. They chose to sing "Row, Row, Row Your Boat" in unison. Next, Siegel asked the participants to sing something in harmony. They arranged themselves into sections and without rehearsal sang "Amazing Grace" in four-part harmony. The audience was then asked, "Which of the performed songs reflected the highest functioning and was the most pleasing to hear?" Obviously, the response was "Amazing Grace," in which separate and individual parts were unified.

With this principle in mind, one can find many other examples in the world where complexity with integration is a system's highest functioning. The human body is a sophisticated and complex system made up of individual and specialized parts. When these parts operate as a whole, the human body functions at its best. Our entire natural world is also ordered around complexity and integration. The eco-system of our planet is based upon complex components, with individual characteristics, combining to form a varied and sophisticated system.

This same complexity with integration concept is the foundational component which produces mental health through Lifespan Integration. Even a difficult experience when integrated will enhance the whole. When aspects of self are not integrated, they work against the internal system rather than working in unity with it. No matter how traumatic or distressing the dis-integrated piece may be, drawing that piece into the whole system, and integrating it through the timeline, will increase the system's overall well-being and level of functioning.

Outcomes

When integration begins taking place with Lifespan Integration change is generally observed in three categories:

1) *The presenting problem resolves.* It is common for this to occur within two to ten sessions. Of course a blanket statement cannot be made about how long therapy will take for various individuals. With LI, change occurs more quickly than with most other therapies due to the mind-body integration. For example, when a client walks into a therapist's office with an anxiety problem,

he or she will probably notice an improvement within
a few sessions of Lifespan Integration. However, it
should be noted that fully resolving a client's anxiety is
dependent upon the client's strength of self-structure.

2) *Clients increase their emotional and cognitive awareness.* If
resolution of the presenting problem does not occur
right away, clients report greater insight about the
nature and contributing factors to their problem, as
well as their role in the difficulty. One young woman
came to therapy to address issues of emotional intimacy. After a session targeting an emotional problem
at work, she came back to therapy understanding—for
the first time—the link between a childhood trauma
at age four and difficulties with her boyfriend. The
trauma at age four was cleared with LI. When secondary issues are integrated and resolved, significant
change is possible for the presenting problem.

3) *Positive results begin to appear in areas that seem unrelated
to the presenting issue, including more secure attachment
styles and intimacy with others.* Occasionally, these seemingly unrelated shifts are the first noticeable changes
from Lifespan Integration. One male client came in
seeking help for his anger. His wife called during the
next week to report that for the first time in 30 years
her husband began sleeping restfully through the
night. After eight sessions of LI, this man continued
to sleep well and also got some relief from the anger
that initially prompted him to seek counseling.

It is reasonable to expect resolution of the presenting problem, greater self-awareness and/or other positive outcomes for
the client after every session of Lifespan Integration with a well-
grounded therapist. An exception to this might be when a target
cannot be cleared due to time restrictions, requiring a second session on the same target. In this case, a therapist will ask the client

for an update on the target from the previous week, which will become the starting point for the current session. Often—even with time restrictions as a factor—the integration has continued to progress between appointments and the target has resolved on its own before the next session.

Finding Targets

Lifespan Integration therapy generally begins with a combination of three methods. In most cases, one of the following will be employed at the beginning of a client's therapy. Advanced protocols are also part of the LI repertoire, but customarily are not applied until the client is well established in LI treatment. These three basic methods for finding LI targets can be used repeatedly and may constitute the entirety of a client's LI experience.

The target for each session of Lifespan Integration may be found via:

Standard Protocol. Clients focus on the emotion of their presenting problem and point to the place in their bodies where they feel the emotion. By focusing on the body feeling, clients let their bodies lead them to an earlier, associated memory. This is called an "affect bridge." Through this method, clients find an earlier memory which has the same emotional derivative as the presenting problem. Integrating the earlier memory with LI will bring appropriate empowerment to the client for his or her current concern.

Another form of Standard Protocol begins with a client choosing a specific, remembered event. LI therapy begins with the client recalling how the event was experienced followed by the remaining steps of Standard Protocol.

Generally, once the earlier scene or ego state is identified, the therapist asks the client to enter the situation, make imaginary interventions if necessary, and assure the younger ego state that "what was happening then is not happening now," followed by the timeline. This process is repeated until distress for the younger ego state is completely gone. As mentioned, the work of LI appears to prove to the body that difficult experiences have passed. Our experience tells us that we can eliminate the distress of a remembered event because the event is not happening in current time. The remainder of this book will give evidence and understanding to this process.

Birth-to-Present Protocol (BP). The LI therapist guides the client through repetitions of his or her lifetime starting at birth. This process decreases dissociation. Some clients are so emotionally fragmented that it is hard for them to target specific memories because their memory bank is overloaded with trauma and the mind-body system is holding information in disconnected ways. With continued sessions using BP, the ability for a client to move smoothly through the self-system increases and they become more emotionally whole.

Posttraumatic Stress Disorder (PTSD) Protocol Sometimes a client's specific traumatic memories must be resolved with LI before other protocols are employed. In such a case, we begin LI treatment with a form of timelines which includes many details of an identified trauma. Rather than increase distress by asking the client to remember the trauma, the repetitions of the detailed timeline proves to the client's body that the traumatic incident has passed and permanently reduces the client's anxiety about the difficult event.

Each of these protocols is more fully developed in a dedicated chapter.

Some terms and concepts of Lifespan Integration overlap with other therapies, while other phrases are specific to LI. The most important aspect of LI is the timeline of memories and is the starting point for definitions.

Definitions

Timeline. This is the process in which a trained therapist asks the client to recall a memory for each year of his or her life by systematically reading memories from the client's pre-written cue sheet.

The cue sheet includes one or two specific items the client actually remembers for each year. The client usually compiles the list of memories between sessions, but the client and the therapist may choose to compile it together in some cases. During a session, the therapist reads the client's pre-written cue sheet of memories one at a time, beginning after the targeted memory. The timeline is the unique, therapeutic change agent of Lifespan Integration and is the main component of LI therapy.

Even though a pre-written timeline of memories is used, negative associations will be among the first feelings to surface during the repetitions of the timeline. Pace suggests this occurs because a primary human instinct is to defend ourselves against negative experiences. Keeping these memories forefront in the mind is imperative for defense. When difficulties happen to a powerless child, he or she will develop a defensive coping mechanism to use in the future as protection should something like that incident reoccur. However, after several repetitions of the timeline, neutral or increasingly positive associations arise from the same cues that at one time prompted negative associations. Additional positive memories continue emerging as clients experience more repetitions of their timelines. Therapists may have to reassure clients that the difficult memories are a sign the therapy is working and promise them that repetitions of their timeline will get better as they continue.

The pattern of negative to positive memories can be likened to a flight attendant walking through a plane with a garbage bag after the snacks have been served. When finished, why are we eager to throw our garbage into the bag? Because it is sitting on our trays and we would like to be free of it. This appears to be the same process that causes negative memories to be the first to appear during the timeline phase of Lifespan Integration. Once clients rid themselves of negative associations, the positive memories always appear.

A target incident can usually be cleared within 3 to 12 repetitions of the timeline. Each repetition of the timeline creates shifts in the ego state memory. If a client is very emotional about an old memory when tapping into it, a therapist might lead him or her directly into a timeline without talking about the upsetting incident. After two or three timelines the client will be emotionally stabilized and able to talk about the upsetting memory in new ways. This makes Lifespan Integration very different from other therapies. In many cases, no amount of talking will resolve old traumas. Getting into the right 'ring' and proving to the mind and body that the trauma is over appears to integrate and forever transform the memory. The science behind this outcome will be presented in Chapter Two.

Ego states. Though the focal point of many therapies, in Lifespan Integration ego states are thought of as self-states that hold emotional, mental, and sometimes physical, experiences. Through imagination and body-based emotion, we can find the ego state holding specific data. For example, an adult remembering a birthday party can find within himself a child ego state who feels, remembers, and thinks about the experience. The adult can report the child's 'ring' of experience with accuracy because it is contained within the self of the adult, and will be re-experienced when the adult reaches back into that childhood 'ring.'

In Lifespan Integration, sometimes an ego state is used to describe a part of us that is responsible for a behavior or way of being. We naturally talk about the "part of me that is eager to go" and "the part of me that wants to stay home." Or, some people talk about "the part of me that purges after a binge." By referring to these 'parts,' we are not implying a case of multiple personality. All individuals can notice within themselves varying aspects that want and feel different things. These numerous feelings and perspectives reflect different ego states, and some individuals have more integrated ego states in their self-system than other individuals.

Lifespan Integration is exceptionally effective at integrating these distinct states. When various self-states understand they all belong to the same person who has resources beyond the limitations of one ego state, collaboration occurs within the internal self-system. This can be likened to the work of a jury. Different voices have different perspectives but the jury has one goal. All members of the internal jury must reach a collaborative decision for the client's greatest well-being. In LI, this is generally done through the Standard Protocol and Birth-to-Present protocol (BP) methods of LI and are described in detail by Pace. After overall integration is apparent, the Parts Model may be applied to a specific problem, such as anorexia. Pace has worked with anorexic clients who have shifted their behaviors after as few as one or two sessions. This behavior shift is only seen after the ego state responsible for limiting food intake understands that it is part of a bigger, more grown-up system. Chapter Eleven discusses the Parts Model of Lifespan Integration.

Internal dialogue. In Lifespan Integration, the therapist coaches a conversation between the adult-self and the younger-self. In this dialogue, the therapist tells the client helpful information to share with the internal ego state. The client repeats the therapist's coaching to his or her internal self. Although quite helpful, internal dialogue is not the primary method for change in Lifespan Integration and should be kept to a minimum during the early repetitions of the timeline. Painful memories are transformed through timelines more than dialogue. If resistance occurs during the internal dialogue, therapists guide clients through the timeline rather than attempting to convince the ego state that things have changed. Resistance decreases with every repetition of the timeline.

Ego states often do not believe what the adult-self is telling them, which is why the internal dialogue is secondary to the timeline. As far as it knows, an ego state's ring is the only ring or the outer ring of the tree. Depending on the trauma, it is possible for the ego state to be unaware that life has moved forward. The ego state also may not realize that additional internal resources are now available to help aid in resolution should a problem reoccur. Because ego states fiercely hold onto their protective and defensive roles, the timeline—rather than conversation—will be the only way to impact them. Once an ego state understands its particular problem is over, internal resources are redistributed to serve a more adaptive role.

For the internal dialogue, the therapist suggests something to the effect of, "Tell your eight-year-old self that you know it was really scary when you were left alone, but you are safe now." The therapist waits while the adult repeats this phrase to the internal ego state. Then the therapist suggests the next important piece of information. After briefly introducing a new and important concept, the therapist leads the client through a timeline of his or her life. These therapist-guided interventions are generally focused on validating the child's feelings, explaining that the child is currently safe, and affirming that there was nothing the child could have done about the problem. Timelines then prove the troubling event is over.

Distress abates for the ego state in direct correlation to the number of timeline repetitions; with each repetition of the timeline another piece of distress dissipates. After each timeline repetition, the adult-self and/or therapist discern the needs of the younger-self and address these directly in subsequent internal conversations. An ego state may be numb, angry, hurt, or scared when first encountered by the client. The ego state might be hiding somewhere and afraid of the adult-self. These conditions are resolved with the internal dialogue and timeline.

Affect bridge. The process in which a client identifies a current problem and its associated body feelings, and then follows the mind-body system to the appropriate neural networks associated with the problem. This is done by having clients focus on their emotions related to the problem and noticing where in their bodies they are holding these feelings. The therapist is particularly looking for clients to access body feelings located in their cores—the area of the body from the gut to the throat. As clients pay attention to their presenting problems and accompanying core body feelings, they generally remember an earlier memory. It is significant to note that the previous memory does not always have an obvious connection to the presenting problem from a client's or therapist's view, but is always relevant to healing the client's current distress. The mind-body system can be trusted to identify which historical memories need to be healed before the client's presenting problem will resolve. Sometimes the memories are traumatic and sometimes they are not. An affect bridge to a previous memory followed by the timeline is how we create remarkable changes for clients.

It should be noted that some clients will not be able to access feelings in their cores and instead will identify feelings in their extremities. These clients should experience the Birth-to-Present protocol for several sessions before using the affect bridge method for finding earlier memories. Clients are generally not aware that problems distressing them in the present have roots in previous life experiences. The way clients handled former problems influences how they cope today. This is sometimes hard for clients to understand because they do not feel like separate ages or ego states— they are just upset. Many cannot understand how solving an old problem will change the current one. But, after clients experience this process, they become convinced.

Throughout the case studies presented here it will become evident how this process leads the client to deep healing. In one of the cases, a 65-year-old man named Franklin kept talking about his car accident as if he had been in a bombing. He did not link the trauma from his car wreck to his childhood. However, when guided through the affect bridge process, the feelings and body sensations of the accident led Franklin to remember a previous trauma which he had not mentioned at the intake session, nor consciously linked to his accident. The distress for the accident would not resolve until the childhood trauma was healed. Although the memory was quite difficult, healing the ego state took about 30 minutes and did not re-traumatize Franklin in any way.

Franklin's story depicts the essence of Lifespan Integration. Resolving painful memories through repetitions of a timeline changes a client's life. Therapists learn how to guide clients to associate current feelings and body sensations back to their related root issues and clear them through the timeline process. It appears that neurological change is created by the timeline, producing positive and lasting change for the client.

An Example of Lifespan Integration

At age 41, Jennifer came to counseling for help dealing with a husband and son who frequently engaged in near-violent arguments. Jennifer had been married to Tom for seven years, and her 17-year-old son Jeff was Tom's stepson. Jennifer felt powerless to do anything about the distress between the two men she loved. Rather than problem-solve with Jennifer—which is traditionally part of talk therapy—we focused on her primary emotions and body sensations. Jennifer described herself as "angry, caught in the middle, divided, and heartbroken" about having to choose between them. She pointed to her stomach, indicating these feelings were in her gut. I asked Jennifer to close her eyes and let the feelings deepen while she focused on her emotions and stomach. I guided Jennifer to follow the affect bridge to an earlier time when these same feelings were present in her life. After a few moments Jennifer began to cry and said, "I see myself standing in the backyard having to choose between my mom and dad who are getting a divorce. The court has decided that I will choose who I'm going to live with and I'm heartbroken. I don't want my parents to get a divorce. I don't want to lose either one of them. I have to choose between two people I love."

"How old are you in this image?" I asked.

"Seven," Jennifer replied.

Following the steps of LI, I coached her saying, "Bring your adult-self into that situation with the child. Tell her you are her grown-up self and you are here to help her. Tell her you know she's really upset because she has to choose between her parents, but that is over. She will never again have to choose between two people she loves because she has grown up to be you." After a brief pause in which the adult Jennifer spoke internally to her younger-self, I said, "Take her to an imaginary safe place like the ocean or a peaceful forest. Tell her that you are going to prove to her that this is over and it's not happening in the present."

I began reading through Jennifer's pre-written timeline and asked her to acknowledge when she recalled the memory. "We're not going to stop on these memories," I instructed. "I just want you to remember what I mention from your cue sheet." Starting with age eight, I began leading Jennifer through the timeline. At each age, I paused until she indicated she had the memory in mind until we reached her adult age of 41 years old. "Show her where you live now and that she lives with you," I instructed. After a brief break I instructed Jennifer to imagine the seven-year-old in the back yard again.

She offered, "When I see her there my stomach is still hurting, but not as much. The little girl understands that she's not alone but she still doesn't want to hurt one of her parents."

"Bring your adult-self into the scene again and tell her, 'I'm here to help you. What happened here is not your fault. You did the best you could have done and there's nothing wrong with you.' Tell her you're going to prove to her it's over. Take her to the peaceful place again and tell her she has grown up to be you. If anything like this happens again, you, as an adult, will take of it," I coached Jennifer. After a silent pause in which the adult-Jennifer repeated my words to her younger-self, I added, "And tell her you are going to show her the pictures again that prove she grew up to be you."

I began reading Jennifer's cue sheet again starting with age eight, one year after the memory scene. At the end of the timeline, I instructed Jennifer to bring her child-self into the present and show her where she lives now. After a brief break, I asked Jennifer to check on the seven-year-old in the backyard again. "How is she doing now?" I asked.

"She's doing well. She's looking up at me instead of at her parents. She's feeling warm and comforted. There is not the same degree of distress, but she's still sad that it happened," Jennifer said. Because some degree of sadness was still present for her younger-self we repeated the internal dialogue and timeline. After the third timeline, I asked Jennifer to check on the seven-year-old in the backyard. She said, "I'm holding her now. Everything seems good. It's a huge relief."

During the three timelines, the memories became consistently more positive and afterwards there was no distress in Jennifer's stomach area when she remembered the event. Jennifer also reported that the child was feeling no distress either in the back-yard or in the present. Because no distress remained for the child, I asked her to consider the current problem which brought her to my office. "Knowing what you know now, what are your current thoughts about what is happening between your husband and son?" I inquired.

"I'm going to go home and tell them I will not put up with this," Jennifer immediately replied. "If they continue to do this, I'm going to leave the home when they begin to argue." Jennifer effort-lessly generated an appropriate, empowered adult response to her problem because she was no longer activated by childhood thinking and emotions from her parents' divorce in which she had to choose between two people she loved. In our session, Jennifer's mind-body system led her to a memory with a similar feeling tone to the cur-rent problem she was experiencing between her husband and her son. When the childhood feelings associated with the memory were resolved, Jennifer easily solved her own current problem. Not sur-prisingly, the next week Jennifer followed through with her plan and left the home twice when the two men began to argue.

When we met one week later, during our debrief Jennifer

offered, "My husband Tom is not only verbally abusive to my son Jeff, but he is also verbally abusive to me." We targeted Tom's verbal abuse of Jennifer in our second session. Once again I asked her to notice the emotions and body sensations associated with the verbal abuse from Tom, and she followed the affect bridge to an earlier time when she felt the same way. In Lifespan Integration, we do not ask the client to analyze the source of his or her distress. Instead, we follow the body to the right source memory for healing.

Jennifer remembered the verbal abuse from her father. She described a specific memory from her childhood and I coached her to bring her adult-self into that situation. Following the steps of LI, we continued to have Jennifer's adult-self intervene in the childhood situation, followed by repetitions of the timeline, until no distress remained for her younger-self in the memory scene. At the end of the session Jennifer said, "I'm going to have a family meeting and let them know I will not stay here if they are going to act this way. I cannot tolerate this from two people I love." Jennifer followed through with a family meeting and established appropriate family rules.

I talked with Jennifer on the phone one month after our two sessions. Due to scheduling challenges she was not able to keep her follow-up appointment with me, but she enthusiastically reported, "Things are a lot better at my house and I'm doing really well. Even my neighbor is commenting on how well I'm doing, and she knew me in the worst of my despair. I have a new job now and my husband and my son know the rules at our house. Things at our home are a lot better."

Why did two sessions of Lifespan Integration create this significant change? We hypothesize that integration, created by the LI timelines, allowed Jennifer to approach the problems in her home as an adult, without the childish thinking of her internal seven-year-old who was sad, frightened, and powerless to prevent her parent's divorce. As a child, Jennifer was powerless to stop the conflict between her parents, yet she was directly affected by it. When the conflict first emerged between Tom and Jeff, although Jennifer was in an adult position to do something about her problem, she acted in a powerless way and became depressed. *Because the brain uses the past to select behaviors for the present,* Jennifer automatically fell into a weak, childish position when Tom and Jeff argued. Resolving the child's powerlessness enabled Jennifer to be assertive and advocate for her needs in the current problem. In LI, we find that healing the underlying situation which prevented a client from being appropriately empowered is more effective than outlining behavioral steps for solving the presenting problem. In most cases, clients generate their own appropriate problem-solving strategies once their underlying, childhood feelings of powerlessness are resolved.

The foundational hypothesis underpinning Lifespan Integration is twofold: 1) Earlier memories influence how the brain processes current events, and 2) A client who is stuck in troubling thoughts, feelings, and behaviors can solve current situations by resolving earlier memories. Collective clinical data from the LI community informs us that remembered events can completely resolve through repetitions of the LI timeline. This is a bold statement, but our experience supports this tenet. My personal therapy practice substantiates our observation that the emotional distress of a single remembered event, no matter how horrific, can be resolved with enough repetitions of LI timelines. The pain associated with the trauma drops away and healthier behavior follows when survivors of war, abuse, or traumas large and small experience enough timelines to integrate their difficult experiences,

Some forms of therapy keep clients in their distressing memories for an extended amount of time. In contrast, Lifespan Integration briefly touches on traumatic material then integrates it through the timeline into the self-system. In some cases, a specific memory can be integrated within a standard counseling session through the use of internal dialogue and the timeline. This method causes change to occur rather quickly without re-traumatizing the client.

The Lifespan Integration method for clearing trauma also appears to prevent the clinician from experiencing secondary trauma, which is the residual impact on therapists from hearing horrific stories. With LI, even though clinicians hear details of very painful events, they are seldom left with residue. This is a very different scenario than other forms of trauma treatment.

Pace's workshops teach Masters and Doctoral level therapists the tools for using Lifespan Integration. In the beginning of her work, Pace developed a method for helping clients take the 'bad stuff' out of their minds and bodies, even if they had been holding difficult memories for years. The Standard Protocol and the Birth-to-Present methods of Lifespan Integration are the primary tools for creating these results. As she continued in her work, Pace expanded her methods to include LI methods that seem to increase clients' internal attachment styles. Once thought very difficult to repair, the modified methods of Lifespan Integration appear to impact the way clients connect with themselves and others. The basic steps of Lifespan Integration are taught at the Beginning Level workshop and the more reparative tools are taught at the Advanced Level workshop.

Lifespan Integration is effective for couples, children and adults. Chapter Twelve is devoted to case studies on children. With children the timeline is shorter and there is less material to integrate than most adults, but their traumas and difficulties are real nonetheless. I am thrilled to have an easy and gentle therapy to use with them that enables children to integrate the bad things that happened to them before they create a lifetime of dissociation, defensive strategies, and negative self-beliefs. The transformation that follows children's healing through LI is moving.

Lifespan Integration changes the beliefs adults and children hold within themselves. When people think about themselves differently they have a new experience in the world. In the case study in Chapter Nine entitled *Dog Attack*, a woman finds the world reorganizing itself around her as she changes her internal beliefs.

By sharing many of my clients' experiences with LI, I hope to give readers, clients, and therapists practical knowledge about how LI has consistently worked to change people who come for therapy. Case studies from my clinical practice are examples of the various ways and many issues in which Lifespan Integration has been used to transform people's lives. Although all the case studies are derived from real client stories from my counseling office, quotations from other experienced LI therapists are included throughout the text. Therapists and clients around the world give testimony to the power of Lifespan Integration. With LI, the outcomes are long lasting and are quite often quickly achieved. It is evident that clients get well using Lifespan Integration faster than with most other therapies. Since I have been in the helping profession, I have not experienced a tool for emotional healing that compares with Lifespan Integration.

2. The Science Behind the Success

What is a brain? Can a brain be remodeled?
The human brain is a sophisticated mass
somewhat like Play-Doh. From birth through
childhood the brain subdivides into various
sections and evolves into a variety of mainly
electrical functions. It develops a complex filing and communication system which uses
chemical secretions and neural firing patterns to keep its system
operating. A healthy brain is a powerful search engine which can
find, decode, and build upon life experience and learning. As it accu-
mulates information, the brain interprets, categorizes, and stores
the data it receives.

Generally, the brain catalogs according to emotion (Gerhardt,
2004). Memories with similar feeling tones appear to be organized
together in the brain. Therefore, a new loss in a person's life will
activate previous grief due to the brain's organizational system.

For most of the scientific age the brain has been somewhat of
a mystery. It was considered to be the thinking part of the human
machine, supported by a body which carried around this all-impor-
tant command center. In recent years, a greater understanding of
the brain and body has emerged. More sophisticated brain imaging
has given us accurate data about the function and nature of the
brain. Today we know that the brain and body are one interrelated

system considered the *mind*. Some consider the mind to be the sum of the self's processing system which occurs throughout the body as well as within the cranium. Previous beliefs that the mind only consisted within our skulls is being replaced with evidence that the human thinking and perceiving system is much more than the neural patterns that fire within our heads.

Scientists now tell us that neurons fire within the heart and gut as well. The heart brain is as large as many key areas of the brain in the head and has powerful, computational abilities. The magnetic field generated by neural firing in the heart is 5,000 times greater than the magnetic field produced by the brain. The intestinal tract has more neurons than the entire spinal column—about 100 million of them (Cooper, 2001).

The mind is defined as the process that regulates the flow of energy and information throughout the body and interpersonally between humans (Siegel, 2010). Lifespan Integration is a mind-body therapy even though a clinician does not touch the client. Instead, a therapist guides the client to find within his or her physical body the sensations associated with a problem and trusts the client's mind to find the associated memory which needs healing to resolve the current distress. If the client can point to the place in the body, especially in the core, where there is sensation related to the problem, the brain and body will take the client to the previous memory that needs healing. This method of finding root causes is much more accurate than asking clients to name the derivative of their distress. The body tells no lies. It can be trusted to guide a client to exactly the right place to start healing, thanks to its emotionally-based filing system.

An example of the accuracy of this process can be seen in the story of an experienced young doctor named Fernanda. She came to therapy wanting to address the anxiety she felt about getting pregnant for the first time. In talking about this anxiety, Fernanda said, "I think it's related to my mother's cancer 15 years ago." I assured Fernanda that there might be a connection between her mother's cancer and the current anxiety, but informed her that we were going to trust her body to lead us—by way of the LI process—to the right place for healing. She closed her eyes, pointed to the center of her body as the location of her anxiety, and arrived at a memory within a minute or so. The memory was of an inpatient mental hospital ward where Fernanda worked during her residency. Patients in the ward were on suicide watch and occasionally became violent. Fernanda was alone in the ward regularly for night shifts. As a young trainee she felt unprepared for the challenges in the ward and felt worried about her own safety. Using the method of LI, in one session we cleared Fernanda's body-based anxiety about being in the mental inpatient ward alone at age 27. Even though Fernanda was certain her anxiety had to do with her mother's cancer, when we focused on her body as it related to her past and current distress, nothing about her mother's cancer entered into our session.

At the next session, Fernanda reported that her anxiety about becoming pregnant was gone and she felt excited about the possibility of having a child. The place in her body where she previously felt anxiety about pregnancy, and her night shifts in the ward, was still completely clear. When I commented that our session had not taken us back to her mother's cancer as she suspected, Fernanda replied, "I guess that's because I know my mother's cancer is resolved. She's doing fine ten years later. Apparently I had not let go of my fear of being alone in the ward at night taking crisis calls and managing the suicidal people in my care."

As the previous example portrays, Fernanda's anxiety problem was in her mind—in her brain and in her body where she felt distress. Lifespan Integration is a therapy that works with the whole self-system to create integration and resolution of thoughts, emotions, and body sensations. This method goes beyond the emphasis of correct thinking, which is the focus of many talk therapies. With LI, we seek to create integration in the mind-body system as a whole. To do this, repetitions of a client's timeline are used to connect previous thoughts, feelings, and body sensations to the present. As earlier memories are healed, the mind and body adapt to a more effective way of functioning.

The Science Behind the Success

Fernanda's case highlights the three scientific components which we hypothesize create change through Lifespan Integration. Each aspect will be more fully developed later. In brief the three components are:

1) **The brain is changeable.** Unlike the perspective of previous years, scientists now confirm that the brain is able to be changed throughout a person's lifetime. Transformation is possible due to the plasticity of the brain. New information from Fernanda's life 15 years after she was a medical resident in a mental ward, plus repetitions of her timeline, appeared to change the way her mind and body held a difficult memory.

2) **Neurons that fire together, wire together.** Hebb's hypothesis tells us that neurons firing at the same time build a connection to one another (Doidge, 2007). With Fernanda, it appeared that each time I led her through a repetition of her timeline, neural networks from the mental ward months were being connected to neural networks that had developed since that time. Repetitions of her timeline strengthened these new connections.

3) **An integrated brain is a healthy, high function-ing brain.** Through Fernanda's example, it appears that her frightening mental ward experience became integrated with up-to-date information about her cur-rent life, specifically that she was no longer singularly responsible for many challenging patients. Integrating these two periods of her life through neural con-nectivity caused the mental, emotional, and physical

stress of anticipated pregnancy to dissipate, affording Fernanda a healthier perspective on her present life.

The concepts presented here occur in virtually every Lifespan Integration session. After watching two videos at a Beginning Level workshop, one man laughingly commented, "Can you show me a video where this doesn't work?"

"I'm afraid I can't," I countered. "This outcome happens consistently due to the integration created by the timelines."

"And when the client comes back with the same problem will you do the same thing again?" he asked.

"The client won't come back with the same problem," I promised. "The changes created from the timeline method don't go away." We observe lasting outcomes from Lifespan Integration which we hypothesize are caused by neural integration.

The Changeable Brain: Neuroplasticity

A few decades ago, a high school biology teacher with an advanced degree emphatically stated that the human brain developed by age five and did not change thereafter. A psychology teacher in the school expressed the same perspective. He also said that a child's character and personality were formed by age five. He reinforced the notion that the brain was locked into its structure before kindergarten was over. Being one of those learners, I was discouraged by the news. Were the pre-kindergarten years really a template for the rest of my life? Would the years leading up to age five be as good as life could get?

Fortunately, the scientific facts taught in the 20th century have since been updated due to new research findings. Extensive imaging shows that the brain can indeed be changed—sometimes in major ways. Scientists have discovered that the brain can remodel itself when change is required. Schore (2003) discussed how new discoveries in the field of neuroscience have confirmed that the cerebral cortex is able to reorganize itself throughout the lifespan. Neural networks are not static, but rather dynamic and changing.

Many cases of this brain change are available in scientific literature. A few examples of the brain's capacity for change are presented here to support the consistent scientific finding that the brain is changeable.

Current research tells us that if one part of the brain is damaged or unused, the brain will re-organize its real estate to best suit current needs. According to Al-Chabali et al. (as cited in Badenoch, 2008) when brain surgery damages a child's language region, the brain rewires itself and moves the language center to an undamaged part of the brain, restoring function and near-normal development. Begley (2007) wrote about adult volunteers with normal sight who participated in a study where they were blind-folded for five days. Their vision was fully restricted so that no light entered their eyes. At the end of the trial, MRIs showed that the part of the brain responsible for seeing had already adapted to perform feeling and hearing tasks since seeing was no longer an option. Many other research projects confirm that it does not take long for a brain to redistribute its resources when change is required. Stroke victims are recipients of this miraculous reassignment process. They can often regain the motor functions that were impaired due to the stroke by influencing their brains to develop new pathways for accomplishing old tasks. Doidge (2007) supported these newly discovered brain facts and stated:

> ...unexpected discoveries...showed that the brain changes its very structure with each different activity it performed, perfecting its circuits so it was better suited to the task at hand. If certain 'parts' failed, then other parts could sometimes take over. (p. xix)

Brain changes occur due to *neuroplasticity*—the term scientists have given to the brain's impressive ability to change its structure and function in response to experience. *Neuro* is for the neurons which are the nerve cells in our brains and nervous systems.

Plastic means "changeable" or "modifiable" (Doidge, 2007, p. xix). Therefore, neuroplasticity is the condition which enables the brain to modify itself in response to various stimuli. Neuroplasticity is defined as the "capacity of neurons and *neural networks* in the *brain* to change their connections and behavior in response to new *information*, sensory stimulation, development, damage, or dysfunction" ("Neuroplasticity," 2012). In simple terms, a neuron is a single nerve cell comprised of a cell body with a nucleus (center), dendrites, and axon. The rounded, central part of the neuron is the cell body. Branching out from the cell body like coral lace are *dendrites*. The farther dendrites extend, the finer their filaments become. Their purpose is to find other cells with which to communicate. Dendrites gather information through their association network and shuttle it into the cell body. When enough information passes through the dendrites into the cell body, a signal is sent out through the *axon*. The axon is a long, tube-like extension from the cell body. It carries a message to the nervous system with instructions to initiate an action. In humans, an axon can be several feet long. Some sensory nerves have two axons. In these neurons, a signal travels up the first axon, into the cell body and down the second axon until it reaches the far end, where it can be transmitted to other cells (Badenoch, 2008).

Nerve cells connecting to one another form a neural network, also called a *neural net.* They group together and exhibit the capacity to learn. Research confirms that humans can rewire their brains. Dispenza (2007) stated:

> For a long time, scientists believed that the brain was hard-wired; meaning that change is impossible and that the system of responses and tendencies you inherited from your family is your destiny. But in fact, the brain possesses elasticity, an ability to shut down old pathways of thought and form new ones, at any age, at any time. Moreover, it can do so relatively quickly… (p. 29-30)

Begley (2007) explained how the "brain can undergo wholesale change...the brain is capable not only of altering its structure but also of generating new neurons, even into old age. The brain can adapt, heal and renew itself after trauma..." (p. i). One of the many ways the brain can change is through focused attention. Clinicians have documented this truth by recording the changes using brain imaging maps of patients' brains (Nicholson, 2011). Brain scans have shown long-standing, physical changes in brain areas after test subjects intentionally worked to change their thoughts.

For Lifespan Integration, the brain's capacity to change is at the heart of our hypothesis that new information from current experience, plus integration from repeated timelines, causes lasting change in the brain. We consistently observe anecdotal evidence to support this perspective. The reported data from our clients, plus the latest information from neuroscience which tells us the brain is changeable, leads us to believe that Lifespan Integration changes the brain and therefore creates lasting emotional and behavioral change as well.

Rewiring

In 1949, behavioral psychologist Donald O. Hebb suggested that learning linked neurons in new ways:

> He proposed that when two neurons fire at the same time repeatedly (or when one fires, causing another to fire), chemical changes occur in both, so that the two tend to connect more strongly. Hebb's concept—actually proposed by Freud sixty years before—was neatly summarized by neuroscientist Carla Shatz: *Neurons that fire together, wire together.* (Doidge, 2007, p. 63)

Michael Merzenich substantiated Hebb's hypothesis through neural mapping on monkeys. By using sophisticated equipment, he was able to pinpoint which part of the monkey's brain was activated when it moved its fingers. The area of the monkey's brain dedicated to finger movements is a neural map. Merzenich systematically limited the movement of the monkey's fingers, and in doing so re-mapped the monkey's brain. No matter which way he forced change in the monkey's movements, the brain mapping always changed in correlation. Merzenich observed that the part of the brain which initially lit up when the monkey moved its fingers one way went silent and dark when the monkey could no longer repeat the action.

> By doing multiple mappings over time, Merzenich observed that the new maps were changing their borders, becoming more detailed, and even moving around the brain. In one case he even saw a map disappear altogether…It seemed reasonable to assume that if totally new maps were forming, then new connections must have been forming among neurons. (Doidge, 2007, p. 63)

Merzenich's mental mapping led him to develop methods to help people overcome disabilities by deliberately forcing their brains to rewire. Since neural reconfiguration occurs, he proposed that people could overcome learning problems, stroke symptoms, and emotional problems by deliberately causing healthy neurons to fire and wire together.

Physical input is proven to change the brain. The fact that stroke victims can force their brains to reacquire motion in disabled limbs is one example of how the brain can change with input. Researchers at Washington University School of Medicine (2000) performed a study where the non-impaired limb of a stroke victim was physically restrained so it could not perform its normal function while the patient was guided through physical therapy to induce re-use of the limb damaged by the stroke. Over time, the malfunctioning limb increased in useful function, and in some cases returned to complete function. If we could see inside the brain during this process, we would notice that the brain map for the good limb is quiet while it is inactive, but neurons are firing and rewiring in response to signals generated from the impaired limb. The researchers discovered that through focused attention, stroke victims experienced decreased swelling in the impaired limb and adaptation of neural networks in the brain. The observable return to function of the disabled limb was a direct result of change in the brain.

Similarly, emotional changes can also manifest from intentionally firing and rewiring brain neurons. Nicholson (2011) reported on a mindfulness meditation program from Massachusetts General Hospital in which 16 participants meditated 30 minutes a day. The participants focused on nonjudgmental awareness of sensations and feelings. Brain images were taken before and after the training. Scientists found increases in gray-matter density in the hippocampus—an area responsible for learning and memory. They also found decreased density in the amygdala—an area in control of anxiety and stress responses. Nicholson (2011) reported, "All this reminds us of two things: 1) The brain is much more plastic than scientists thought even just a decade ago, and 2) The way we feel—calm or nervous—can be correlated with real structural indicators in our brains." While Richard Davidson was a graduate student at Harvard, he focused his research on the science of emotion. Davidson hypothesized, "…we can think of emotions, moods, and states such as compassion as trainable skills….we know that experience can induce changes in the structure and function of brain regions involved in regulating emotions" (as cited in Begley, 2007, p. 221).

The outcomes from Lifespan Integration indicate that neural reconfiguration is happening through the therapeutic process. We do not yet have brain imaging to verify our hypothesis, but the lasting emotional improvement reported by clients, in addition to the scientific research available on neuroplasticity and brain change, implies that their brains have changed. When we guide a client to remember a traumatic event, the memory will briefly be activated once remembered. A systematic repetition of the client's timeline from the traumatic event to the present reduces the emotionality of the remembered event as the session progresses. Clients consistently report that highly traumatic events, which at one time kept them from normal functioning, become non-emotional, remembered events after the Lifespan Integration process.

Repeatedly activating neurons together strengthens their connection. Doidge (2007) stated, "When we say that neurons 'rewire' themselves, we mean that alterations occur at the synapse, strengthening and increasing, or weakening and decreasing, the number of connections between the neurons" (p. 54). In 2000, Eric Kandel won the Nobel Prize for proving that when people learn something, the wiring in their brains change:

> He demonstrated that acquiring even simple pieces of information involves the physical alteration of the structure of the neurons participating in the process. Taken broadly, these physical changes result in the functional organization and reorganization of the brain. This is astonishing. The brain is constantly learning things, so the brain is constantly rewiring itself. (Medina, 2008, p. 54)

Given the plasticity of the brain and its capacity for rewiring, the theory behind LI is the concept that a difficult, emotional memory can be wired to newer parts of the brain that have developed since the difficult memory was initially stored. It appears that rewiring takes place through the LI timeline method and is reinforced with each repetition.

Integration

Integration is the third component in the hypothesis that repetitions of the timeline change the brain. Siegel (2010) stated, "... Integration is the key mechanism beneath both the absence of illness and the presence of well-being. Integration—the linkage of differentiated elements of a system—illuminates a direct pathway toward health" (p. 65). In essence, integration is mental health. Siegel's clinical work has developed into methods of mindfulness with the purpose of increasing neural integration. Begley (2007) also made statements that can be seen as an endorsement of integration equaling mental health. Begley said:

> ...neurobiology suggests that no one is a single self, but rather that health lies in the harmonious flow among our many selves, so that they can wax and wane within a wide window of tolerance in response to life's stresses and delights. (p.148)

Simply expressed, a system must have integration of its various components in order to function at its best. There is no upward limit to how much complexity a system can tolerate as long the system is well integrated. In other words, it does not matter if a system has few parts or many parts. The quality of the system depends on how successfully the parts work together—how well the parts are integrated.

Humans are complex, multi-layered systems and the human brain is comprised of a multiplicity of neural networks. The interconnectedness of these neural networks appears to be the basis of emotional health. Our experience with Lifespan Integration suggests that repetitions of a client's timeline appear to increase neural network connectivity. The outcomes from LI give evidence to this thesis.

Tracy, an artistic and bright woman with a Bipolar diagnosis, drew a series of images to support this thesis. In her first LI session, Tracy spontaneously drew a metaphoric representation of her brain. Over twelve sessions Tracy drew three drawings (Figures 1, 2, and 3) which portrayed her progress from a lack of integration in the first session to a complex network of integration by the last session.

I gave Tracy a rudimentary description of the brain in our first meeting to which she replied, "Oh, this is how my brain works… can I draw a picture for you?" Figure 1 is Tracy's conceptualization of her brain at session one.

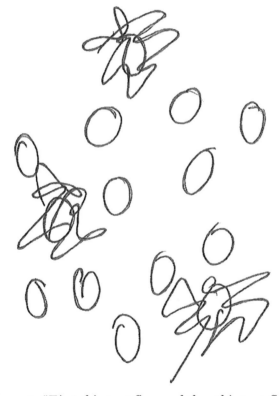

Figure 1: "First this part fires and then this part fires…"

To begin her diagram, Tracy drew the separate circles as seen in Figure 1. She took the pencil, scribbled completely over one circle and said, "This part fires, and…"filling in another circle, said, "…

then this part fires." She continued to scribble over the circles, indicating that the circles only fire one at a time and did not seem to have any impact on one another. They appeared to lack integration.

After five sessions of Lifespan Integration, I asked Tracy to make another drawing to represent how she conceptualized her brain. Tracy enthusiastically drew the diagram in Figure 2 without any influence or input from me. When she was done, Tracy showed me her work which was a beautiful portrait of brain connectivity—a visual representation of integration.

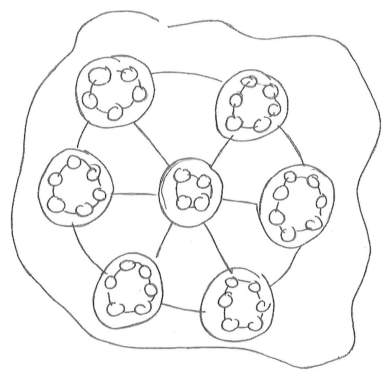

Figure 2: After five sessions of LI

In her second drawing Tracy drew an icon for integration. Rather than separate parts that fire independently as in her first drawing, Tracy's second drawing represented a connective brain system with integration among its parts. After five sessions of

Lifespan Integration, primarily using Birth-to-Present protocol, there appeared to be a change in the way Tracy's brain functioned. This was evidenced by her metaphoric drawing of brain parts (circles) that contained circles within circles and connection from one part to another.

After five sessions, Tracy noticed a positive change in her life. For the first time, she consistently experienced the ability to delay gratification. She said, "I told my mom that if I get an idea or a feeling, now I think to myself, *Well, that's important, but I don't have to do something about that right now. I can wait a bit and see what I need to do over time."* The integration in Tracy's drawing, and the discovery that she could wait before acting on an impulse, implied that other parts of her brain were connected to and influencing the new ideas that emerged within her brain. The drawing in Figure 1 showed no indicator of connection in which one brain system mitigated another. After five sessions of LI, Tracy reported increased self-control and conceptualized her brain as an integrated, organized, inter-connected set of systems within systems. Tracy's second drawing shown in Figure 2 suggested that other aspects of her brain weighed in when she got an idea, feeling, or impulse. Impulse control is a major challenge for Bipolar clients. For Tracy, the circles with interconnection paralleled her increased self-control and awareness.

At the end of the twelfth session Tracy offered to draw another conceptualization of her brain. "Could you make a copy of my last drawing?" she asked. "My brain is still like the previous drawing, except it has more connections now. I would like to add on to what I did before." I made a copy of Tracy's drawing from our fifth session and she began increasing the circles and connective lines. Tracy said, "I could draw more circles on this but here's enough to give you an idea of how my brain seems now."

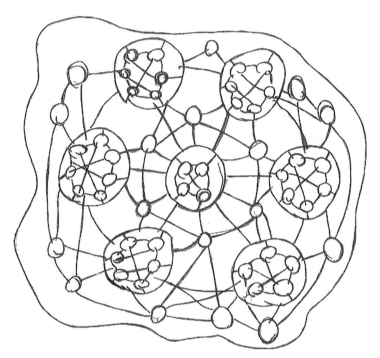

*Figure 3: "I could draw more circles but this gives you
an idea of what my brain is like now...."*

It is apparent in Tracy's third drawing that she perceived her
brain to have more integration and connectivity after additional LI
sessions. She said, "Now if I get an idea to do something musical I
stop and think hmmm, what could I do that's musical and still get
to school tomorrow? I know, I'll go to karaoke with my friends.
That would be fun, social, musical, and I could still get my home-
work done." Tracy's comment is quite a departure from the excessive, risky behavior of Bipolar clients. Tracy's drawing implies that
other brain systems influenced her when she had a creative impulse.
We find LI to be a very effective therapy for Bipolar clients, which
will be discussed more fully in Chapter Ten.

Over and over again in Standard Protocol LI sessions we hear
clients say, "The child that is *x* years old in my memory had no idea

she had grown up to be me!" This happens so consistently that it informs us the brain holds memories in separate neural networks which do not appear to have a relationship to one another. After multiple repetitions of one's timeline a client will say, "Now the child understands she is a part of me," at which point the emotional and bodily distress of the memory is completely gone. This consistent outcome suggests that integration has taken place.

Referring back to the rings of the tree analogy, people are a composite of their experience over a lifetime. Like the rings of a tree, one layer which had a certain experience in life may not have contact with other layers within the same tree, even though together they make up the overall unit. A cross-section of a tree tells us which years the tree experienced fire, drought, or abundant rain. Together, all the rings comprise the overall well-being of its structure.

With humans, we can guide them to go back into a neural network, figuratively equal to the ring of a tree, and heal the fire or drought that took place at a given time in their history. After the neurons holding the memory have been activated, the client can be guided to input appropriate healing language and imagery into the difficult scene. The brain does not differentiate between real or imagined experience. Other therapies use similar visualization, but the exponential difference with LI is the repetition of the client's timeline after the imagery work, which appears to integrate the memory into the whole self-system.

A famous set of brain scans depicting the way the human brain experiences real and imagined images was published in Time Magazine ("How to Read a Mind," 2007). The MRI results from the volunteers showed that actual experiences and imagined experiences activated the same area of the brain. The only difference between brain scans was the level of activation in the brain activity. Actually viewing the place or face slightly increased the amount of activation, but the areas of impact were the same for imagining and actual viewing. Many other scientific studies substantiate the findings that the brain can learn from imagined experiences. Schwartz and Begley (2002) discussed Pascual-Leone's 1995 research which demonstrated that imagined movements create changes in neural networks in the same way, but to a lesser degree, that actual physical movements do (as cited in Pace, 2009). As mentioned, with LI we follow a positive, imagined experience with timelines to integrate the brain activation caused via imagination.

An example of integration can be seen in the story of Kaeli who was temporarily separated from her mother at birth. She was whisked away to receive medical treatment immediately after delivery. Four hours later, Kaeli was returned to her mother who had been anxiously waiting. The mother attempted to nurse her baby, but Kaeli had a difficult time. When Kaeli's mother brought her in for Lifespan Integration at age eight, she mentioned that Kaeli had some anxiety, ADHD, and was dealing with her parents' divorce. Kaeli's mom described the birth experience and we began there. I asked big-girl-Kaeli to imagine herself while I described the details of her birth, followed by the rest of her timeline. Kaeli and her mother were both seated on the floor during this phase of our session.

By the sixth repetition of her timeline, Kaeli had crawled into her mother's lap with her long legs hanging over her mother's legs. The muscles in her mouth moved in sucking motions when I mentioned nursing as a newborn baby. As we progressed through her timeline other memories evoked physical feelings in Kaeli's body. After the eighth timeline Kaeli was very tired and said the newborn baby knew for sure she had grown up to be eight-year-old Kaeli.

Two weeks after that first session, Kaeli's mother left me a voicemail. She said Kaeli had not wet the bed once since our Lifespan Integration session, even though bedwetting had been a problem throughout her childhood. These results occurred simply from the integration of Kaeli's newborn-self into eight-year-old Kaeli via repetitions of her timeline.

After three sessions of Lifespan Integration using the same

methods from our first session, Kaeli's mother said, "I have taken Kaeli to many therapists over the years and they have proposed simple, cognitive behavioral therapies. They didn't go deep enough. I knew we had to get deeper to heal Kaeli's anxiety and fears. Lifespan Integration has done this." Kaeli's mom began to cry and said, "I have waited eight years to get help for my daughter. This is the healing work I hoped for." Through LI, integration and rewiring of the changeable brain appears to have provided the depth of healing Kaeli's mother was seeking.

Research

The first completed Lifespan Integration research project was conducted by Bethany Balkus in 2011 at Hope Place, a residential drug, alcohol, and domestic violence treatment program for women in Seattle, WA. Seventeen women volunteered for the study. They were asked to identify a single trauma from their lives which was treated with two Standard Protocol Lifespan Integration sessions. Results were measured by the Impact of Events Scale (IES) by Horowitz (2011), which separately scores a client's report of avoidance about the trauma and the level to which he or she experiences intrusive thoughts related to the trauma. The IES was administered three times to each participant: before the treatment, after the second session, and one month after the second session.

The residents at Hope Place generally have a history of trauma and abuse coupled with their alcohol and drug addiction. For the study, participants chose a single trauma such as bludgeoning a partner to death after he apparently killed her child and threatened to kill her as well, witnessing a shooting, robberies at gun point, and childhood rape.

According to the scored results, each of the participant's trauma level was considered severe. At the beginning of session one, the mean scores for Avoidance and Intrusion were each approximately 28 out of 30. At the end of session two, Avoidance and Intrusion were each approximately 7 out of 30. One month after session two, with no intervening LI, the scores continued to decrease to approximately 3.75 out of 30. These outcomes are considered to be statistically significant.

When asked about the overall finding on the study, Balkus said, "Our IES data suggests that Lifespan Integration has a long-term effect for individuals struggling with severe trauma."

When I asked if Balkus was surprised by the results, she said, "At first I thought maybe I had tabulated the results incorrectly because the findings were so clinically significant. My advisor reviewed and checked the compilation and said my results were accurate. I was very surprised, though, by how incredibly grateful the women were when they realized it worked. Some of the women cried at the end. They said, 'I haven't felt this good in a long time.' Some women came back and said things were much different for them, such as the perspective on themselves and how much control they actually have in their own lives. They described having a stronger sense of self and being more empowered. Half the clients I worked with came back and asked for more LI."

In referencing their empowerment, Balkus said, "When these women came in initially, their perspective on what happened to them was distorted. A lot of it was turned on themselves. They felt as if they were completely responsible for an aversive event they had no control over. After the two sessions of LI, there was clarity on the reality of the situation and the women were able to place the blame on the perpetrator instead of on themselves. They were able to say, 'I did the best I could in that situation. I can't believe I blamed myself for something I had no control over.'"

Carol Lindlow is the Counseling and Domestic Violence Track Coordinator at the Hope Place treatment program. She was one of three therapists who conducted the LI sessions for the project. Lindlow noticed that the women who participated in the study became more proactive in their overall recovery and more aware of their own needs and rights as members of the community. She said, "Our treatment program is long term. Guests stay in the program from one to three years. They are recovering from drugs, alcohol, and domestic violence. Most of our women have complex PTSD, or years of domestic violence and childhood abuse. For example, one woman grew up in a drug house. Using LI, the memories that traumatized her resolved and she became more stable. We find that LI increases stability which improves guests' recovery."

Balkus added, "The women who enter our program are fragmented by trauma. Those who got LI sessions were able to understand their trauma without being stuck in it and become more integrated. Noticeably, the LI participants were better able to handle their transition back to the outside community. The women we have here are going back into difficult situations. If we can help them go back into life with a more integrated self then we are setting them up for success."

Lindlow concurred. "One client said to me, 'The LI you did with me was the most significant thing that happened for me in this program. It made the most lasting difference.'" Lindlow continued, "We have a population where every individual is 100 percent traumatized. By clearing their traumas with LI, we increase their capacity for emotional regulation, and this helps people maintain their sobriety." Experts agree that emotional regulation is the key to long-term sobriety (Clements, 2011).

Addiction specialist Mate (2010) summarized the connection between trauma and addiction:

> Chronic substance use is the addict's attempt to escape distress...Addictions always originate in pain, whether felt openly or hidden in the unconscious...Most hard-core substance abusers come from abusive homes...A *hurt* is at the center of *all* addictive behaviors. (p. 35-37)

Given the connection between trauma and addiction, Balkus' research implies that healing trauma with Lifespan Integration enhances addiction recovery. The volunteers from Hope Place evidence this outcome through their personal testimonies. The women who received LI as part of their addiction recovery generally had better-than-average success when transitioning out of the treatment program.

Summary

In review, three main principles underlie the hypothesis for change through Lifespan Integration:

1) ***The brain is a living and changing organism*** *that creates new neurons throughout life—contrary to the previous theory that the brain became fairly solidified once it reached adulthood.* This adaptive, changing nature of the brain means it can be rewired and literally restructured through intentional thought changes. We believe repetitions of the timeline are an interactive process that changes the brain in an enduring way.

2) ***The changes created by the timeline*** *most likely occur because neurons that fire together wire together according to Hebb's hypothesis.* Applying this principle to the timeline, we hypothesize that neural networks from one period of life are systematically fired along with neural networks holding memories from subsequent years when clients are guided through a timeline of their lives. Neurons from separate years wire together when clients are prompted to remember the years of their lives. Repeatedly firing these neurons together strengthens their connection until a new way of thinking develops regarding former problems. Circumstances that provided negative emotional triggers at one time lose their emotional charge when tied with more adult, up-to-date thinking through the neural reconnection.

3) ***Integration is mental health***. All parts of a system must be working together in order to have the optimum functioning of the system. When one part of the brain is overloaded with emotional material, the whole brain system and its functioning is reduced. In order to return the brain to its optimal level of functioning, difficult or dissociated 'rings' must be re-integrated into the system. This is accomplished through the timeline. If a difficult experience occurs at a young age, the brain may be holding the information out of consciousness or in an isolated, protected way. Joining the neural networks that hold the isolated memory to years of life that have occurred since the event integrates it and increases the brain's overall functioning.

Mental integration, neurons firing together, and the changeable nature of the brain combine to create lasting emotional change through Lifespan Integration. It is suggested that these results occur because the brain is actually rewiring with repetitions of the timeline. The results from LI reflect a level of emotional healing we have not seen before. It is hypothesized that these changes are due to neural integration.

The Lifespan Integration method of counseling is different than talk therapy because it does not rely solely on the client's intellectual understanding of issues, but rather goes back to the source where beliefs first developed and gives clients the opportunity to rethink what they know and believe. The timeline integrates the new ways of thinking. All people process emotional distress with their young minds by assuming the challenges they faced were due to something wrong with them. This developmentally appropriate self-centeredness leads to wrong conclusions when things go awry. We can change thinking that developed in childhood, or previous 'rings of the tree,' by integrating the thoughts, feelings, and beliefs that were formed in earlier years.

By helping clients identify the body-based location of their feelings and guiding them through an affect bridge followed by timelines, we can help individuals heal on a profound level. When the adult-self goes back to enter a memory scene with a younger-self and speaks the words of healing, clients are able to grasp their experiences with new understanding and form new conclusions about themselves. We hypothesize that the timeline integrates this work and causes new neural pathways to be formed. Anecdotal evidence supports the hypothesis. Research will continue to substantiate our hypothesis that Lifespan Integration appears to create integration, and integration is mental health.

Pages and pages could be written about the science supporting the tenet that brain change occurs with Lifespan Integration. Until we have brain scans to support our theory, we can hypothesize from client's reports and observable clinical data that brain changes occur for clients through LI. Current scientific findings and research on the brain align with what our clients tell us: their lives are changed in lasting ways through Lifespan Integration.

Many of our clients have experienced other therapies but have not achieved permanent relief from the problems they addressed with other therapies. With the tools of LI, we go back to a source memory, input the needed information, and resolve physical and emotional distress with repetitions of the client's timeline. The results clients experience appear to last.

People go from being highly activated to calm—and they stay calm. It holds. They say, 'I used to be in this situation and it bothered me, but now it doesn't.'

Evelyn Schmechtig-Cochran, LI therapist

3. Standard Protocol

Four-Phase Pattern

Most Standard Protocol LI sessions have a common four-phase pattern that begins with the younger ego state being frozen and/or quite emotional when first identified. The intervention for the first stage is for the older-self to briefly state that the difficult circum-stance is over, create an imaginary intervention such as calling the police or forcing an abuser to stop, and quickly take the younger-self to the peaceful place. In the imagined peaceful place, the older-self can briefly express again that the trouble is over and it was not the child's fault, followed by the timeline. This stage usually needs to be repeated two to five times.

The second phase occurs when the younger ego state is no longer in the same heightened distress. The adult-self then enters the scene and expresses anger on behalf of the child. Virtually all difficult situations have an anger component in them. The anger may not be recognizable until the initial frozen, traumatized state is briefly accessed and resolved with repetitions of the client's timeline. The second phase also requires approximately two to five repetitions.

The third phase occurs when the child-self has become more integrated with the older-self through the timelines, and can express his or her anger directly toward a perpetrator in the presence of the empowered adult. All children are powerless. They cannot stop abusive behavior from adults. They are not old enough or strong enough to defend themselves in traumatic situations. In phase three of Standard Protocol the child himself is given the opportunity to hit back, shout back, and defend himself through imaginary behaviors while the empowered adult-self supports him. It may seem counter-intuitive to some readers that we guide victims into hurting others, but this provides a safe way for the body to release its unexpressed, instinctive self-protection—something which is necessary for complete integration. In review, the third phase usually takes two or three repetitions and includes giving the child an opportunity to say whatever he or she wishes to the offender.

The final phase involves an imaginary, positive repair of the troubling event. For example, if a child was left out of social circles or bullied, a positive repair would be coaching the child, with the adult-self present, to have friends and safety. Playing this out in the client's mind creates neural networks of the experience, almost to the same degree a real version of it would.

Standard Protocol LI ends when there is no bodily or emotional distress for the younger-self when the original scene is remembered without the adult-self present. We check the original scene without the adult to make certain that the original neural networks which loaded the painful memory are fully resolved. If the adult is present during this assessment, the client will report a different level of activation than if he or she remembers the difficulty as it actually occurred. Fortunately with Lifespan Integration, we can bring any incident to complete, body-based resolution due to the integration created by repetitions of the timeline.

The four-phase process described here is not a cookie-cutter recipe intended for identical replication in every case where Standard Protocol LI is used with clients. Lifespan Integration is a live, interactive exchange between a younger ego state and adult-self coached by a psychotherapist. The therapist's attunement through the process is an essential component of LI's success. The four-phase process is a guide to the common pattern of Standard Protocol LI, and not a set of directions that can be followed verbatim. LI requires a therapist to pay attention to the internal experience of the client and one's self in order to successfully guide the LI process. Lifespan Integration works best when the therapist trusts the client's body and allows the client's neural networks to lead. When done correctly, the Standard Protocol will help clients fully resolve any distressing memory.

Parenting Teens

Mary Beth came to see me through the Crime Victims Compensation program because she had been robbed in a parking garage after an evening function. Mary Beth was about to open the door to her car when a man wearing a mask demanded her wallet and fled. We met for five sessions of Lifespan Integration and her distressing symptoms following the traumatic incident completely resolved.

As I knew her in that context, it was clear that Mary Beth was a smart and likable young woman. She told me that she had a son and a daughter two years apart in age. From her description of family life at that time, it sounded like Mary Beth was quite involved in her community and in her children's lives. She appeared to be a well-balanced mom who gained a lot of joy from parenting, her social network, and her professional life. I was quite impressed by Mary Beth's warmth, intelligence, and high level of functioning.

After we resolved the trauma from the assault in the parking garage, Mary Beth said she would contact me again if anything about it bothered her in the future. Eight years after the assault Mary Beth called to schedule an appointment. In our first meeting she said the robbery still did not bother her and she was very grateful for the change Lifespan Integration brought into her life. "It worked so well for me," she said, "I think I'm back for more. My children are teenagers now and I'm struggling. Janet is 15 and

Chase is 13. Our family life is not going well." Mary Beth continued describing the problems in her household. In my estimation, the problems she faced fell into the challenging end of normal behavior for adolescents. Nevertheless, the situation was quite disturbing for Mary Beth. She explained that Chase was experimenting with drugs and Janet constantly rejected her. Mary Beth began to cry and said, "I think the hardest part is Janet's rejection. I feel rejected as a mom."

I thought, but did not say, *Welcome to parenting teenagers. Of course your daughter is rejecting you. She's 15.* The situation Mary Beth described was much more complicated than I initially perceived. Throughout the intake session I got more information about her family struggles. At the end of the session, I gave Mary Beth instructions for filling out a cue sheet at home.

When she returned, Mary Beth said again that the most distressing part of her story was the rejection she felt from Janet. Using Standard Protocol, I asked her to point to the place in her body where she carried the feelings of rejection. "It's right here," she said, crying and pointing to her stomach, heart, and throat.

"Let your mind be quiet," I guided, "and see what comes up."

In a few moments Mary Beth opened her eyes and said, "It's about my feelings as a mom and not being able to conceive my own children. I feel so rejected by Janet. I see myself at age 28 not able to get pregnant. Janet and Chase are adopted. We had two years of infertility struggles while all of our friends were getting pregnant. They said things like, 'It's God's will for every woman to get pregnant if she wants to.'"

My compassion for Mary Beth deepened. "What image do you see right now when you think of those years?" I asked.

"Walking to the hospital for infertility treatments. We had two awful years." Mary Beth cried as she filled in details of her story. Rather than spend much time telling the details, I asked her to bring her adult, 43-year-old self into the image with her 28-year-old self.

"Can you see them together?" I asked.

"Yes," Mary Beth answered through her tears.

"Tell her you are her grown-up self and see if she will go to a peaceful place with you," I guided.

"She will," Mary Beth quietly answered.

"Tell her this is how everything turned out. Ask her to watch these pictures. It's the story of how she became a mom," I instructed. I began reading Mary Beth's cue sheet starting at age 29, one year after the age of her source memory. At the end of the timeline I asked Mary Beth to bring her 28-year-old-self into her current home and show her the bedrooms of Chase and Janet.

"She can't believe it's true!" Mary Beth exclaimed.

"You mean she doesn't know that you have children?" I asked.

"Yes, that's exactly right. She's dumfounded! She's looking in their bedrooms and has no idea that I have children," Mary Beth replied.

"Well, let's keep showing her how it happened," I said. "See yourself again at the hospital where you went for infertility treatments. Can you see her there?"

"Yes," she responded.

"Point to where you feel something in your body," I told her.

Mary Beth again pointed to her stomach, heart, and throat area. "It really aches," she said.

"Bring your 43-year-old-self to her again," I coached, "And tell her that she has two beautiful children now. Take her to the peaceful place."

When Mary Beth acknowledged that she and her younger-self were in the peaceful place I continued, "Explain to her how things worked out." Mary Beth was silent for a few minutes, explaining the circumstances to her younger-self. She and her husband were at the birth for both of their adopted children. They loved their babies from the moment they were born. The 28-year-old was astounded to hear the stories of her children's births. After a few minutes I led Mary Beth through her timeline again. Her cue sheet contained many memories with their children. Some of her cues were, "taking the kids to Disneyland for the first time," "vacation at a family camp," "Janet's first day of kindergarten," and "Chase getting stitches and shopping with Janet for a prom dress."

When she brought her younger-self into their home again, Mary Beth said, "This is the same house we lived in when we were struggling to get pregnant. Now it's filled with teenager stuff. I'm showing her around again. I'm showing her the kids' rooms. She loves it. She's so happy about all this."

Once again I queried, "And she didn't know you had babies and had been parenting for 15 years?"

"No, she had no idea! That's kind of weird. She likes it, though," Mary Beth answered.

I acknowledged, "Yes, it is kind of weird, but this happens all the time, over and over. The younger-self doesn't know what the older-self knows. That's why this works. We get them connected through the timelines and things change."

I guided Mary Beth back to the image of the hospital and infertility treatments. "When you see her there now, tell her that she does get to have some wonderful babies,"

"She's beginning to believe it," Mary Beth replied.

"Take her to the peaceful place and explain how it happened. Tell her that Rachel selected you out of all the parents she could have chosen to love Janet and Chase. Let her know that you were at their births and you've been their mommy from the moment they were born."

"She didn't know any of this," Mary Beth said incredulously.

"Let's show her the timeline again," I guided.

In the present home, Mary Beth imagined that her younger-self joined them at the table for a family dinner, participating in the conversation and laughter. "She loves this!" Mary Beth said. "She wanted nothing more than to be a mom and she is one."

"Is she beginning to understand that she is the same person you are?" I asked.

"Yes, she's beginning to get it. My stomach is relaxing and I don't feel the same tightness in my heart and throat," Mary Beth replied.

"Let's go through the pictures again while everyone is eating and talking at the table," I said. Beginning with age 29, I led Mary Beth through her timeline again while she imagined they were both in the present. This is an optional, adaptation of Standard Protocol. When we finished the timeline, I asked, "What's happening now? Is everyone still at the table?"

"No, the kids are showing her their rooms and stuff. She's interested in everything about them," Mary Beth answered. Then she added, "I was a really good mom. I've had a great relationship with my kids. We really love each other and have had a lot of fun as a family." I validated her because I perceived Mary Beth to be a conscientious and involved parent. "Janet and I have been close. We've had a good relationship over the years." Mary Beth said.

"See your 28-year-old self at the hospital again," I instructed. "What do you get now?"

"I think she understands that even though infertility was hard, we have a good family," was Mary Beth's reply. Her remark indicated that the first phase of LI standard protocol was accomplished because her younger-self understood that her hard circumstance was over.

In Mary Beth's case, since her younger-self was beginning to understand that she was part of a family with two teenagers in it, I guided her into the second phase by having her adult-self express anger on behalf of the 28-year-old. Some very hurtful words had been said to Mary Beth and her husband throughout the two years in which they struggled with infertility. "Where do you need to express anger?" I asked Mary Beth when she and the 28-year-old were in the present.

"To the people who said it was God's will for every woman to have a baby if she wanted one," Mary Beth answered.

"I trust you know where to find these people in the memory?" I asked.

"Yes," she replied.

I guided Mary Beth to imagine her adult-self entering the situation where she heard the hurtful remarks. "Do you know what you would like to say or would you like my coaching?" I asked.

"I would like your coaching," Mary Beth answered.

Here again we find the importance of attunement to the client. I needed to generate truthful phrases for Mary Beth to say to her offenders, while keeping in mind her perspectives and values. If a therapist proposes words or interventions that are not in keeping with the client's truth, the client will generally push back—though some things need to be stated even if they are not in the client's frame of reference. In Mary Beth's case I encouraged her to express anger, not forgiveness, toward her offenders. Later, after resolution is complete for clients through the LI timelines, they may wish to express more compassionate sentiments toward their offenders. For the purpose of healing, Mary Beth needed to express and integrate the hurt and anger she felt when others made well-meaning, but inappropriate remarks. After the older adult expressed anger on behalf of the 28-year-old, I led her through another repetition of her timeline. With the younger-self in the present, Mary Beth said, "Wow, that feels really good. Have I been holding this for 15 years?"

"Yes, you have," I answered. Returning her to the memory scene, I asked, "Who else do you need to speak to?"

"My husband," Mary Beth answered. "I said some rather unkind things to him in those years. I was distraught and angry. I would like to go back and say I'm sorry."

"Do you need my help?" I questioned.

"No, I can do this one," she replied. Mary Beth closed her eyes and took a few minutes to speak to her husband in her imagination.

When it appeared she was done speaking, I said, "Ready for the timeline?" She nodded. When the adult and 28-year-old were in the present I asked if the younger Mary Beth understood that she was the same person as the older Mary Beth.

"Yes," she answered.

"When you think about the infertility years, and see yourself at 28 going for treatments, what do you get in your body now?" I inquired.

"Nothing. It feels fine," responded Mary Beth.

"Are your gut, heart, and throat okay?" I asked.

"Nothing feels distressing there"

"Is anything upsetting in the memory when you think of it now?" I questioned.

Mary Beth reflected and quietly said, "That was a really hard time for me. I thought I must have jinxed myself or not been good enough to get pregnant. Now I understand it was a biological issue that nothing could have changed. And look, now I have these amazing teenagers!"

The check list for knowing a Standard Protocol session is complete when there is:

1) No distress when the client remembers the scene without the adult present,

2) The body scan is clear, and

3) The younger-self understands she is the same person as the adult and lives in current time with the adult-self. Mary Beth met all these criteria.

"Could you imagine that your younger-self merges into you in your present home?" I asked.

Mary Beth closed her eyes and imagined that the 28-year-old was melting into her 43-year-old self as she sat in the living room watching TV with her children. She was peaceful and quiet when she opened her eyes. "I was afraid of losing my children as toddlers," she said. "I was afraid that when they reached independence they wouldn't choose me. Now I see that we are very attached to one another and this is normal teenage stuff we are going through."

I agreed. Mary Beth continued, "It's unbelievable that my 28-year-old didn't know I had children. How is that possible?"

I reassured Mary Beth that it was normal for younger selves not to know anything about older aspects of their lives. I told her that this repeated itself in every LI session. The transformation with LI comes through integrating younger states into the current adult-self. In this way, younger-selves get to release everything they are holding and let an older-self solve the problems.

"It feels better doesn't it?" I asked Mary Beth.

"It's unbelievable," she said again.

Mary Beth came to the next session and said, "Since last week, I've been able to roll with the kids' rejection of me. I'm not completely impervious, but it's much less of a crisis for me." By integrating Mary Beth's distress about not getting pregnant, she felt more empowered to weather the moods and rejections of her adolescent daughter. Riding the waves of adolescence with Janet and Chase wasn't the same problem as struggling to become pregnant. Mary Beth remembered the infertility problem through the affect bridge because it had a similar emotional tone to her current concern of losing the daughter she loved. Mary Beth's distress about not having children fueled her heightened sensitivity of Janet's rejection. After the early memory was integrated, Mary Beth was able to respond to her daughter's age-appropriate separation without the added angst of losing her toddlers. Mary Beth's children were securely attached to her and appeared to be going through normal adolescent separation and independence.

When the work of LI was finished for the session, I talked with Mary Beth about some parenting strategies. This conversation could not have been absorbed by Mary Beth if she had still been reacting from the struggling 28-year-old. For this reason, we use LI to resolve underlying stressors first so clients can solve their current problems with age-appropriate maturity.

In reviewing Mary Beth's case according to the four-phase

guideline for Standard Protocol LI, the initial timeline repetitions were about proving the infertility years of her life were over and integrating the emotional distress held in her body from those years. As Mary Beth aptly stated, the 28-year-old had no idea she had grown up to be 43 years old. The second phase of Mary Beth's session was about the adult expressing anger to those who hurt her. The third phase consisted of the 28-year-old speaking to whomever she wished in the memory scene, via her imagination. Mary Beth chose to respond with kindness, instead of anger, to her husband. We did not need the fourth repair phase for this session because Mary Beth's body naturally integrated the truth that she had children and was present at their births. Once again, every LI session is different and needs to evolve in response to the client's neural networks.

Financial Issues

Jay, a 53-year-old man, struggled for several years with financial stresses. He was a hard-working contractor whose work was somewhat seasonal. Although Jay had income throughout the year, he became very anxious three to four times a year fearing he would not have enough money to meet expenses. Jay's income had risen throughout the years, but he was not able to change the emotional tone regarding his finances. A high level of anxiety was normal for Jay, which he attributed to his career choice. His family however, was affected by his anxiety and was eager to see a change.

To begin Lifespan Integration, I asked Jay to describe his problem with finances. Jay was baffled by the financial problems because he was confident that he wanted to be financially successful. In his way of thinking, circumstances outside of his control were the problem in his financial situation. Once Jay described the presenting issue, I asked him to point to the place in his core where he felt something associated with the problem he had just described. Following the affect bridge, Jay remembered a time when he was a young boy working on a model airplane in the basement of his home. "Our home wasn't a very happy place for me," he commented when he first saw his younger-self in the basement.

"Bring your adult-self into the scene," I coached.

"I can see myself with him in the basement, near the washing machine and clothesline. He's working on the model and doesn't really acknowledge me," Jay explained.

"Tell him that you are his grown-up-self and you have come down to help him. Will he go to a peaceful place with you or does he prefer to stay there?" I inquired.

"He wants to stay there, working on the model."

"Okay, tell him you are his grown-up-self. He can keep working on his model while we go through the pictures that prove he grew up to be you," I instructed. Since the little boy in the basement was seven years old, I read Jay's cue sheet beginning at age eight. After each cue, I waited until Jay—the adult sitting in my office in front of me—acknowledged each memory. We proceeded through the timeline up to his current age of 53. "Bring him into your current home," I prompted, "and show him where you live now. Ask him if he has any questions."

Jay relayed to me that his younger-self did not believe he lived in the present home with Jay. "He thinks he still lives with his parents where finances are very tight. My parents were constantly talking about the depression era and how tight things were financially. It makes me mad. We always had enough money for everything, but they acted like we would never have enough."

Seeing the emotional charge in his body, I asked Jay to return to the memory scene of the little boy in the basement. "Point to the place you feel something in your core when you see this memory," I instructed.

Jay pointed to his gut, and seeing the boy in the basement he said, "The little boy is mad. That's why he's ignoring me. He's lonely and he's mad. He's down in the basement because he doesn't want to hear his parents talking about money the way they do. He's sick of it."

"Bring your adult-self into the scene," I said. "Tell him you understand why he's upset. It's okay to be mad about all the times your parents said they didn't have enough money. Tell him you are going to go upstairs and express anger for him."

"That makes him feel better," Jay replied.

"Does the little boy want to go with you or stay in the basement?" I asked.

"Stay in the basement," he answered.

"Do you know what you want to say to your parents on his behalf?" I questioned.

"Yes, I do," Jay answered authoritatively. The adult Jay went upstairs. I gave him permission to yell at his parents and tell them how they were hurting his child-self. Jay followed my directions. After he yelled at his parents, he said to me, "The fear about money was always worse than the actual condition. My parents were endlessly talking about doom and gloom. No wonder I'm discouraged!" I guided Jay back to his younger-self in the basement to show him the pictures again about how he grew up to be the adult Jay. In his current home, Jay reported that his younger-self felt relieved to know he didn't have to live in his parent's home anymore. He also liked seeing the sports equipment Jay's sons played with in their backyard.

"Tell him it's your plan to always have enough money to take care of him. He doesn't have to worry about money anymore. Everything about money is your job," I coached.

After the internal conversation, Jay released a large sigh. "That feels so much better," he said. In the current home I asked Jay if his child-self would like to say something to his parents. "I'm not sure," he answered. When we returned to the basement for the third time, the little boy was still involved in his project at the worktable but was glad to have the company of his grown-up. He was pleased that his older-self had stood up to his parents for him.

"With you by his side, is there anything he would like to go upstairs and say to them?" I asked.

"Yes, he would like to tell them that it's really boring here and he would like to do what other kids do. He's mad that he can't spend the night with his friends or go places with their families. He wants to be like other kids," Jay shared.

"Take him upstairs and give him a chance to say these things," I guided.

Jay imagined that he stood near the child while the little boy expressed anger to his parents. "He wasn't even allowed to climb a low tree in the yard," Jay told me in anger.

"Did the little boy say what he wanted to say to his parents?" I asked

"Yes," Jay said.

"Now take him out to the yard and let him climb the tree. Lift him up if he needs help. Stand by and enjoy him in the tree," I said. "Your parents can watch from the window and there is nothing they can do about it. You are there to decide what he can and can-not do," I said.

"He loves it," Jay responded.

"Let's show him the pictures while he's in the tree," I suggested and I read Jay's cue sheet to him.

When Jay entered the basement for the fifth time he said, "My younger-self is a bit shy but he wants me to like him." I was trying to figure out the relationship between Jay's child-self in the base-ment and his current financial distress. Jay arrived at the basement memory through an affect bridge, which meant that something about this memory was connected to his current financial problem. I was having trouble deciphering the connection between these two, but the goal of attunement guided me to move in the direction of the child's need as presented.

A phrase I often repeat at the Beginning Level LI training is, "If you don't know what to do, do a timeline." Something always changes as a result of another timeline. I followed my own advice in this case and asked Jay to tell his younger-self how great it was to be with him.

"He loves my attention," Jay reported.

"Does that communicate how likable he is?" I asked.

"Yes, he's thirsty for this kind of attention," Jay said. We followed with a timeline. By the seventh time we entered the basement, Jay's younger-self was feeling better. He was still somewhat frightened that his family would not have enough money for food or clothing based on the conversations he overheard from his parents.

"Tell him that you're in charge of money now because you are his grown-up. Things are very different from when he was a little boy. Tell him you make enough now to take care of your family and your business." Jay told me the little boy was very interested in the timeline.

At the end of the timeline, Jay relayed the child's perspective on current finances. "He likes what he hears about me making enough money. His parents were raised in the depression and they were always talking about not having enough money. Everything was tight and I hated it."

"Tell him he doesn't live with his parents anymore," I said, "He lives with you and you can have plenty of money. Tell him the depression is over and he doesn't have to live like that anymore. Tell him it's okay now to have more than enough money."

"He doesn't believe me. He only believes his parents," Jay informed me. I suspected the adult client didn't believe me either. He and the younger ego state were one person so it is understandable that they would think alike.

"That's okay," I politely countered. "Ask him to watch the pictures." All resistance is best countered with the timeline. Trying to convince a younger ego state of the truth is useless without the timeline. Occasionally a self-state will refuse to watch the pictures. Proceeding with the timeline will still impact the younger child. Jay saw his younger-self building a model at the workbench again while we went through another timeline using every other cue on his sheet beginning with age 25.

When we returned to the basement after the seventh timeline, the adult client approached the little boy. "He would like my help with the model he's making like my grandfather helped me. I'm going to help him do what he can't do by himself." This interaction represented the repair phase of Standard Protocol LI.

"Bring something out that you purchased for him. Show him that you have enough money to meet his needs. Do you know what you should offer him?" I asked.

"Yes, building models would be a lot easier with a Dremel tool," Jay said.

"Show him that you have one just for him. Bring the tool and show him how to use it," I instructed.

"He's thrilled," Jay told me. "He's really happy that he didn't have to wait for Christmas or his birthday to get something he really wanted."

"Tell him you can provide everything he needs. Does he know how to use the Dremel tool?" I asked.

"He's pretty sure he can do it, but I'm helping him," Jay replied.

"While you're doing that," I proposed, "ask him why it's better to not have enough money—to think like your parents."

Jay was quiet for a bit, interacting with the little boy, then reported the situation, which he knew firsthand. He said, "My mother and her brother were both raised in the depression. Her brother became a businessman and a millionaire. Uncle Frank bought a new Cadillac every year, which I admired every time they came to our home. Whenever I commented about Uncle Frank and his lifestyle, Mom chided me and said 'We don't need those things.' I sensed an air of superiority from her as if it were actually better to be financially strapped than to live like Uncle Frank. As I grew up, I wanted to live like Uncle Frank but I sensed my mother disapproved."

In time, via many repetitions of his cue sheet, Jay had discovered and revealed to me the connection between his source memory and his current financial struggles. The little boy in the basement was aligned with his mother and her belief system. When Jay's adult-self got too far ahead financially, this young ego state took him back to loyalty to his mother. Jay had previously described his earning pattern alternating between the gas pedal and brake. I sensed that whenever he got a little bit ahead monetarily, he backed off on his production until the finances dipped.

At the end of the eighth timeline, when Jay had his child-self in the present, I said, "Ask the little boy if he would like it to be different now since he lives with you and you are grown up like Uncle Frank? Tell him that you don't live with Mom anymore and you can make as much money as you want without upsetting her. Tell him you own a business, too, and you would like to be success-ful—so successful that you don't need to worry about money." Jay expressed these ideas to his internal little boy-self and we showed him another timeline of how he grew up to be the adult. The images from the timeline began to change to more positive images of Jay's life, an indicator that integration was taking place.

In our final visit with the boy in the basement, Jay assured him that the adult-self was equipped to handle everything about money and that the little boy did not need to worry about it at all. Jay began to appear more centered in his adult-self rather than his child ego state. The little boy wanted to concentrate more on his model-building and other interests and was happy to surrender the financial issues to his adult-self.

After the tenth timeline, Jay asked the little boy what he wanted to do for fun in the present. The seven-year-old said, "I want to go on a trip." Jay had made vacation suggestions as a little boy, but his mother always countered saying his suggestions were too expensive.

Jay liked to travel and asked his younger-self, "What trip would you like to take? We can go anywhere." The little boy was thrilled and suggested they go to a friend's cabin in the Adirondack Mountains of upstate New York.

"Take him there. Spend some money on your trip. Show him that you can afford things that are important to him," I coached.

"We're going to fly to New York and I'm going to rent a car at the airport. It's going to be a cool car," Jay said.

Through his imagination, Jay and his younger-self traveled to the friend's cabin. They canoed, hiked, and played in the mountains. When Jay put the little boy to bed at the end of a magical day, I said, "Tell him you can always provide experiences like this for him. You are his grown-up and you want him to be happy. You have plenty of money to take him on trips." We followed with the eleventh repetition of his timeline.

At this point, the little boy from the basement believed he was the same person as the adult Jay. After one of the timeline sequences, Jay had shown him that he had the boy's dremel tool in his current garage. "See, you live here with me," Jay said. The boy believed him.

This case evidences all four phases of Standard Protocol Lifespan Integration. We proved that the lonely and angry child's distress was over, the adult expressed anger on behalf of the child, the younger child was given an opportunity to express his feelings toward his parents, and three positive repair scenarios were enacted in Jay's imagination between his child- and adult-self.

It is important to note that we did not imagine scenes in which Jay's parents were different than they actually were. With LI, we do not change the facts about clients' childhood experiences. Instead, we create opportunities between the child-self and adult-self so the child can receive what he or she needed.

We were finished with the session when there was no emotional or bodily distress for Jay's younger-self in the basement without the adult present, and the child understood he was living in present time with the adult Jay. The two symbolically merged in Jay's home. Jay's session took 90 minutes and involved eleven timeline repetitions. Most Standard Protocol sessions require 5 to 15 repetitions of a client's timeline intermixed with appropriate interventions. A month after this session, Jay reported that things were looking up financially for him. He came to a few more sessions over the next year and reported an overall improvement with his finances.

Internal beliefs play a major role in the quality of our lives. Jay's belief, which he initially denied, aligned with his mother's attitude towards money. What Jay learned over the years about money became incorporated into his internal belief system and neural networks. Unbeknownst to Jay, a child ego state in his self-system was dutifully operating to maintain family loyalty—a very powerful motivator for a child. When the child-self understood how Jay had grown up, he was willing to relinquish his parents' perspective, which he did not like in the first place.

The adult Jay was baffled in the beginning of our work and thought his financial stresses were completely outside of his control. It is true that finances were out of Jay's control as a child. The inner child's perspective was manifesting through the adult. After the child's restrictive view—which had evolved during his younger years—was integrated within the greater adult self-system, Jay was able to create a different reality for himself.

Humans are a composite of their life experiences. When Jay, and Mary Beth from the previous case study, were freed to approach their situations with more adult thinking, they self-generated empowered solutions to their problems. Such is the gift of Lifespan Integration. Joining neural networks that developed in childhood with more empowered adult thinking creates long-lasting change for clients.

To see a client come in angry, detached, and wanting to damage her tender side (she wanted to throw her imaginary baby-self), then to transform into tender, full and abundant life—free from damaging relationship styles—has been fabulous for the client and myself. This particular client referred four of her friends to me for therapy because it was fabulous for her.

Genevieve Rideout, LI therapist

4. Birth-to-Present Protocol (BP)

When using her new method, Pace discovered that most clients were rapidly changing through the Standard Protocol of Lifespan Integration. Yet Pace also noticed that some clients had difficulty compiling their list of memories because they remembered so little of childhood or every memory brought a high degree of distress. It became apparent to Pace that some clients needed a soothing, overall integration process to help them before they could use Standard Protocol or other LI methods. In response to this need, she developed the Birth-to-Present (BP) protocol which is a prescribed way of leading clients through their lifetime from the day they were born to the present. It does not begin with a specific target or source memory as in Standard Protocol. Instead, the counselor guides the client through imagery based on the known details of the client's birth, followed by the timeline, and ending in the present with the client's current age.

Joan's Story

Joan's story is a brief introduction to the Birth-to-Present process. Joan came for therapy to resolve the trauma of having her house burglarized when she was at home. After a few sessions, her distress about the burglary was completely gone but it became apparent that Joan lacked a positive sense of self even though she was highly educated and successful. She was born to an 18-year-old high school girl who was forced to marry her high school boyfriend—Joan's biological father. "I never felt wanted," Joan reported. The emotional atmosphere of her childhood home supported Joan's internal belief that she was nothing but an annoyance with whom her mother had to cope.

To repair Joan's early emotional distress, and build in the capacity for self-soothing, I guided her through the Birth-to-Present protocol. Initially, we imagined that I was holding Joan's baby-self in the imaginary scenes of being born, bathed, and taken to a safe and peaceful place. To make the experience real, I asked Joan to open her eyes and observe me actually holding a baby doll about the size of a newborn infant in my arms. I said aloud to the baby, "It is wonderful that you are here. You are perfect and special. You belong in the world and grown-ups will now make sure you are safe and loved." We followed with Joan's written timeline and repeated the exercise until our session was complete. After three sessions of the Birth-to-Present protocol in which I held the doll and spoke to Joan's imaginary baby-self, she said, "This is the most profound thing I have ever experienced in therapy. If you as a baby know someone takes delight in you, the world is a different place. It is invaluable to know someone sees the light in you!"

As I held the baby doll and affirmed Joan's worth, she created a positive feeling state inside herself which we integrated through the timeline. Through BP, the feeling state became an internal resource which could always, and automatically, be accessed by Joan. Because it was within her, the new state was not dependent on me as the therapist. Joan left my office with a more positive self-state inside herself, which became part of her ongoing, internal resources.

I find it interesting that Joan considered the experiences through the Birth-to-Present protocol more significant than resolving her trauma from the burglary. The burglary was very dangerous for her, yet once it was resolved, the impact of seeing herself as a valuable and lovable baby was more outstanding. The impact of LI on Joan's life is typical of the profound effect we observe when clients experience BP.

Not all clients need the repair from the Birth-to-Present protocol. Some clients were securely attached to their caregivers and are able to form healthy intimate relationships in their adult lives. Yet others, like Joan, find their worlds dramatically changed by multiple sessions of the Birth-to-Present protocol.

As mentioned in Chapter Two, science now tells us that the brain cannot distinguish between a real or imagined experience. As Joan's story portrays, in BP we guide a client to imagine his or her baby-self being soothed and connected to an important adult, which causes neurons to fire and load the imaginary experience into the brain. The counselor then guides the client to integrate the positive new state through a repetition of the timeline. During a BP session the client sees and feels his or her baby-self being cared for and loved repeatedly. Each imaginary scene is followed by the client's timeline. Many sessions of the Birth-to-Present protocol appear to aid clients in constructing a more solid internal self. With this method an important foundation, which may have been missing from a client's childhood, can be rebuilt. Through the BP process, clients learn how it feels for a caring adult to respond to their needs and attune to their various feeling states. The infant within the client becomes soothed. Clients also experience the perspective of a grounded, coherent therapist guiding them through the exercise, and this solid, coherent state becomes a resource within the client as well. Positive states are created and integrated while difficult body-held memories are resolved.

Outcomes

The Birth-to-Present protocol has several overlapping outcomes for the client: soothing for earlier internal states, increased emotional regulation, overall integration, and the clearing of birth trauma.

These are the main outcomes we see when using BP, but there are secondary gains as well. Other challenging aspects of a client's life often spontaneously resolve simply through the BP process. Even though the change may seem unrelated to the birth experience, it is not unusual for a client to report that a negative situation or behavior is noticeably different after BP. Traumas which have occurred over a client's life may lose their impact simply from repetitions of BP. Anxiety symptoms fall away after BP even though anxiety may not have been targeted directly. We believe addiction recovery is enhanced through the BP process. Mate (2010), an expert on addiction wrote, "...there are two ways of promoting healthy brain development, and both are essential to the healing of addiction: by changing the external environment and by modifying the internal one" (p. 361). Birth-to-Present protocol supports addiction recovery because it appears to positively modify a patient's internal environment as Mate recommends.

Over ten months, Pace conducted nine Birth-to-Present protocol sessions with a client who weighed approximately 300 lbs. During the ten months she lost 50 pounds. Pace reported, "I am still working with her and she is still losing weight. She no longer has panic attacks and doesn't think much about food, nor does she dissociate when eating. It has been the consistency of BP that has brought these results." Pace's clinical experience endorses the findings of Mate (2010) that modifying the patient's internal environment is an essential element to healing addictions and other emotional issues.

The results from BP can be very profound for clients who missed important nurturing experiences or who experienced trauma as they came into the world. This method of Lifespan Integration gives us the tools to go back to the very beginning of life and repair what was missing or traumatic. As a result, clients become more emotionally stable and are able to process and resolve issues with which they may have struggled for a lifetime.

Self-Soothing and Emotional Regulation

Current research in the field of human attachment informs us that children learn to manage their emotions and develop a sense of self through the relationship to their caregivers. It is vital for children to experience parents soothing them, validating their presence, and keeping them safe. In the parent-child relationship, the child's brain formats its structures for self-soothing based on the parent's own ability to self-soothe. Just like children learn the native language of their parents by living in the home environment, they also learn the complexity of emotion through their caregivers. We are born with certain temperaments, but children learn to navigate the emotional world based on their parents' capacity to manage emotions. A parent who is able to accurately attune to his or her child helps the child learn that distress—and other reactive emotions—can be managed and soothed.

Children have a difficult time developing affect regulation and a positive sense of self when their environment includes trauma and abuse. A young brain dealing with chaos and violence is at a disadvantage for learning healthy, emotional self-management. Trauma decreases a child's capacity for developing emotional intelligence. If a parent or caregiver cannot create a safe environment, or manage his or her own emotional world without violence, the child will not receive the necessary tools to internally manage his or her world.

Emotional regulation is recognizing and appropriately managing one's emotional states. Some people reach adulthood highly capable of responding to the internal and external emotional world. Yet as Lifespan Integration developed, it became apparent that many individuals needed help developing greater capacities for emotional regulation. Some clients found themselves being emotionally high, low, and states in-between within a matter of hours or minutes. They observed the emotional roller coaster they were on, but could not change it. The methods of BP increase a client's ability to regulate emotion. Clients also report that the Birth-to-Present protocol of LI brings down the automatic swings observed in Bipolar Disorder, which will be covered in Chapter Ten. Emotional regulation is important for every stage of life and many people benefit from building a more resilient internal system through repetitions of BP.

One new client came to therapy when her husband was facing a severe, potentially terminal, cancer diagnosis. The best treatment I could offer her was the Birth-to-Present protocol of LI. She said it calmed her down unlike any other resource in her life, and helped her understand that she had a life within herself from which she could draw strength to survive whatever the future held. With all the medical appointments, household responsibilities, and her own work to manage, the client prioritized coming to our appointments because the BP process created a deeper connectivity to herself. She concluded most sessions with a phrase like, "Wow, I feel really different than when I came in here! Thank you. I think I can go on now." The work accomplished through BP strengthened her own internal structure, which made her a stronger resource for her husband's cancer diagnosis and its ramifications.

Overall Integration

As mentioned, the Birth-to-Present protocol enhances overall integration, and as Siegel (2010) proposed, the overall functioning of any system is based on its level of integration. If an individual cannot remember large segments of his or her childhood, it means the individual's experiences, and thus memories, are not well integrated. The individual's overall sense of self is compartmentalized and he or she does not have sufficient internal connectivity between memories, feeling states, and actions. In this condition, a person may feel like an out of control observer to his or her own experience. This person may rage at a customer service employee, walk away, and ten minutes later wonder, *Where did that anger come from?* It may have come from a younger, unresolved ego state which got activated during the conversation and escalated during the exchange. LI integrates these younger aspects so that the adult can respond to the outside world without being hijacked by younger, frightened states within.

Another indicator of the need for overall integration is apparent when clients having difficulty recalling sections of their lives. These clients will have LI memory cue sheets with gaps of time where no cue can be recollected. When clients cannot recall years of their life, we know that aspects of those years are dissociated and need the overall integration of BP. Lack of overall integration also manifests when clients have some recall of their histories, but the details may be foggy and emotional aspects of events are missing or consistently overwhelming. In these cases, the stabilizing repair of the Birth-to-Present protocol helps individuals develop internal connectivity between their memories, feeling states, and current adult capacities. Repetitions of BP show these individuals that their lives happened to one person, over time, through many experiences. People are fragmented to varying degrees and many need the foundational rebuilding which appears to occur through the Birth-to-Present protocol.

Birth Trauma

Some people are born with Posttraumatic Stress Disorder (PTSD) which means they faced a serious birth circumstance in which they thought they would die. Ben, in the case study presented in Chapter Six, was stuck in the birth canal for several hours. When I used the Birth-to-Present protocol with Ben, he reported that his baby-self did not know he had lived through his birth. Ben's body was still holding the fear that he would die where he was trapped. When we completed enough repetitions of BP, his challenging behavior problems disappeared. Ben's mother did not know that birth trauma was the cause of the difficult behaviors, but Ben's emotional challenges were so hard to explain and manage that his mother brought him to therapy.

Birth trauma can be overlooked as the root issue because this type of trauma can erroneously appear as Attention Deficit Disorder (ADD), hyperactivity, and other difficult behaviors in children and adults. In contrast, clear connections can often be made between impairments adults and children exhibit after a known trauma. For example, a car accident may cause adults to fear driving. After sexual trauma, children become withdrawn and frightened, thus changing their normal behaviors. War trauma causes survivors to suffer impairments for many years after they have returned from war. Experiencing LI corrects all impairments listed in these various examples of 'known' traumas. Similarly, birth trauma has a myriad of implications that we are just beginning to recognize. Through Lifespan Integration we can also heal birth trauma and watch the road of life smooth out for children and adults. Even if birth trauma occurred but is not known, the thoughts, feelings, and symptoms associated with birth trauma can be healed through Lifespan Integration.

Advanced Applications

In the Advanced Level LI workshop, Pace teaches therapists tools for using adaptations of BP with clients diagnosed with Dissociated Identity Disorder (DID). What was formerly called Multiple Personality Disorder is now included in the spectrum of the DID diagnosis. Lifespan Integration is incredibly healing for clients with DID, although it may take many, many months for thorough integration to take place. At the advanced workshop, Pace shows DVDs of a client with DID who transforms into a fully functioning adult through many sessions of Birth-to-Present protocol over several years. Integration truly is mental health.

The advanced workshop also trains therapists in ways to help clients increase their ability for long lasting, meaningful relationships through the Attachment Repair protocol—a more developed application of the BP method. Although we have not researched this hypothesis yet, Pace suggested that a client's ability to form secure attachments can be increased through Lifespan Integration. Even though LI is just beginning to be researched, anecdotal evidence suggests that Pace is right. Clients repeatedly report better relationships and a higher capacity to manage themselves in stressful situations after LI sessions of the Birth-to-Present protocol. After BP, clients report an increase in ability to stay in relationships and function in healthy ways, rather than escalate, withdraw or become emotionally flooded.

Damon's Story

Damon traveled 300 miles round trip to experience Lifespan Integration with me because he heard about the power of this therapy from a family member. After our first session Damon was convinced about LI's effectiveness. Damon saw me for eleven sessions over nine months. At the beginning of our last session he said, "The deep sadness and grief I have been carrying around is 90 percent gone; only a sliver of grief remains." For our final session we targeted Damon's deep fear which he had identified was present from birth. By the end of the session we were able to clear Damon's remaining grief and conclude our therapeutic work together.

Damon's story encompasses several of the typical outcomes therapists see when using BP with clients. Damon needed help with emotional regulation, he was having trouble maintaining close relationships, he had severe trauma from his birth, and he needed the capacity for internal self-soothing. Damon had carried grief and sadness in his heart from the day he was born. He was a very likable, kind man who radiated love and compassion for others. Yet he described the ways in which his life was chaotic and filled with repeating patterns of self-destruction. With women Damon was passionate, distancing, volatile, dependent, and angry. His behavior in these relationships signaled the need to repair earlier attachments to people he loved in order to help him gain a greater capacity for managing his emotions in relationships. Thankfully, we can accomplish this much needed change through the Birth-to-Present protocol.

At the intake session, Damon described his growing up years starting at his birth. Damon was born with a grave medical problem and was transported immediately, and alone, via ambulance to another hospital for emergency surgery. The doctors predicted a 20 percent chance of his survival. Damon described his mother as non-nurturing, cold, and lacking in affection. He continued, saying, "My mother is strong, but also very weak and subservient. Her main requirement is that no one rocks the boat." The relationship Damon described with his mother played out in all of his romantic relationships. Over two decades Damon had received feedback from women that he was too dependent and needy, while also being too independent and overly sensitive at times. Damon said, "In relationships, when someone wants me, I step back; and when they step back, I move forward." He said that one woman told him, "You're too needy and you're constantly rejecting me." Damon continued, "I can be soothing and nurturing in relationships, but when I fall apart I want the woman to be there for me. But then I treat her disrespectfully. I'm angry at Mom for being so non-assertive, yet I was non-assertive when I dated Rebecca."

Damon was describing aspects of an insecure-avoidant attachment style with the women he loved. The foundation for this style was evident in Damon's birth and early years in which he was alone for life-saving surgery and not well nurtured by his primary caregiver—his mother. The rage Damon felt about his abandonment and unmet neediness from infancy was still active in his brain and acted as a template for his adult romantic relationships. It appeared that Damon's romantic relationship pattern closely followed his early life experience and could be summarized this way: "I need and want you, but I'm furious at you. Please stay and comfort me in my anger. If you distance from me I will feel abandoned because I need you desperately."

One of the areas Damon hoped to heal through therapy was

an obsession with his previous girlfriend. She had since begun a relationship with another man and refused to interact with Damon. Even though they had broken off the relationship one year previously, Damon pursued her and thought about her every day. He wrote her letters, sent emails, and phoned her. One day Damon appeared at his ex-girlfriend's door and she refused to let him in, saying, "I tried, but I just couldn't help you." In the Lifespan Integration model, in order to give Damon the changes he was seeking in his adult life, healing needed to occur where the injuries first took place—his birth and the infant years where neediness and dependency are developmentally appropriate. Damon had experienced other forms of therapy preceding LI. Although he gained insight into his relational patterns through other counseling, he had not been able to successfully change them.

I began the second LI session by guiding Damon into the Birth-to-Present protocol. I knew the details of Damon's traumatic birth: how he was expected to die; his lonely, frightening ambulance ride on the first day of life; and the days he spent alone in the neo-natal intensive care unit. To create a positive first-week-of-life experience that Damon missed, I guided him to imagine that I held his baby-self immediately after he was born and bathed him peacefully in warm water. While the imaginary baby Damon relaxed in the water as I carefully bathed him, I spoke loving words of affirmation and acceptance to him. After gently drying and dressing the baby, I held the baby and asked the adult Damon to guide the three of us to a peaceful place where we could comfortably be together. He chose a beach in the Caribbean. In the peaceful place I reassured the baby again, aloud, that he was valuable, precious, and very wanted. I promised baby Damon that he would live and grow up to be a good man. I commented on the warmth of the tropical air, the fragrances he could smell, and the sound of the birds flying overhead.

"How is the baby doing?" I asked Damon.

"He is very, very afraid. I'm totally tense right now. Everything in my body is tight. I can feel the fear right now, right here," Damon told me, pointing to his chest and stomach. His body was connecting to the implicit memory from his first few days of life.

"What happened then is over," I promised him. "We are going to show your baby-self what really happened and how he grew up to be you." I began the timeline with the details of his actual birth and paused to make sure Damon was imagining the events as I mentioned them, such as, "Your mother is afraid. There's no time for her to hold you and you are whisked away to a waiting ambulance."

"I've got it," Damon replied. We continued through Damon's surgery, the four weeks in the hospital following surgery, and an experimental treatment. The day of the treatment the administering doctor recommended that Damon's parents begin funeral arrangements for their son. He did not anticipate that Damon would survive the night. When the doctor came the following morning to check on his young patient, he was shocked to discover that Damon was alive and growing stronger. Damon's thoughts, feelings, and sensations from his birth trauma were all loaded into the young neural networks of his brain. They became the foundational layer for his experience in the world.

We continued through Damon's timeline. After several cues, I asked Damon to imagine the peaceful place again where I soothed the baby through touch, and reminded him to feel the air on his baby skin, hear the birds, listen to the waves, and so on. I spoke loving words about his safety and value before returning to the cue in Damon's timeline where we had paused momentarily in order to reconnect with his baby-self in the peaceful place.

The adult Damon cried throughout the timeline. At the end of the timeline I guided him to visualize taking us into his current home while I continued to hold the baby in my arms. Afterwards we took a break and Damon said, "In the beginning of the timeline I was so powerless. I felt panic in my gut when you said the cues about birth. Later I felt angry. I was dependent and my mom was not nurturing. The baby looked grotesque."

It is not uncommon for adults to feel rejectment toward their infant-selves and see them like monsters. When clients have been neglected or abused, they dissociate from the infant's distress and hate the infant for what he or she is holding. They may view the infant as an ugly being rather than a real baby. For several sessions of BP, a dissociated client may hate the baby and encourage the therapist to hurt or abandon the infant also. For this reason, it is imperative for the therapist to hold the baby during BP sessions so the client can absorb and integrate the positive feeling states which are created through the therapist's care and attunement to the infant. When the client has progressed to truly loving his or her baby-self through many repetitions of the timeline the client may hold the infant during the BP process. When clients truly love their infant-selves, it is a signal that they may not need the Birth-to-Present protocol any longer and the therapist can move on to attachment repair, or other LI protocols.

Damon's description of the baby's grotesque appearance indicated a detachment from his actual internal baby-self and informed me that I needed to be the loving caretaker of the new baby for several more sessions. We repeated the BP process three more times, exactly as previously described, and Damon silently wept through each repetition.

Two weeks later, at the beginning of the third session, Damon said, "Since we met I have been sleeping better. I'm more relaxed and I'm noticeably more optimistic. I was really lost for a year, but now I can see myself getting back on track." Damon was referring to his current adult life but I heard these words in the context of his infant-self. "Sleeping better," "more relaxed," "getting back on track," and "more optimistic about life" are all outcomes for an infant who thought he was on the verge of dying but discovered, through integration, that he made it through his near-death ordeal. Damon's entire self was more optimistic because he was beginning to understand on a cellular level that he was no longer in danger of dying. His body was beginning to understand that his trauma had passed. Damon also reported that his obsession for his ex-girlfriend had noticeably decreased. One session of BP reduced his longing for a woman he could not have, which would be very similar to the feelings of a distressed infant who could not be with his mother. Resolving the newborn distress appeared to have a direct, diminishing effect on Damon's urge to get his former girlfriend to re-engage with him.

Damon also spoke more about his relationship challenges at the beginning of our third session. He said he wanted to be more comfortable with himself and more accepting of the women he dated. He categorized himself as perfectionistic, which translated into high self-standards and an overly-critical view of others. "I want to be with someone perfect," he summarized. Damon's perspective belied a childlike, naïve, and unrealistic hope for a female relationship. I guessed he was still trying to find the ever-present, ideal mother figure, but I did not share my thoughts with him. Analysis is not a component of LI. We do not need to psychoanalyze clients because their bodies hold their issues and we can use LI to resolve whatever their bodies are holding.

I used the BP protocol for the focus of the third session. Once again I asked Damon to imagine that I was present at his birth, received his baby-self from the doctor, and lovingly soothed and bathed him. We went again to the imaginary peaceful place where I continued looking into baby Damon's eyes and told him that he was perfect and special. To show the infant the timeline, I began with the events of his birth as they actually occurred, including the frightening ride in the ambulance, surgery, and the plans for his funeral. Infants have the capacity to sense the mood and feelings of others around them, and Damon needed to integrate all the difficult experiences which he held in his body from birth. I intentionally included the most difficult parts of Damon's story. They were already loaded into his brain and body, and my goal was to help Damon integrate, rather than avoid, these distressing events. Approximately every ten cues I reminded Damon to see us together in the peaceful place as I held his infant-self, then we returned to the timeline until we reached the present. Damon showed us around his home again and we took a break. Apart from our opening conversation, our entire third session consisted of four repetitions of Damon's life from his birth to the present. Once again Damon cried throughout the process.

Four weeks later Damon described the changes he observed after two sessions of BP. He said, "The obsession about my previous girlfriend is holding at about 50 percent less and I'm happier than I have been in years. I notice that I feel less shame. My body image is better and I'm more comfortable being myself. I don't feel the need as often to put on a front or project something to people. I'm coming from a less fearful place." The repetitions of Birth-to-Present protocol were resolving his infant trauma and helping to build a more unified core from which Damon could be himself in the world.

We continued with BP for our fourth session. Damon said he was aware of shame connected with his infant-self. As we progressed through the steps of BP as previously described, I focused on attunement to Damon's infant-self. Lack of attunement exacerbates shame. *Attunement* means that one human being is attending with compassion to the needs, wants, and feeling states of another. I repeatedly assured Damon's infant-self that his adult-self and I were focused on him as a whole person, and that grown-ups in his current life, specifically the adult Damon, would be able to respond to his every need. He alone was the center of our focus, and we would make sure he felt cared for and safe. The tears Damon cried during session four were tender and different from the weeping of the previous sessions.

Damon traveled for a month before our next session. When asked how things were going he said, "I'm shocked. I'm handling things surprisingly well. I'm doing a personal cleansing and putting everything in my life in order. I've straightened up my finances, I've cleaned out boxes that have been closed for decades, and I'm giving away lots of unneeded stuff."

"Did you know that is related to the work we've been doing?" I asked.

"I thought it might be," he replied, "But it's weird. There is a very important project related to my business that I've put off for five years. During the last month I got my accountants working on it. I should have everything wrapped up within the month. And one more thing," Damon added with surprise, "the stuff about my old girlfriend is still fading. Instead of playing on high volume inside of me it's on very low volume. I might be willing to start dating again."

The outcomes Damon described meant that deep, internal changes were taking place inside him. The trauma Damon experienced at birth was clearly beginning to heal, but it had many layers and facets, all of which needed integration before our work would be finished. I guided Damon into the Birth-to-Present protocol again. After the first timeline in which I held the baby, Damon asked if he could hold his baby-self. For the second repetition of BP, after I guided him through the imagined birth, Damon received his newborn-self from the doctor and gently bathed him in warm water. After Damon dried and gently dressed the baby, I handed him the baby doll in my office. While physically holding the baby doll in his arms, with eyes closed, Damon took his imaginary baby-self to the peaceful place. I coached Damon to tell his baby-self that he is valuable and precious. At times Damon opened his eyes and gently caressed the baby. Tears slowly trickled down his cheeks. "Would you like to tell him that you love him?" I asked.

"I would," Damon replied.

"Tell him that he's safe now, and he made it through the trauma." After a pause, giving Damon time to repeat these words to his baby-self, I added, "Tell him he will never, ever be alone. You are his adult-self and will always take care of him. If anything frightening or lonely happens again, you, as his adult-self, will take care of it." Damon's shoulders noticeably relaxed with these words and he let out a sigh.

"That feels really good to my baby-self," Damon reported. "He was scared and everyone around him was scared. Knowing that he doesn't have to figure anything out really helps him."

"That's right. He doesn't have to figure anything out. You will always be with him to protect him. He can relax and do what babies do—needing people to love and pay attention to them. It's all about him," I affirmed. We proceeded through another timeline, after which Damon took his baby-self into his adult home. "How is he doing?" I asked.

"He's asleep. He's very peaceful. Those words about not having to figure anything out really helped him. He fell asleep as we were going through the timeline," Damon answered.

"Can you imagine holding him on your chest in a comfortable chair in your home while he sleeps?" I asked. Damon shifted his position in my office and lovingly placed the baby doll on his chest. With eyes closed, he sighed again. "Yes, we're resting in my recliner. He's breathing very peacefully," Damon replied.

"Notice what this feels like in your body," I said. Several minutes of silence passed as I let Damon take time to absorb the sensations of his baby-self sleeping peacefully in his care. To integrate the physical and emotional state Damon was experiencing in his home, I began another timeline and said, "While you're holding him in your recliner, I want you to imagine the day you were born. We're going to go through the timeline again as it actually occurred. It's okay that he's asleep. He will get the benefits of the timeline because you share the same brain." I mentioned every difficult experience on the timeline. At the end of the timeline I inquired again how his baby-self was doing in his home.

"His eyes are open. He's peaceful. He gets it. All that stuff is over. He knows that I'm going to take care of things," said Damon.

"What did you notice about the memories during the timeline?" I inquired.

"Some of them were the same, but others showed more self-sufficiency. Even though it's not on my timeline, when you mentioned moving to Virginia I thought about the thousand mile bike ride I took by myself. Other stuff like that came up, too," Damon answered.

"Like what?" I asked.

"Oh, other times when I was able to make really good choices or handle things well...more self-sufficiency in a good way. When I went to a new school I made friends easily. When I was 23 I started a business that became very successful. Stuff like that..." Damon replied. Because his imaginary baby-self was relaxed and trusting in Damon's arms, and the memories that arose during the time-line were shifting toward positive ones, I knew that a significant amount of integration had taken place. A final way to check the level of integration was to check Damon's experience of his body in the present.

"Do you remember where you felt something in your body when we first started doing BP? I asked."

"Definitely. I was tense all over, especially right here in my chest and gut," Damon said pointing to his core.

"What do you get in your body now when you think about your birth?" I asked. Damon, who was very body-aware, ran an internal scan.

"Not much. Just a little tension in my stomach, I guess," he said.

I asked Damon to focus on the area where he had pointed and I guided him through the Birth-to-Present protocol again. He held his imaginary baby-self as soon as the doctor delivered him and I gave Damon the baby doll after the infant-self was bathed and dressed. I directed Damon to take the baby to the peaceful place again, and I prompted him to say the loving words of reassurance and care. Damon spontaneously told the baby how much he loved him and how proud he was of the infant's strength for living. He had beaten the odds and survived, and Damon was grateful. Watching him through this exercise, I could feel his devotion and care for his infant-self. "Now we're going to show him the pictures again about he grew up to be you," I told Damon. I mentioned every traumatic aspect of his birth and the days that followed. The adult Damon appeared focused as I observed him. Sometimes his brow furrowed at certain memories, but he also looked peaceful. At the end of the timeline, when Damon and his baby self were in the adult's home, I inquired about the child.

"His eyes are open. He's awake. He's got it. During the last timeline, I felt a lot of warmth in my heart area," Damon told me.

"See if he could blend into you," I suggested. Damon's face had a peaceful smile. I waited quietly.

"As I'm holding him in the recliner he just melts into me. That was cool. He just went right into my chest," Damon said.

It is important to notice that I did not ask Damon to merge with his infant—self in the previous sessions. Until all the signs of integration are present, we do not ask clients to symbolically become one with the infant. For Damon, the signs of full integration were present: no distress when remembering his birth scenario, positive memories emerging during the timeline, a clear body-scan when remembering the traumatic birth, and the adult had genuine love for his baby-self. If Damon had not reported a genuine care and love for his infant-self we would have used the Birth-to-Present protocol again, with me holding Damon's imaginary baby-self and the baby doll, until the above outcomes were achieved.

Damon scheduled his next appointment for two months later. When he returned to my office he said, "Regarding my former girl-friend, I'm glad she's out of my head. I'm actually relieved we are not together." He mentioned some other difficult aspects of his life which we targeted with other LI protocols.

The Birth-to-Present protocol is the beginning of the LI process therapists can use to help clients repair what was missing from their childhoods. Pace discovered that we could remove trauma as well as help clients create positive internal states. Integration through the timeline appears to make these changes permanent.

Since Damon appropriately loved, and was able to merge with his infant-self, the next steps in his therapy required the Attachment Repair process for other early childhood ego states. The lack of attention and attunement during much of Damon's first three years of life meant that other developmental phases needed healing. It was vital to heal the trauma of Damon's brand new baby-self, but loneliness and disconnection were present at many points in his zero-to-three years. By using Attachment Repair, we were able to supply Damon with an even greater capacity to connect with others and respond to life with healthier, higher functioning ways.

Adoption

This book opened with Becky's story of healing from PTSD after surviving the 9/11 attack. In a handful of sessions, Becky was free from all the PTSD symptoms that had crippled her for five years. She summarized her experience by saying, "This therapy really works for me. Not only did I get my life back, but it opened the door to other healing." Becky was adopted at three years old and had never told anyone about her adoption. Her shame about being an adoptee from another country kept Becky from revealing this personal detail about herself. A year after her successful treatment from the 9/11 attack, Becky contacted me to heal the impact of being adopted.

During our treatment for the 9/11 PTSD, I led Becky through a few repetitions of the Birth-to-Present protocol to calm her whole system. During that time Becky had expressed feelings of sorrow, loss, anger, and shame about being separated from her family and country-of-origin at age three. The complicated circumstances of Becky's adoption left her afraid and unable to trust people in close relationships. Her adoptive parents divorced when Becky was 35. She said her initial gut response to their divorce was, "But who will take care of me?" which hearkened from the frightened three-year-old inside her. Later, Becky laughingly answered herself, "Oh, I guess I will." After Becky returned to Lifespan Integration to heal the heartache of her adoption, she answered her own question with the voice of her solid adult-self.

Since Becky came to the U.S. at three years old, she remembered aspects of her life before she was adopted. Becky maintained some connection with distant family, but had never met her birth mother from whom she was separated in the first few days of life. To heal her early years, we had many sessions of Birth-to-Present protocol and some sessions of Attachment Repair in which we created imaginary, healing scenes for Becky's inner child. Throughout the weeks of therapy focused on her adoption, Becky's self-confidence grew, she made positive changes to her living situation, and she entered into a long-term romantic relationship. In Becky's case, the work addressing her adoption and early trauma took eight sessions.

Several years after Lifespan Integration for her adoption, Becky said she was still in the long-term relationship which began after the therapy, and she was involved in a volunteer organization for adoptees from her country of origin. "Now everyone in my life knows I'm adopted," she said. "I don't know why I was so afraid of telling people before. When I talk about my story at adoption gatherings I seem to have more peace and resolution than most people there. I think all adopted people need this work." Of course I agreed with Becky.

Some clients need many, many sessions of BP in the beginning of their LI therapy. The power of this tool cannot be underestimated. Birth-to-Present protocol may erroneously appear as a simplistic method, but clients report monumental shifts inside themselves as a result of the process. Those internal shifts have proven to be positive and lasting changes.

The Aftermath of Birth-to-Present Protocol

Birth-to-Present protocol is very helpful to clients, but it may also be challenging for them. Metaphorically, it can be like reorganizing the garage by taking many things off the storage shelves at once. Temporarily, the shelf contents may be disorganized on the garage floor until time is allotted to get them reorganized. The reorganization creates a cleaner, more efficient system to access important items. Outdated items that have been stored in the garage for a long time can be evaluated with current perspectives to see if they are still needed for current life. We hypothesize that the BP process is similar to this garage-cleaning metaphor. Through repetitions of the timeline during BP, long-held contents of the brain are forced into connection with new memories. This process of self-reorganization and integration of new information takes time, just like a major room cleaning project takes time. Fortunately, when the brain is forced to reorganize, it always does so at a higher level. An individual can assess and assign meaning to all the contents viewed in the BP timeline and organize them into a meaningful, more accurate format.

The disorganizing and reorganizing of BP can leave clients feeling fuzzy in their heads, emotional, or very tired. I have known clients to sit in their cars for 45 minutes before driving away from the office. Highly dissociated clients may leave a session feeling extremely emotional and need someone else to drive them home. This is not the typical condition at the end of a session, but the Birth-to-Present method is a powerful change agent. Over time, as the new neural pathways are established and reinforced, the BP process becomes easier and the post-BP impact also decreases in severity. A light snack immediately after an LI session helps some clients feel better after the work. BP is a process that requires a good amount of brain fuel. Replacing that fuel immediately after the session can be helpful.

Birth-to-Present protocol is a foundational component of Lifespan Integration. Along with Standard Protocol, BP is taught at the Beginning Level workshop. Therapists who complete the beginning level training are equipped to use Standard Protocol and BP as the beginning of their LI work. Many therapists use the Birth-to-Present protocol early in therapy to introduce Lifespan Integration to clients, help them become stronger within themselves, and assess the client's need for birth healing, attachment repair, and levels of dissociation. As evidenced by Damon's story, many seemingly non-related aspects of a client's life can be positively healed by repetitions of the timeline from birth to the present.

In my practice, the biggest difference LI has made for me is with those folks who come for help with anxiety. Traditional treatment models are very painful or uncomfortable for clients with anxiety. With LI, in a few sessions, it's relief or full recovery.

Zandra Zimmerman, LI therapist

5. Anxiety

Three Root Causes of Anxiety

Pace conceptualized the source of anxiety into three categories: 1) birth trauma or early separation, 2) over-responsibility in childhood, and 3) specific, unresolved events in the client's life. Birth trauma and early, traumatic separations from the mother create distress in a client's young body which he or she carries throughout life into adulthood. As mentioned, humans are a composite of their experiences beginning in utero. As an infant forms in his or her mother's womb, the infant loads sensory and emotional material into his or her developing brain and body. This unconscious material can be triggered at any point without the client being able to locate a historical source of his or her distress. When we observe generalized anxiety occurring in a client's life, and the client cannot name a specific starting point for the distress, it is very likely that he or she had birth trauma or early, traumatic separation from the mother.

Generalized anxiety is consistently resolved with BP. A client's generalized anxiety tells a Lifespan Integration therapist that early trauma occurred for the client before conscious memory was formed. It is likely that the early trauma occurred during the birth experience or resulted from difficult separations from the parent early in life. Damon's story from the previous chapter is a clear and typical example of the resolution of generalized anxiety that occurs when clients experience the Birth-to-Present protocol with a coherent, emotionally solid therapist. The distress Damon experienced about his impending death and separation from his mother at birth never left his body until we completed many repetitions of his timeline from birth to his present-day life. It appears that we integrated the early distress through the tools available in LI.

Many clients know the stories of their birth separations and traumas. When we start the LI timeline at birth and follow the specific steps outlined in the Birth-to-Present protocol, we help create lasting resolution for clients' generalized anxiety. The same is true for separations that happen at a young age, such as an infant's surgery at ten weeks old. In such a case, we begin the LI process by asking the client to imagine being ten weeks old and going into the hospital for surgery. The neural networks holding the client's body-based memory will activate, which allows resolution to occur with imaginary interventions and repetitions of the client's timeline.

Over-responsibility in childhood is another source of anxiety for clients. This condition is not based on a single experience or set of memories which can be treated with Standard Protocol LI because it was the child's ongoing reality from which he or she could not get relief. Over-responsibility generally occurs through many years of a child's life and is characterized by powerlessness coupled with responsibility.

One anxious adult client told me of the time when she was required to watch her three-year-old sister and infant brother in the car while her mother shopped in the grocery store. The client was an eight-year-old at the time. When she protested about being left alone with the younger children, her mother slapped her and told her to stay in the car while she was gone. The adult client remembered that her mother was gone for a long time; although she admits the perspective of a child would make any amount of time seem lengthy. Eventually, the client's baby brother became restless and her three-year-old sister said she had to use the restroom. The eight-year-old decided to take her siblings into the store to find their mother. When she finally found her mother, the three-year-old had wet herself. The client's mother was enraged and yelled at the client. This is an example of a child having responsibility for a problem, but being in a double-bind when attempting to solve the problem.

A ten-year-old client described his anxiety, and in so doing explained that before he was adopted he was left in an apartment at night with two younger siblings while his drug-using birth parents went out. He said the three of them slept in one small bed and he was terrified that someone would come into the apartment and harm them. He had responsibility for the welfare of his younger siblings, but not enough resources to meet his and their needs. After his adoption, he had trouble sleeping, and was afraid to be separated from his parents at night.

Responsibility, coupled with powerlessness, creates an ongoing state of anxiety. This form of anxiety is also treated with the Birth-to-Present protocol of LI. As clients move through the steps of BP, their minds and bodies activate the neural networks holding the many incidences of over-responsibility and integrate them with timelines in the presence of a compassionate, grounded therapist.

The third type of anxiety Pace references is based on specific, remembered events and can be cleared with body-based, Standard Protocol or the PTSD protocol. This type of anxiety is differentiated from the others because clients remember not being anxious, and note that something changed and they became anxious. Often clients can name the source of their anxiety, but occasionally they cannot. In the following case, Cynthia was not anxious up to a certain point in her life and then began to be anxious. It took a handful of sessions to uncover the origins of Cynthia's distress, but since the body tells no lies, we were able to find and resolve all roots of her distress through an affect bridge and timelines. If Cynthia had been able to name a specific trauma we would have used the PTSD protocol, which is described in Chapter Six.

Unfriendly Skies

Cynthia was a regional sales manager for a small company that expected all employees at her level to travel a significant amount. Her company referred her for counseling because flight anxiety was interfering with her work and impacting her associates. Due to Cynthia's anxiety, other team members were shouldering her portion of out-of-town trips. Cynthia had become so anxious about flying that two to three days before a trip she would be unable to sleep, have diminished productivity at work, feel irritable at home, and consistently drink too much the night before flying. On the day of a scheduled flight, Cynthia regularly arrived at the airport three hours early, drank two glasses of wine while waiting to board, and took a prescription anti-anxiety medication right before take-off. She tried to be the last person to enter the plane, and once in her seat she could not read, sleep, or work during the flight. Twice Cynthia had major panic attacks in flight. I met with her seven times, using Lifespan Integration sessions.

In our first session, Cynthia could not recall exactly when or why the flying anxiety began. She guessed, "It started about five years ago, around the time our youngest son was born." Before that Cynthia could fly easily, completely free of anxiety. She remembered working and reading comfortably during former flights. She gave a personal history, a brief family history, and details about the worst and most frequent symptoms associated with her anxiety. In the last 15 minutes of our session, I used LI to target the worst flight anxiety episode Cynthia had experienced, which was five years earlier.

In the second session, we targeted Cynthia's guilt which was her predominant feeling associated with flying. Locating this in Cynthia's body, we floated back to a time when she was 12 years old and was forced to baby-sit, without any compensation, for her parents and their friends who often played tennis. She was angry and resentful at her parents' level of control which required not only that she baby-sit her siblings and the children of family friends, but she also had to attend church three or four times a week and regularly attend confession with a priest who yelled at her. Using Lifespan Integration we cleared the distress held by the 12-year-old ego state.

By session three, Cynthia could not identify any change in her flying anxiety but reported being noticeably calmer with her two children at home. Situations that normally caused her stress seemed much easier to handle. She found herself being more confident and at ease in her parenting. It is very common when using Lifespan Integration for the first positive outcome to be seemingly unrelated to the target issue. As mentioned previously, the client's mind-body system can be trusted to guide the process. The improvement in Cynthia's home life was the first noticeable, positive change from her therapy.

When I asked her to focus on her flying anxiety in the beginning of session three, Cynthia described herself as "stressed out like usual." I asked her to identify the worst part of flying and she named the morning routine of getting herself ready to go to the airport in the dark while her children slept. Cynthia hated the loneliness associated with leaving her family. I asked her to find this loneliness in her body and she pointed to her gut and upper chest area. "It's in my heart," she sighed. We floated the body sensation back to a 27-year-old Cynthia who was angry with herself for being afraid and not wanting to go on trips. Cynthia had a good job traveling but an introverted personality. When it came time for the 27-year-old to travel, she was torn between the comforts of her home with its weekly activities and the demands of her job. In the early years of her marriage, Cynthia and her husband hiked every weekend with their golden retriever. Since they did not have any children in those years, Cynthia's husband perceived her job as an opportunity for them to build financial security. He did not understand or sympathize with her distress about traveling and disregarded her feelings. Cynthia joined her husband in denying her feelings, which was a contributing component to her anxiety. During the repetitions of the timeline I coached her to validate, comfort, and encourage the 27-year-old until her distress regarding that time was over.

At session four, Cynthia reported that the outbound flight from the previous week was the best she had experienced in a long time. She had not used any prescription medication or alcohol before the flight. Cynthia admitted that she was, "a little bit antsy, with some anxiety," before flying, but not the usual, horrible longing to go home that she had previously experienced on her business trips. Before the return trip however, Cynthia argued with her husband over the phone, and during the flight she felt the "trapped" feeling associated with her airplane anxiety. We targeted the trapped, hopeless feeling, floating back to a two-year-old ego state who got in trouble with her highly controlling parents. We cleared this memory with LI. During the processing, Cynthia became aware of two other major episodes of feeling trapped in high school. When Cynthia's two-year-old-self was no longer in distress, we cleared the high school episodes with LI during the same session. One of these was an abortion, which Cynthia described as "the worst time in my life."

Due to Cynthia's work schedule, we were not able to meet for a month. At the fifth session, I asked Cynthia to check on the high school incidents. She replied, "I know I would handle that differently now, but I did the best I could at that time." She was calm and peaceful when remembering the high school situations. During the fifth session, Cynthia said she had recently gotten anxious at work when they started planning the management team's travel schedule. Targeting these anxious feelings, we floated back to an incident from elementary school. As Cynthia was walking to school, her older brother turned to her and said, "Today Mom is going to give our dog away." Cynthia ran home and found strangers with her mother, taking the dog. She loved the dog very much but the older brother tormented the dog until it bit him. Because of the biting,

Cynthia's mom made arrangements for the dog to be taken away. We processed this memory with LI. During the repetitions of the timeline, Cynthia exclaimed, "I remember when my flying anxiety began!" Once she entered the dog memory, Cynthia's brain made a connection to a repressed incident which was directly related to the flight anxiety. It's hypothesized that this occurred because the two memories had the same feeling tone and were separate, but connected, neural networks in Cynthia's brain.

Cynthia recalled one of the mornings she was traveling. After dropping her son at his day care, a shooting occurred in a government building within a block of the childcare center. The police barricaded the area. Due to security restrictions, parents were not able to retrieve their children from the facility until late evening. Cynthia learned of her son's situation when she was 1,200 miles away on the west coast. Cynthia's husband was not able to pick up their son until 10 pm. Alone in a hotel room, while her son was in a police barricade, Cynthia was distraught and anxious, fearing she might not see her son again. She tried to book a return flight after hearing the news of the shooting, but was unsuccessful in returning home that day. As the memory surfaced, Cynthia remembered working with ease on the outbound flight, but "being a wreck" on the trip home, which took place the day after the shooting.

Here again, we see the wisdom of trusting the emotions and body sensations to lead a client and therapist to the targets associated with anxiety. Losing her dog unexpectedly while innocently walking to school was similar in feeling tone to the possibility of Cynthia losing her child through a shooting while she traveled across the country. Resolving an old memory created the pathway to heal Cynthia's current distress. When Cynthia first described her flying anxiety, she did not remember the childcare incident, but guessed her anxiety began somewhere around the time her second son was born. This was quite true, but she was unable to find the root memory until healing of other memories took place.

Even though a significant memory emerged regarding her

son's danger at daycare, we continued processing the elementary school memory of the family dog being given away until there was no distress for the elementary-aged Cynthia. I assured her we would target the shooting incident next time. It is important to clear target memories once begun, even when more distressing memories surface, because the initial target memory will continue to be distressing until fully resolved through enough timelines. Even though we did not begin targeting the shooting story in the session where she remembered it, I suspected Cynthia would experience some relief in her distress by clearing the dog incident and identifying the underlying core feeling associated with flight anxiety.

For sessions six and seven, I used the LI PTSD protocol to target Cynthia's experience from the shooting. When we finished with session seven, Cynthia was looking forward to flying and was eager to schedule some trips for work. She occasionally won vacations through sales incentives, but Cynthia had not been able to use them because of her anxiety. Cynthia was anticipating the pleasure of taking her family on these free vacations. She concluded her therapy at that point, feeling confident that she could go back to flying with the same ease she experienced before the shooting incident.

Generalized Anxiety

Engaged to be married, Monica wanted to resolve her debilitating anxiety before her wedding. She was afraid to enter malls, be in large stores, drive over bridges, or be alone in public settings. Monica guessed that her anxiety began four years before coming to therapy when she was overseas. She did not remember being anxious before then. Monica thought her first panic attack occurred in a European hotel. Two months previous to the European trip, she had been with her family at a Jamaican resort when their suite was burglarized as they were sleeping.

We targeted the burglary with Standard Protocol Lifespan

Integration. I asked Monica to take her current, adult-self back to the memory of her younger-self asleep in the resort bedroom when a burglar quietly entered through the sliding glass door. Through repetitions of the timeline, I guided Monica to show her younger-self that she was now safe and living with the adult Monica in the present. As we moved through the timelines, fear for the younger ego state dissipated. After this session, Monica was able to enter a large warehouse store for the first time in three years, and she commented that her mom was noticing a difference in her.

At the next session, Monica recalled that her first panic attack had actually occurred prior to the burglary when her dog was diagnosed with cancer. It is common for additional information to surface as distressing memories are resolved. Monica remembered details from the day she received the news that her dog had a terminal diagnosis. She described the shock, devastation, and grief that accompanied the difficult news. I asked Monica to notice the feelings in her body associated with the news about her dog. Using the steps of Standard Protocol again, we resolved the distress of her younger-self holding these feelings. At the end of the repetitions of the timeline I asked Monica to imagine her younger-self in the present. Monica said she could imagine that her younger-self was very content in the present, holding the client's real new puppy.

Monica came to the next session reporting that her anxiety had increased somewhat during the week. This was not surprising to me since we had entered her internal system where the emotionally intense dog memory was stored. I guessed that other feelings about the dog, like his actual death, might need to be processed as well. If additional feelings about the dog were stirred up and unresolved I knew it would be possible to also clear these unprocessed feelings.

Instead, Monica attributed the anxiety feelings during the week to her wedding and issues about her brother being in town. I asked her to focus on these emotions and feelings in her body. She floated back to a memory from high school which involved her brother and we cleared the distress with LI. This highlights again that the client's mind-body system is a reliable guide to the best path of healing. When trusted, it will lead the client to the right derivative memory to heal current distress.

After that session, Monica experienced "an uneventful week in which she felt more confident at work." She also had been to a nearby mall and said being there was fine. Monica experienced some anxiety before she left for the mall, repeatedly asking herself "what if" questions. She called this her habit of "borrowing trouble." Using the affect bridge again, Monica found a five-year-old version of herself around the time her younger brother was born. Monica described her child-self as "prepared." When her baby brother was born, Monica assumed it was her role to strengthen her relationship with her dad since her mom was involved with the new baby. Monica developed a special relationship to her father that in some ways usurped her dad's relationship with her mother. Monica wanted to help in every way possible and took leadership in the family over her mom and brother. One goal of this behavior was to please and help her dad. Monica was fearful of disappointing her father, and in her words, "stayed ready as best she could to help him."

Monica's childhood description fell into the "over-responsible child" category. I began to suspect that although she came to therapy due to acute anxiety that surfaced as her wedding approached, she had probably carried a certain degree of generalized anxiety throughout her life as well. When I asked Monica more about her childhood she said, "I lament the responsibility and worry I felt as a child. It was quite cumbersome." Monica's remarks led me to the conclusion that we needed to use Birth-to-Present protocol to address the underlying, generalized anxiety which was probably a result of over-responsibility from her childhood. We moved into the BP process. At the end of the final timeline repetition Monica said, "It's such a relief to know I can stop worrying about my baby brother and mom." Monica was not aware of any specific birth trauma or extended separations from her mother as an infant, yet the BP process integrated the neural networks which held distressing feelings from her childhood, probably those pertaining to over-responsibility. We did not have to know specifically which memories or feeling states were being resolved because the timeline repetitions accomplished their function and gave Monica relief.

Monica described the following week as "great, with a huge step forward." She said, "It's awesome to know I don't have to be responsible for another person's life." Monica reveled in how wonderful it felt to walk around the mall by herself.

Monica was experiencing significant relief from her anxiety when she met an acquaintance on the street who said she was considering a late-term abortion. After their conversation, Monica entered a large bookstore and was surprised that she was overcome with anxiety about getting out of the store's parking lot. Her anxiety shifted to sadness when she took the time in the store to reflect on her body-based feelings. She said, "I took the time to focus on what was happening to me, especially in my body, and I realized I felt a profound sadness at the potential loss of my friend's baby." As soon as Monica identified the feeling, her anxiety disappeared, but was replaced with encompassing sadness. I suspected that this feeling was somehow personal for Monica and not just about her friend's baby, evidenced by the way the emotions overtook her. I wondered if her mother considered an abortion which would have been loaded into Monica's neural networks in utero. Fortunately, with LI, psychological hypotheses like these are not important. I did not mention to Monica what I was thinking. Instead, I guided her through the Birth-to-Present protocol for the remainder of our session.

I saw Monica three more times after the second BP session. She came to those sessions reporting that all her anxiety was gone. Monica found herself consistently able to go to malls, drive across bridges, and shop by herself for the wedding. The final three sessions were primarily focused on conversations about pre-wedding arrangements and new-bride jitters.

Monica's story portrays the way in which generalized anxiety can be transformed via integration and the emotional regulation which comes from the Birth-to-Present protocol. Often clients have birth trauma or over-responsibility issues which need to be resolved before their anxiety symptoms will clear. In this case, I used a combination of Standard Protocol and Birth-to-Present protocol to give Monica relief from her anxiety symptoms.

Teen's Anxiety

Sixteen-year-old Joel came to therapy to resolve grief related to his mother's death in a car accident. Over several months, we used the PTSD protocol and other LI methods to help Joel manage his grief and rebuild a life without his mother. Near the end of therapy, he said the only problem remaining for him was his anxiety. It had been an ongoing problem throughout adolescence, and was the only target not yet resolved in our work together. Since the anxiety was present before his mother's death, I did not expect it to disappear during the repetitions of the PTSD timeline. After Joel's trauma symptoms were resolved, the anxiety felt quite acute to him.

To begin targeting the anxiety, I asked Joel to notice where in his body he felt sensations related to the anxiety pattern. He pointed to his stomach. I decided to begin with the feelings in his body as a way to get an overall sense of the anxiety problem. Joel did not report any birth trauma and his father confirmed that his birth was normal. Nevertheless, I suspected that we might need repetitions of Birth-to-Present protocol and Standard Protocol with specific targets to clear his anxious feelings.

We started with Birth-to-Present protocol in our first session addressing Joel's anxiety. As we progressed through the BP process, Joel reported that the feelings in his stomach initially became more intense, but lessened with each repetition. After four BP repetitions Joel was quite sleepy and said, "There's just a little bit of tension left in my stomach." He was gradually sliding down the back of his chair into a more prone position after each repetition. I coached Joel through one more timeline. Joel was very tired at the end of the fifth timeline, and reported that his anxiety was gone. At the end of the session, I encouraged him to rest if he felt tired after our work as the integration continued. That evening his dad left a voicemail on my answering machine saying, "Joel was really tired after his session with you. He was quite impacted and went to bed about 8:30 pm. I guess (with a question in his voice) it's a good thing?"

The next week when Joel returned, his dad said Joel had also gone to bed early the second night after our session. "He's doing better now though. We've really seen an improvement in Joel since he began working with you, but we saw a really big change last week after he got over being so tired," Joel's dad told me.

Alone in our session, I asked Joel about his anxiety. "It's gone," he said.

"Completely gone?" I asked. "Check your stomach, okay?"

Quietly going within, Joel did a body scan and replied, "Yeah, I don't have any anxiety." I mentioned a few of the topics related to his anxiety that had come up during our work the previous week and Joel said, "None of that stuff bothers me anymore."

"Hmmm. What do you think happened to it?" I asked.

Puzzled, and pausing for a moment, Joel said, "I don't know." He appeared to be surprised. Joel was apparently noticing for the first time that he had been without anxiety for the week. "That's weird," he added.

"What do you think happened?" I asked again.

Not making any connection to the LI repetitions, he said, "I think I just slept it off."

"Sleeping probably helped," I suggested, "but the timelines we did about your anxiety probably also made a big difference in your anxiety."

"I don't think it was that," Joel countered. "I'm pretty sure it was because I slept so much last week."

Rather than argue with Joel, I was pleased that he had experienced an anxiety-free week. "What should we focus on today?" I asked. Joel could not think of anything that was bothering him. I specifically asked about the depression, which was his main reason for coming to therapy, and he said it was virtually non-existent. "Anything else you're anxious about?" I queried, once again checking in on the anxiety topic. Joel had listed anxiety and depression as his reasons for coming to therapy and I wanted to make sure we covered each aspect fully.

"Nope," came the short, typical teenager reply.

"Then I guess we're done," I offered.

"Cool," he answered.

Joel and I spent his final session reviewing the changes in his life and talking about the ways Lifespan Integration had helped him. In eighteen sessions over six months Joel had gone from being a depressed, anxious teenager back to his normal, under-communicative self. Even Joel's short answers were endearing because the light and vitality had come back into his eyes. Joel was making positive movement regarding the loss of his mom. It is possible that Joel would face brief episodes of grief about his mother's death in the future, but his resilience and developmentally appropriate teen behavior had returned. The anxiety appeared to be gone.

The final clearing of Joel's anxiety in one session is a bit atypical, but it followed seventeen previous sessions of LI. Joel was a young, smart client who had many unprocessed feelings. Some of these were resolved through the PTSD protocol about his mother's death, and the Birth-to-Present protocol.

Anxiety responds well to treatment with Lifespan Integration. Specific phobias can be cleared with LI, and generalized anxiety is greatly reduced through timeline methods. Anxiety from birth trauma is always resolved with LI. Whatever the cause, we can generalize that LI is highly successful for phobias, generalized anxiety, birth trauma, and most other forms of anxiety. Joel thought two nights of good rest cured his five years of anxiety, but I'm quite confident Lifespan Integration also played a major role.

It's amazing to watch a client move, in the course of an hour-and-a-half, from a traumatized state into observation, then into appropriate feelings like anger or sadness, then to neutrality and comfort, and finally into an expansive sense of relief and joy. Clients often spontaneously begin talking about their lives as if the trauma never happened.

Sharon Eiler, LI therapist

6. Posttraumatic Stress Disorder (PTSD)

Bombed

Franklin was a 65-year-old man, who had Posttraumatic Stress Disorder (PTSD) from a car accident, which totaled his car. The attorney who referred Franklin to me was quite familiar with the criteria for PTSD and I agreed with his diagnosis. After the accident, Franklin found himself too anxious to drive in situations where he was previously comfortable and he avoided freeway driving because it was intimidating. If Franklin's only route to his destination included a highway, he was reluctant to change lanes or merge with other traffic. Franklin was nearing retirement and feared a future in which he was afraid to drive to the many activities he was anticipating for his later years. Although neither he nor I knew it at the time, Franklin described his accident using phrases that disclosed a deeper trauma, which also needed healing. The language of the deeper trauma is evident throughout this narrative of Franklin's crash.

The accident occurred on a rural two lane road as Franklin was driving to a friend's home. As a musician, Franklin joined his friends weekly on Friday nights to play music and relax in the country. This was often the high point of his week. On the night of the crash, another driver lost control and crossed into Franklin's lane.

Franklin described the driver coming at his car "like a Kamikaze pilot." He had nightmares about the crash and quit going to his friend's home because it required him to drive through the accident scene, which Franklin described as a nuclear war zone. The accident took place one year before Franklin saw me. I met with him a total of five times, the first being an intake interview of the accident.

At the intake session, I wrote down the events of the accident starting with the few moments before the accident occurred. I wrote down the first thing Franklin thought when it appeared he would be in a crash. I listed everything Franklin remembered from the accident, such as how the collision occurred, where the car stopped, who responded, what the other driver did, and other details until he fell asleep that night. Then I wrote several events for the next day. I asked for cues for the next few days. Then I asked Franklin to remember something from each week in the first month that followed the accident. Finally, I asked for two memories from each month until we filled out the remainder of the year.

To begin the PTSD protocol, I asked Franklin to imagine himself right before the accident. Then I read each of the cues from the memory list and asked him to nod when he remembered the cue I mentioned. There were approximately twelve cues for the day on which the accident occurred. Next, I read four cues for the day following the accident. I read a cue for each of the next five days and then began reading the cues for each week following the accident. After we covered approximately two months, I read the two cues for each of the following months until we completed the year.

Taking clients methodically through timelines from a trauma to the present enables them to process the thoughts, feelings, and body sensations which are stored in neural networks during a difficult event. The PTSD protocol of Lifespan Integration—after enough repetitions—leads to neutral or positive responses to a difficult incident without re-traumatizing the patient.

After the first repetition of the timeline, Franklin reported that he had a slowed-down, frame-by-frame sequence of the accident. "This is a moment out of time," he said. "At first I thought I would die. Now I understand I'm going to live." We repeated the timeline sequence from the few moments before the crash up to the present three more times in the initial session. Franklin was very tired from the process when we closed our 90 minute session.

At the beginning of our second session, Franklin was fixated on, "the frantic few seconds when you know a collision is coming.... when you're not sure you'll be alive." He described himself as a victim. Franklin was angered that a maniac lost control and relieved that his affairs were in order because he thought he might die. After the second timeline of the session Franklin remarked, "There's so much pain in my body! I'm going to have so many things to deal with!" He described the pain and anger at the other driver for the physical and financial repercussions which followed this event. Even though the accident was not his fault, Franklin had other driving citations, which he feared would put him at risk for losing his auto insurance. We proceeded through his accident timeline four more times. After the sixth and final timeline Franklin said, "I've survived worse than this. This is nothing."

One week later I asked if anything remained from our session the previous week. Franklin replied, "No, the impact isn't too bad now because I know I lived. Maybe I've worked through all the bad stuff." Beginning the PTSD protocol again, Franklin focused on the image of going home from the accident and the regret at losing his car. We proceeded through the same timeline we had previously constructed, beginning right before the accident and continuing to the present. Throughout the session Franklin reported shifts such as, "I feel like a detached observer," "This doesn't affect me in any profound way," and "It already feels like it's over."

At the beginning of the fourth session Franklin told me that he was on the freeway more than once and was not troubled by merging or changing lanes. He described his distress about the accident as "the feeling of being bombed." He was angry and felt like a victim because he had already been through so much in his life. Sometimes it's helpful to heal earlier events that have a similar feeling tone to the recent trauma. Franklin's recurring reference to "I've already been through so much," prompted me to switch to the Standard Protocol of LI. I asked Franklin to focus on his body sensations. Following the affect bridge, he remembered a time during World War II when he was a child living in a small town near London. One evening, as Franklin was coming home from a friend's house, German airplanes appeared overhead and dropped a bomb in their district. Franklin ran to a bomb shelter and spent the night with strangers, wondering whether his family was alive. The next morning Franklin's family came and found him asleep at the shelter. Because the brain stores memory according to its feeling tone, Franklin's narrative about the car accident matched this World War II memory because the two events apparently had similar emotional qualities and evoked one another.

I asked Franklin to take his 65-year-old self to the frightened little boy he had described in London. He pictured his eight-year-old-self running with others into a bomb shelter while strangers wailed and shouted, frantically searching for loved ones. The adult Franklin assured the child that this nightmare was over and proved it to him with visual memories from his life. After four or five timelines, the young boy was relieved to know he was the same person as the adult Franklin. In the beginning of the timelines for this session the younger-self wanted to know, "Am I going to die? Is my family alive?" After the repetitions, the younger-self said, "Everything is fine. I'm all right and so is my family." Franklin reported there was no distress for the little boy in the past or present; an indicator that the target was completely clear. Healing of this memory took about 30 minutes and did not in any way re-traumatize Franklin. Instead, it healed a longstanding trauma, which had become associated with the recent car accident. At the end of the session I asked Franklin to imagine the original car accident scene, which he said was without distress. I suggested that he drive through the scene of the accident between sessions if he could, and make notes about what was still difficult for him. Franklin was interested in joining his friends again for music on Friday nights. Since he was more confident with his driving, he hoped to drive into the country again for the regular musical evenings.

When Franklin walked into my office for the fifth and final session, he began by stating, "My distress about the accident is completely gone." He told me he had driven through the accident scene twice over the weekend and forgot to notice he was in the area of the crash. Franklin was at his final destination when it occurred to him that he had passed through the accident scene without noting whether anything about it still bothered him. We concluded our therapy at this point. Franklin was driving easily in all weather conditions and was looking forward to the years ahead. As for freeway driving, Franklin said, "Yesterday, I drove for 70 miles on the freeway and didn't give it a second thought."

The PTSD protocol of LI is remarkable for clearing recent and long-held trauma. It is relatively gentle for the client to experience and brings relief immediately. If time permits, a clinician should prepare for ten or more repetitions of the trauma-to-present timeline during each session. The timeline should include many cues surrounding the traumatic event and conclude in current time. It is not necessary to bring the younger-self into the adult's home because repetitions of the timeline are sufficient to heal the trauma. Extended sessions of 75-90 minutes provide the opportunity for multiple repetitions of a client's timeline. It is common for a major trauma to require more than one session. In such a case, our goal is to activate the neural networks holding the trauma and complete enough repetitions of the timeline so the client can leave in a somewhat resolved state. Between sessions the trauma will continue to resolve. In following sessions we can repeat the PTSD protocol until the trauma activates no distress for the client consciously or unconsciously.

Franklin was a high-functioning professional with stability in other parts of his life. Franklin's rapid healing from the trauma is a normal outcome for LI, but it was aided by the health of his life in general. Clients that are highly dissociated or have other major stressors can take more than five sessions to completely heal their traumas. Nevertheless, the PTSD protocol of Lifespan Integration brings relief and all clients report improvement within a session or two.

Dog Attack

Nancy came to therapy to resolve a dog attack that she experienced while opening the gate to her driveway. The incident was so severe that Nancy believed she would die from the vicious attack by her neighbor's dog. Using Lifespan Integration, I helped Nancy piece together a timeline from the moments before the dog attack to the present. Nancy was visibly emotionally distressed when recalling the trauma, but within 30 minutes we were able to create a detailed list of memories from the attack. The timeline began with Nancy getting out of her car, then approaching the gate, and seeing the dog coming toward her. The cues for the first day ended when Nancy went to sleep after visiting the emergency room of a hospital. We added at least one memory for each day of the two weeks following the attack and something for each following week. The incident occurred twelve weeks before I saw Nancy for her first session.

After composing the timeline, I read the memories from the cue sheet, and Nancy signaled when she had each memory in mind. The PTSD timeline was relatively short so we were able to complete six repetitions before the end of the session. Pace stresses the importance of completing enough timeline repetitions so that we do not leave the client too activated after compiling their trauma cue list. Nancy dissociated during the timeline sequences, but was diligent to follow the instructions. Near the end of our time she said it was impossible for her to complete any more repetitions during the first session, but she was willing for us to meet again.

Nancy and I briefly talked in the beginning of each of the next two sessions about the circumstances related to the legal resolution of the dog attack. Then I repeated the PTSD timeline five to seven times per session.

By the third and fourth sessions Nancy reported some changes and admitted that she had initially come to the office completely skeptical that anyone or anything could help her. Nancy agreed to therapy only because she was debilitated, but had no expectation that her situation could improve. I had told Nancy that part of her was still engaged with the dog attack and was vigilant to make sure it did not happen again. By the fourth session she said, "Although I didn't believe you then, now I understand that I really was stuck back there when the dog attacked me."

By the fifth session, Nancy's overall distress about the dog attack was significantly reduced. After four sessions using the PTSD protocol, Nancy said her remaining concern was angst that the Animal Control Agency and county prosecutor were not pursuing her case. She was reluctant to personally sue the neighbor who owned the dog. Nancy was not sure she wanted to hire an attorney because her father had always taught her to return good for evil. Nancy wanted to set a good example for the neighbor about how good neighbors should act. In this case, the idea of setting a good example for a difficult neighbor did not seem realistic to me, so I opted to use the Standard Protocol of LI to look for a previous memory, which was influencing the way Nancy thought about her situation. I asked Nancy to focus on the feelings in her body around the legal issues of the case. We floated this back to a time ten years previously when another incident had occurred in her family that involved the county sheriff. Although the family had been wronged, the sheriff did not do his job of turning the case over to the proper legal agencies, and the case went unprosecuted. Nancy felt bitter and hopeless about that legal tangle and was not expecting good results on the legal outcome of the dog attack. I asked Nancy to take her current-self back to the Nancy from ten years ago who had experienced the legal debacle. I asked her to validate the younger Nancy and reassure her that the incident was traumatic and very upsetting, but that it was actually over. I instructed Nancy to tell her younger-self that she had done everything she could to make the earlier situation better; other people did not do their jobs and she could not control that now. I said, "Tell her to watch these pictures of how time has passed and how she has grown up to be you." I read Nancy's cues starting the year after the incident with the county sheriff and ending in the present. We repeated this process a total of five times until the younger Nancy was at ease in the memory scene as well in the present with her adult-self. The younger Nancy believed she was the same person as the adult Nancy.

The following week, Nancy reported that she had retained an attorney able to help her secure financial damages and stop the neighbors from having dogs on their property. Five years prior to the attack, the same neighbor's dogs killed one of Nancy's goats. Animal Control required the dogs to be removed, but within six months all the dogs were back on their owner's property. Regarding Nancy's recent run-in, the attacking dog was gone but her neighbors had bought a pit bull as a replacement.

During the session, Nancy told me that the most pressing problem remaining from the dog attack was the fact that no one helped her when the attack happened. I heard a "little girl voice" in Nancy's remarks and asked her to explain. She said Animal Control was not returning her phone calls and she called them at least once a week. It was their responsibility to turn the case over to the county sheriff to establish that the neighboring family could no longer own dogs. When I asked about the attorney, Nancy replied that although he was interested in her case, he was not available for several weeks to help with this problem. I had heard the little girl's voice from Nancy before and I suspected it was related to something before the dog attack. To resolve her feeling of help-lessness, I asked Nancy to point to the place in her body where she felt something related to the powerless feeling that remained from the trauma. Nancy pointed to her heart and stomach and I guided her to follow the affect bridge to a younger ego state. Nancy found a little girl hiding under the bedclothes in her bedroom. I coached Nancy to take her adult-self to the little girl and assure her that the adult had come to help her. After Nancy relayed my verbal coaching to the little girl, we proceeded with the timeline to the present. We repeated this four more times. As we went back into the bedroom after each timeline, the younger Nancy was able to explain why she was hiding, why she needed help, and the adult Nancy was able to act on the child's behalf with authority. Nancy proved to her younger-self with each of the timelines that the difficult situation was over. Through my coaching, Nancy repeatedly assured the little girl that Nancy was her grown-up-self and the adult Nancy would handle any problems that occurred in the present.

When verbally coaching Nancy, I instructed her to tell the little girl that even though she currently has the big problem of the dog attack, it is the adult's job to find a way to solve it. She is not a little girl anymore and does not have a mom or dad to take care of things for her. The adult Nancy was a bit resistant to communicate this at first, but the loving truth is the most helpful thing to tell younger ego states. As far as I understood, no one was going to step in and take care of Nancy's dog attack problem, so she needed to be her own empowered advocate. I was seeking to help Nancy resolve the helpless child neural networks so she could move forward with appropriate adult action for her current problem.

Not surprisingly, the next week Nancy came in and reported big changes in the circumstances surrounding the dog attack. First, someone from Animal Control came out to the property twice to check the current status of Nancy's complaint. Second, the sheriff visited once and called twice to follow up on his part in the case. Third, the county prosecutor had interviewed Nancy and let her know that they would be prosecuting the neighbor for the removal of all dogs from the property. The prosecutor had formerly been in criminal law and Nancy was very impressed with her proficiency and thoroughness. Nancy's attorney had not stepped in yet, but Nancy was definitely committed to personally sue the neighbor for medical fees associated with the trauma. Before too many days had passed, the neighbor—who had hired a lawyer to defend her—withdrew her defense.

Nancy did not initiate any of the steps taken by the government officials or neighbor after the session in which we worked to increase her adult empowerment. Even though she had been calling the government agencies at least once a week for many weeks, when Nancy changed her internal world, the outside world responded to her differently. Fortunately, when clients feel stuck, we can help them by targeting their feelings and body sensations related to current stressors even if someone else is clearly in the wrong. Floating feelings back to root issues, followed by timeline repetitions, always produces positive change in the client. Client changes are reflected in the way they respond to the world and how the world responds to them.

Apart from Nancy's childlike powerlessness, I was also concerned with her belief that she should always return good in response to her neighbor's aggression toward her. Nancy told me that her father had taught her this maxim and he was always right. Although I support the principle of being kind to others, I was concerned that her perspective was a bit naïve in the case of neighboring dogs who attack people and kill animals. It was evident that I personally would not be able to convince the client that any perspective was more correct than her father's perspective.

After we targeted and resolved her childlike powerlessness, Nancy's unconscious set her up to address her belief that one must always be kind to others regardless of the personal cost. By the tenth session, the only thing that was troubling Nancy was a dream that kept repeating itself during the two nights before our appointment. Nancy said, "In the dream the neighbor had moved closer and there was no fence between us. The dogs were running around on my property. Both of our entrances were broken down and there was nowhere to get away from the dogs. Her fence was broken down and so was ours." I asked Nancy to focus on the most significant part of the dream for her which was "nothing between the dogs and me." After a few minutes of her reflections on the dream, Nancy thought the dream was about having poor boundaries with the neighbor and the risk it created for her. I asked Nancy to go into an imaginary basement and find the part of her who's open to people who are mean. I assured Nancy that this part of her had really good reasons for not putting up barriers.

In the imaginary basement, we found a little girl ego state who felt sorry for people who needed help. Nancy said she also felt sorry for people like her neighbor who were pathetic and helpless. We began using timeline repetitions with the younger Nancy. We told the younger-self that she could definitely have compassion for others, but no one wanted her to be hurt by people or to keep avenues open for danger. When asked, Nancy agreed that her father would never want her as a child or an adult to be in danger as a result of being kind to others. I coached Nancy to explain this to the internal child, followed by repetitions of the timeline. Between each timeline we gave important and new information to the child ego state. After four timelines, Nancy said, "In my current situation, it's too dangerous for me to set a good example for my neighbor. I could get killed. I'm afraid those dogs are going to kill me. In this case my father was wrong. I think I have to change some harmful ways of thinking." As a result of LI, Nancy was wholly convinced that she would have to develop a new strategy for relating to her neighbor. This was our final session.

In reviewing the outcomes, Nancy was shocked by the success of Lifespan Integration for her Posttraumatic Stress Disorder. Her sleep had improved and was back to the pre-dog attack level. Lack of sleep had become such a problem that Nancy often was too tired to perform her best at work. After LI, Nancy still woke during the night, but it was not the excessive waking she experienced following the dog incident. Nancy reported that her thinking had drastically improved and she was able to remember more events from the dog attack to the present, while also having a noticeably better capacity for thinking in general. I attribute this to Nancy being less dissociated and the decrease of PTSD symptoms. Nancy was thrilled about the fact that her lifetime fear of spiders had unexpectedly diminished after our LI work. She was no longer having panic attacks when she saw spiders. Nancy was also able to get out of her car and open her gate without paralyzing fear. She was still cautious and kept a look-out for the neighbor's pit bull, but Nancy was able to function normally when arriving home. She had a plan to pursue the legal aspects of her case and felt strongly that her neighbors were not suited to own dogs. If the county did not want to follow through on this case, Nancy said she would pursue it with her attorney.

Two months after our last session, Nancy called with an update and said, "Every day I notice a positive difference as a result of our therapy. I can think more clearly now and my husband is constantly thanking me. He didn't do that before. The reason he thanks me is because I can do things I could never do before. I can help him in the barn and with other chores without my old fears. This therapy has really changed my life. Thank you."

Trauma: In the Eye of the Beholder

A familiar expression states, "Beauty is in the eye of the beholder." Our perspective on something makes it beautiful, engaging, or frightening. In the following case, individuals who lived through the same experience perceived and processed it in very different ways. To one person it was exciting, to a second person it was the stressful role of responsibility, to a third person it was the possibility of death and manifested as mild PTSD symptoms, and to a fourth person it was an exercise of physics and expended energy. These individuals were riding in the same car when it hydroplaned on heavy highway rainwater. The driver, Michelle, struggled to gain control as the vehicle thrashed from side to side across the highway.

Michelle's brother, Gary, was seated in the front passenger seat of the van, and her two teenage daughters—16-year-old Isabella and 14-year-old Kenzie—were sitting in the back seat. The girls were each listening to music with headphones when the drama began.

One of the salient points of this experience is the drastic difference in perception reported by each participant. I had the opportunity to speak to the four individuals separately. Each factual report varied in details including: the number of lanes on the road, how many times the car crisscrossed on the highway, the direction of the spin, and the level of perceived danger.

Gary reported that it was raining heavily as they traveled on a four-lane freeway to an extended family dinner. As they headed north, the weather improved and eventually stopped raining, but pools of standing water remained on the road. Michelle was driving at an appropriate freeway speed when the vehicle began to drift to the right. Gary said, "It was clear the van was gliding across the water and the wheels had hydroplaned off the surface of the road." The van was speedily sliding toward the right embankment when Michelle corrected the steering, preventing them from sliding down the hillside off the right shoulder. But the correction caused the van to speed toward the center metal barrier. Michelle corrected again to the right and the vehicle crossed the road toward the right shoulder again, at which point she corrected to the left. Gary said, "As the van was cutting a path to the left for the second time, I think Michelle put her foot on the brake which locked the wheels. The van went into a spin. The van began a full revolution left toward the center barrier and eventually came out of it facing forward in the direction we had been traveling. She did a great job handling it." When Michelle made her first correction, Gary confidently told her, "You've got this!" Later, Michelle told me that Gary's comment was instrumental in her approach to the situation.

Michelle said, "I didn't feel confident or in control, but if Gary thought I was, it meant a lot to me."

After they came out of the spin, Michelle pulled off to the side of the road to let Gary drive. As they were settling themselves, Gary explained why he felt certain that they were going to be alright. He had been an Air Force pilot and perceived the situation in terms of physics and dynamic energy. When Michelle made her first correction to the left Gary said, "You've got this!" because the energy from the moving vehicle was being dispersed with each pass of the tires across the asphalt. As Michelle decelerated and the car gradually slowed, Gary knew that the momentum and energy of the swerving vehicle would dissipate. With less speed and greater control, Gary was confident that time and distance would rectify the situation and all the passengers would be safe. He said, "Even as the car was spinning, energy was being discharged." Michelle said Gary was compassionate and helpful. She later asked him if he had any disturbing thoughts after the mishap and he said, "No, I knew we would be okay. You had things under control." I noted that Gary experienced the mishap confidently based on his many years of driving and physics perspective.

Isabella was in the same, but different, freeway mishap. She said, "I was listening to music in the back when I felt the rear wheels lift off the highway.

I looked up and saw the van swerve to the right, and then go back to the left. Then we went into a spin."

"How many times did you crisscross the highway before the spin?" I asked.

"We went once to the left and once to the right," Isabella answered.

"Then what happened?" I inquired.

"We started to spin to the right. I was sitting in the back, on the right side, and I was getting really close to the metal barrier. We were going to hit it on my side. I was trying to figure out what

I would do to protect myself or how we were going to get out afterward." Isabella said. When Isabella initially told me her version of the story, she very briefly mentioned that she thought she might die or be seriously hurt in the accident.

"When did you think you might die?" I asked.

"When my side of the van was going to hit the metal barrier first and go down the side of the road," Isabella answered. From Gary's narrative of the near-accident, I could not understand why Isabella perceived the situation to be life threatening, so I queried further. Isabella had taken her driver's training about a year before this roadway scare and had been driving on her own approximately six months. She said, "In driver's education we saw lots of horrible videos of people crashing and dying in accidents. They were so bad I couldn't watch some of them. If I did watch, they made my cry. I've never been in an accident before and I don't know anyone else who has been in an accident. I thought all accidents ended in death or people being seriously hurt. We saw movies where people got decapitated."

"So, is that why you thought it was going to end so badly?" I questioned.

"Yes, that's all I know about accidents," she replied. Isabella continued telling me what happened. Inches away from a collision, she thought, "Gosh, I guess this is it. I'm going to die or be really badly hurt." Isabella said the van was spinning to the right and then corrected in a reverse direction. She added with distress, "At one point we were looking straight at oncoming traffic. The cars were heading toward us!" Isabella was relieved and grateful that they did not hit anything. Yet her brain loaded the impending, life-threatening situation as extremely dangerous. To Isabella, the experience meant that she might die or have her life drastically altered. Isabella's fear should not be minimized. The way Isabella processed the mishap from her new-driver perspective influenced the way her brain stored the memory.

Posttraumatic Stress Disorder is not only about what actually

happened to people, it is also about the individual's frame of reference and what *could have* happened to him or her. Isabella perceived
a level of danger that was very different from Gary's well-informed
physics perspective. Even though Isabella and Gary had been in the
same van that glided across the roadway, Isabella thought her life
was in danger and Gary was sure that all would be well due to his
age and experience. They also reported that the vehicle spun in different directions, and came out of the spin in different ways. Gary
reported that the van completed a revolution and Isabella said it
reversed the direction to come out of the spin. Later, Michelle said
she had no idea how the van ended up facing the right direction
after spinning. The four people in the car perceived the spin and
its dangers completely differently. Isabella's sister Kenzie, who was
seated on the left side of the van, said, "I thought it was kind of
exciting. It's not bothering me at all." Kenzie spent the day after
the event meeting friends at a shopping mall.

Less than 24 hours after the incident, I had the opportunity to
use the PTSD protocol with Isabella and Michelle. Gary and Kenzie
did not appear traumatized or feel the need to debrief the experience any further. The single LI sessions for Michelle and Isabella
are described below. As their timeline sequences progressed, it
became evident how Michelle and Isabella processed and stored the
experience differently in their own neural networks. Throughout
these session summaries, we see how the various layers of perception, feelings, and anticipated outcome influence responses to an
incident. Isabella thought she was going to die or be severely hurt,
which made sense from her perspective. Michelle had many layers
of feelings within the memory, which did not appear until several
repetitions of the PTSD protocol.

Isabella's Lifespan Integration Session

In our LI session, I used Isabella's version of the story even though
some of the facts differed from Gary's recall of the event. As clients progress through repetitions of their PTSD timeline, the

facts become clarified and the sequences generally fall into a more accurate order. Isabella's timeline follows:

- I was listening to my iPod when I felt the car lift up in the back.
- Then we swerved to the left and went backwards.
- When the car was swerving to my right I thought, "Gosh, what if this is it?"
- I was thinking, "What would I have done if we had hit the metal barrier?"
- "Was the hillside steep enough for us to roll over?"
- "What would happen if we did roll over?"
- Then the car went straight.
- We stopped.
- Another driver stopped and said something to my mom.
- We had dinner at Uncle Stewart's.
- We played a family game after dinner and dessert.
- We started driving home and I listened to my iPod.
- I tried to sleep in the car.
- I came home really tired and went to bed.
- I woke up and had something to eat…..

Even though the items on Isabella's cue sheet were written in first-person, I read them to her so that they would make sense to her as the listener. I said, "You were listening to your iPod and felt the car lift up in the back." Then, "You thought, *what if this is it?!*" One could read Isabella's timeline and wonder why the experience was traumatic for her. No one was seriously injured through these events. A difficult situation fortunately resolved itself without harm or injury. Yet Isabella truly believed that the situation was life-threatening. As we moved through the repetitions of her time-line, her feelings and perceptions about the experience emerged.

After the first repetition of the timeline, Isabella described in more detail how she assumed she would die or be seriously injured. The videos from Isabella's recent driver training course led her to believe that all accidents end tragically. The written timeline tells the facts of her story, but the repetitions we completed together brought forward Isabella's feelings. She said she was very, very scared about what would happen to her when they hit the metal barrier or rolled down the hillside.

"Did you cry at all?" I asked.

"No, I never did. When we got to Uncle Stewart's I went to my mom for a hug. I wanted to cry but everybody was standing around and I didn't let myself cry," Isabella told me. I validated her feel-ings and expressed compassion. Knowing that timeline repetitions would do more to change her internal state than our conversation could, I moved into the next series of timelines.

After the third timeline, I asked, "What are you aware of now?"

"The sadness is in the back of my head. That's where most of it is," Isabella answered. Occasionally, clients report physical sen-sations in their heads through the LI process. Probably less than five percent of people report this, but those who do appear to be sensitive individuals. The timeline method works whether or not the client can report changes in the head area. I was intrigued that Isabella described activation in the back of her brain which is where trauma is processed. I guessed that not only sadness was held in the back of her brain, but the trauma itself was being reprocessed as we showed her brain the events that followed the most dangerous moments of their spin.

After the fourth timeline Isabella said, "Now the feelings are in my throat and heart." To me it sounded like tears were stuck in her throat. Since Isabella had difficulty expressing feelings at the fam-ily gathering, I thought she might be reluctant to cry with me—a person she did not know well.

I drew a picture of a standard bell curve on a piece of paper which looked like a rounded mountain with a gentle slope on each side. Following the shape of the mountain with my pen, I asked Isabella, "How far have we come in helping you feel better about what happened in the car? Are we here?" I asked, pointing to the gentle upward slope of the mountain, "On the top or down closer to the bottom?"

"Over the top and almost to the bottom," Isabella replied. Her response matched my sense of the resolution we had accomplished together through four timeline repetitions.

"How about if we do one or two more timelines and finish up?" I suggested.

"Okay," she said. "I'm getting really tired."

And you need a big cry, which is probably not going to happen in this office, I thought.

In general, if the therapist moves the client far enough through the emotional matter so that he or she leaves the session on the downward side of the bell curve, the client's mind-body system will continue processing the effects of timeline repetitions outside of the session. Isabella and I both perceived we were at this point and I was quite certain that no tears were going to emerge in my company.

I guided Isabella through one more timeline after which she reported that the sensations were more in the front of her head than in the back, but that her heart and throat still felt something. I suggested that we finish for the day, and I offered to see Isabella again if anything still bothered her about the event.

A few days later I spoke with Isabella on the phone. She reported that after our session she drove straight home and went to bed where she cried and slept soundly. "Is anything still bothering you about the trip to Uncle Stewart's?" I asked.

"No, after I cried I felt a lot better. Thank you," replied Isabella.

Three weeks after our single LI session regarding the rainy day scare Michelle asked Isabella if anything still troubled her about the event. Isabella responded, "No, the method Cathy used really worked. I was really upset about it afterward. Now I think of it as just a thing that happened one day—no big deal."

Michelle's Lifespan Integration Session

For Michelle, the focus of the roadway event centered on the responsibility she felt for the well-being of people she loved. Throughout the ordeal Michelle kept thinking about the ominous possibility that something bad might happen to the people in her car. She feared driving them off the roadway, smashing her van, seriously injuring her family, along with other repercussions from her split-second decision-making. Michelle also kept flashing in her mind to the angry ways her family might respond to her when it was over. Michelle said, "It was no longer raining, but I was still being very mindful about driving at a safe speed. I looked up and saw a sheet of water on the road. Then I felt the car gliding on the water. I felt the back of the car move to the left while the front of the car was sliding to the right. I turned the steering wheel to the left and felt the car turn really hard. Then I corrected again to the right and Gary said, 'You've got this.' I turned left again and we went into a spin. I saw the barrier in front of me and was thinking about my responsibility for the people in the car. Someone in the car cried out and I thought, *We're going to hit!*"

"How did the car get turned around?" I asked.

"I'm not sure how we ended up going in the right direction. When we were finally going straight I looked at Gary and he looked at me. He had a gentle smile that implied, *We made it. Good job.* I continued driving the car forward. I could see that I was staying within the lane lines, but inside I felt like I was still spinning. I pulled the car over to the side of the road so Gary could drive. When we were stopped on the side of the road a driver pulled up beside us. He rolled down his window and said, 'I saw the whole thing. I think you were going too fast for the conditions.' Gary replied, the motorist drove on, and Gary got into the driver's seat," Michelle said.

I began the PTSD timeline repetitions with Michelle based on her reported sequence of events. Michelle's mind–body system had stored the incident in a certain way and I needed to follow the way her brain had loaded the information into her neural networks in order to resolve it. With all PTSD cases, we do not worry if the sequence of events is remembered in the same way by every person who experienced the trauma. With LI timelines, the facts of a client's story will become more accurate in his or her memory over time. Michelle and Isabella's accounts had slight variations in the sequence of events which posed no problem in helping each of them heal.

After the first repetition of her timeline Michelle said, "I feel dizzy when I have my eyes closed going through this." I suspected that she was experiencing and releasing body memory from her time in the near-accident. Dizziness was a component of Michelle's experience immediately after the spin. I told her she was welcome to keep her eyes open during the timeline sequences if it would make her more comfortable.

We began the second timeline repetition and Michelle opted to close her eyes. By the end of the second timeline the dizziness associated with remembering the scene was gone. Michelle said, "The accident itself is not so traumatic now. It's weird that I didn't release the emotion right afterward. My head feels a bit fuzzy, but the dizziness has cleared. I realize I'm worried about what people will think of me."

At the end of the third repetition through the PTSD timeline, I asked Michelle what she noticed when she remembered the accident in the session. She said, "Now I just feel a little bit of the 'Oh no!' feeling when I see that day in my mind. I'm focused on seeing the standing water as I drove into it." Michelle reported that her head still felt a bit fuzzy.

I guided her into a fourth repetition of the accident timeline, expecting some of the fuzziness to turn into emotion and be released. Instead, at the end of the fourth timeline Michelle said, "When I remember that day I'm aware of waiting to be in trouble." I did not know Michelle's family history, but I suspected that the pattern of being in trouble was linked to previous experiences in life which had some commonality with the car accident experience. Having taken many people through the PTSD protocol, I knew that the emotion in Michelle's story was not being fully accessed.

"Does anything about this make you angry?" I wondered aloud.

"No, I don't feel angry about it, just worried about how other people will respond to me," she answered.

Trusting the process, I didn't try to control Michelle's awareness, rather I moved her into the fifth timeline repetition. When we began, Michelle immediately said, "I really don't want the water to be there! I'm really angry at that sheet of water for being on the roadway!" She began to cry heavily and I waited a few brief moments for Michelle's tears, after which I read the cue sheet of her accident. At the end of the timeline Michelle released a deep sigh and said, "I'm also angry at the driver who stopped and said I was going too fast for the conditions! I'd been driving in a downpour for an hour before this happened and I was being very intentional about my speed. Who is he to say I was going too fast?"

"Good point. Let's go through it again. See the driver who stopped and give him a piece of your mind," I guided.

Before we started the sixth timeline repetition, I asked Michelle to imagine she was speaking to the driver who saw her spin and chastised her for speeding. "I was deliberately not going too fast," Michelle said aloud, along with a few other remarks. Without any discussion from me I took Michelle through the sixth and final timeline. She cried again as we proceeded through the sequence. At the end of the sixth repetition Michelle was tired, a bit fuzzy-headed, and peaceful. "I did everything right," she said. "That could have happened to anyone. I'm glad Gary was there and everything turned out okay. I was really worried about everyone's safety but no one was hurt. I still don't know how the van came out of the spin, but I'm grateful that it did. It was a miracle that we made it through without any damage to my car or the people I love." Michelle continued, "Today when I took Kenzie to soccer practice, I avoided driving my car. My husband is out of town so I used his car rather than mine. I don't know how it will be when I have to drive my own car again."

Two days after our PTSD session, Michelle deliberately drove back to the accident scene. She later told me over the phone that the roadway was much smaller than she remembered, and the drop-off on either side was not very steep. She said, "Had we gone off the side of the road, it wouldn't have been serious. There is a rumble strip on the edge of the highway which I would have heard if we had swerved onto the shoulder, so I guess we didn't cross far enough to reach the shoulder. When it was all happening it seemed like we were crossing several lanes of highway. But today it all looked very small when I was there."

"Is anything still bothering you about it?" I asked.

"No, I'm fine. I'm driving with only a little bit of tentativeness which will probably go away with time," Michelle answered. I offered another session to Michelle if her symptoms did not completely clear and she agreed to call me if she was not back to normal driving within a day or two. A few weeks later, Michelle called me and said that she and Isabella were doing fine. Isabella was continuing to drive carefully and deliberately as a new driver, but she was not troubled by the near-accident anymore. Michelle was back to driving her regular mom-taxi service without concern.

Four Perspectives Revisited

It is evident from these accounts that each participant experienced the roadway mishap in very different ways. Trauma is dependent on the way each person perceives and processes his or her experience. It is clear from Michelle's response that issues of "being in trouble" affected the way she conceptualized and stored the incident. Matters of responsibility also weighed heavily on her mind. In short, the accident to Michelle was a matter of staying out of trouble and the fear of others' reprimand. As I heard about the case, I did not perceive it as an issue of others' approval, but one of Michelle's main concerns was disapproval. Something in Michelle's personal history, which she did not need to disclose to me, set her up to experience the accident from this perspective.

From another perspective, Isabella was a new driver who recently saw movies in Driver's Education of decapitation and death, and she feared for her life as the van approached the metal barrier and embankment. Isabella and Michelle were in the same mishap, but Isabella genuinely believed she'd die or be seriously injured. Explaining to Isabella that her notions were incorrect would not have changed what she stored in her brain during the event. The actual way Isabella's brain laid down the experience in her pre-existing neural networks would affect Isabella's response to the accident and future events like it. By resolving the distress of this accident with the PTSD protocol, Isabella was able to grasp the reality of her situation from a broader viewpoint and let go of her belief that all roadway mishaps end in death.

Kenzie and Gary also brought their frame of reference to the rainy day roadway spin. Gary had probably survived more threatening situations than this one and accurately assessed their level of danger, while Kenzie happily listened to music through headphones, oblivious to any potential danger. Kenzie loves rollercoasters and her mother later reported that a few weeks after the accident nothing about it bothered Kenzie. Four people in the same car had four different experiences. Their level of trauma was based on their frame of reference, beliefs, and previous life experiences which were referenced in their individual neural networks.

Validating One's Viewpoint

Especially where children are concerned, it is important to understand an event from their perspective. Something might seem like a minor mishap to an adult, but the way a child perceives the event will be his or her truth about it. I once worked with a young boy named Andy who was too anxious to go to school because he was afraid of vomiting in the classroom. As we worked through his distress, it became apparent that Andy's beliefs made sense based on his perception of the story. Andy approached his father one night at 2am feeling sick. His dad said, "You'll be fine. Go back to bed." Later Andy vomited all over his bed and clothing.

"That's when I knew I couldn't trust my Dad anymore," Andy said during our work. The loss of trust with his dad was at the root of Andy's anxiety. Through LI timelines we brought greater awareness to Andy's vomiting incident and his anxiety about going to school completely disappeared. Finding Andy's view of the problem and resolving this belief where the neural networks were formed brought him relief. Andy's parents had been telling him for months that they were sure he was not in danger of vomiting at school. Andy wanted to believe his parents but their truth was his not his truth. Andy's parents had no idea that the nighttime illness was the beginning of a deep loss of trust for their son. When Andy understood and healed the experience from his perspective, the negative symptoms associated with it disappeared.

Andy's fear of vomiting and Isabella's driving scare show us that what our mind-body systems believe about an incident is more important than what actually happened. Trauma really is in the eye of the beholder. Fortunately, with the LI tools available to us today, we can understand an experience from the beholder's perspective and help them integrate accurate truth into the places where erroneous beliefs hold them back. Isabella continued to feel fine about the accident several months after the trauma, and six years after our work together Andy still had no anxiety about vomiting at school. With Lifespan Integration, we can resolve what happened to clients, what nearly happened to clients, and what they believed happened to them, within a few sessions.

Lifespan Integration: Effective for all Trauma

The trauma cases presented here do not represent the worst traumas that can happen to people, yet the trauma healing method with LI is the same, regardless of the trauma's severity. I have worked with survivors of war and rape, and they, like Isabella and Nancy, also have virtually complete relief from their traumas. The emphasis of trauma healing with Lifespan Integration is on proving to the client's *body* that the trauma has passed. Repetitions of the client's trauma timeline appear to convince the client's brain and body that they do not have to defend against the trauma any longer because it is not happening in present time, rather it is an event from the past which had a beginning, a middle and an end.

LI changed my life. After 18 years of groups and therapy, LI helped me let go of my husband's death and get a new life. As a therapist, I find LI to be a caring and effective way to help people rapidly change.

Beverly Bridge, LI therapist

7. Grief

 Lifespan Integration is an effective modality for change when clients have ongoing struggles with grief. The nature of grief varies, as do the approaches an LI therapist uses to address a client's grief. Just like trauma, grief can be complex and multi-layered. We know that the brain stores memories according to emotional content; therefore, multiple grief experiences will be stored in relationship with one another. As a result, the loss of a pet or loved one can trigger memories of previously experienced losses. To treat a client's grief, the therapist needs to assess the depth and complexity of the client's grieving. Is this primarily a single incident grief, or is it a series of accumulated losses?

We often treat grief with the PTSD protocol, compiling a timeline of the client's experience from the grief occurrence to the present. This may seem like an unusual application of the LI method, but surprisingly, it is a great relief for clients to experience their grief as a mind-body connected story, via the timeline. I have used the timeline with patients a week, a month, a year, or decades after a serious loss and they are always helped by the method. The value of using the timeline in a short period of time, such as a week or a month after a loss, is that the client finds clarity by discovering something has changed about the situation even in the few days since difficult news was presented to them. They may have recollected a bit of themselves after a terrible shock or found resources within themselves to handle the unimaginable. Clients are helped by the timeline even a few days after a difficult event because they can see that the initial shock of the news is over, family and friends may have moved closer to offer support, and problem solving solutions are being generated.

The following story is similar to a PTSD case study, but it was Johnny's grief and inability to move forward in life that paralyzed him more than the initial traumatic incident. Johnny's story is that of a young man whose wife died unexpectedly at home while he was out walking the dogs. It is a single episode of grief which was completely resolved in eight LI sessions over four months. As reported by Johnny, he had no previous history of loss or trauma beyond the level of losing a pet.

Johnson, called "Johnny" by his friends, was 32 years old when his wife Lori died. Within two months of her death, Johnny saw a counselor three times and quit because he said, "It didn't help me at all." Johnny began therapy with me eight months after Lori's death. Johnny's parents urged him to try counseling again because he was depressed, inactive, socially isolated, and afraid to try new relationships. As a 32-year-old man, he could not imagine a future in which he had a good life and a family, even though he desperately wanted both. Johnny was financially stable, but Lori's illness brought monetary chaos into his life and he was fearful that a new relationship would cause the financial pattern to repeat. His experience with Lori colored his view of the future, and he could not imagine any long-term relationship that was different than his marriage which ended one year after it began.

At our intake session, Johnny told me that he lived with his parents because he could not face the challenge of selling or living in the condo he shared with Lori. His finances were wrecked by the cost of Lori's illness, and he could not afford to rent a separate place to live on his own. Lori was diagnosed with Lupus six months into their marriage. She developed complications which required large doses of narcotics as prescribed by her physician. Johnny had a comfortable amount of money in savings before he married, but Lori's treatments depleted it. Out of love for his wife, Johnny kept investing in Lori's well-being and medical needs. It later came to light that Lori may have been supplementing her prescribed medication with street drugs.

Since this was a single incident of grief which occurred eight months previously, Johnny and I compiled a timeline of his life from the morning of Lori's death to the present during our first session. Telling the story was difficult and activated the very grief Johnny was trying to keep at bay. I assured him that we could make a significant difference in the distress around Lori's death if he would stay engaged in the process with me. After compiling the list, I read the cue sheet to Johnny and waited after each cue for him to nod that he remembered the memory on the sheet. Per the PTSD protocol, I began the cue sheet right before Lori's death and included as many details as possible during the days of the trauma, several cues for the next week, at least one cue for each of the following four weeks of the next month, and two or three cues for each month up to the present. I took Johnny through the grief timeline as many times as I could for the remainder of the session. At the end of the session, Johnny said his head was spinning.

"Success," I replied. "I call that the 'head-in-the-blender' feeling. It means a lot is happening in your brain and you will be better this week." I warned that he might have some difficult dreams or strong emotions as his brain continued to process Lori's death. "And please be careful driving. Your brain is not normal right now," I added.

"That's the truth," he answered. Johnny's story can be told through his cue sheet. I read the following cues to Johnny many times in each of our sessions:

FRIDAY, SEPTEMBER 15:

- Woke up in the morning and showered.

- Made lunch and heard Lori sleeping on the sofa in the living room. Sometimes she went out and slept on the couch when she was restless.

- Fed the dogs and said to them, "She's sure sleeping hard right now."

- Took the dogs outside and walked them for about 45 minutes.

- Came in and I couldn't hear the heavy breathing so I thought Lori was awake.

- I went into the living room to say good morning and she didn't look right.

- I knew something was wrong so I went over to her and found she wasn't breathing.

- I began CPR and called 911.

- I continued CPR until the aid car arrived.

- They wanted to pronounce her dead right away, but I urged them to work on her.

- They worked on her for 45 minutes.

- The aid car team called the coroner.

- The chaplain came.

- I went down to a neighbor's while they took the body away.

- Afterward I gathered clothes for a couple of days and put them into a suitcase.

- Took the dogs, locked up the house.

- Went to my parents.

- Around 6pm my mother said dinner was ready but I didn't want to eat.

SATURDAY, SEPTEMBER 16
- I don't remember much from that day. I think I settled in and helped my dad with a household project.
- I took the dogs for a walk and it was raining.

SUNDAY, SEPTEMBER 17
- I watched a football game.
- I called my boss and told her I wouldn't be coming into work the next day.

MONDAY, SEPTEMBER 18
- Made arrangements with the funeral home.

TUESDAY, SEPTEMBER 19
- Talked to the cemetery.
- Relayed information from the coroner's office to the cemetery and funeral home.
- Talked with Lori's parents.
- Her brother called.

WEDNESDAY, SEPTEMBER 20
- Friends came over after work.

THURSDAY, SEPTEMBER 21
- Went to the cemetery, picked out a plot.
- On the way back selected flowers.
- Started a viewing of the body at the funeral home.
- Left at 9pm for food.
- Lori's dad made an inappropriate comment to me.

FRIDAY, SEPTEMBER 22
- Left the house at 2pm for a half day of viewing.

- Had a late dinner with my best friend from work.

SATURDAY, SEPTEMBER 23
- Attended the funeral service at church.
- I passed by the casket first. I touched her hand and it was cold so I couldn't hold her hand again.
- Stopped for lunch on the way to the cemetery.
- Met at cemetery.
- Said goodbye to everyone who attended.
- Left with my parents.
- Family came to my parent's home.

MONDAY, SEPTEMBER 25
- Went to work to get my mind off things.

FIRST WEEK OF OCTOBER
- My parents went out of town and I watched their dogs.

SECOND WEEK OF OCTOBER
- Took out a bank loan to begin some remodeling on the condo to get it ready to sell.
- Went to the condo with friends and family to clean it out.

THIRD WEEK OF OCTOBER
- Lori's mom called and we talked for a while.

LAST WEEK OF OCTOBER
- Professional cleaning in the condo.

NOVEMBER
- Met with a pastor.
- Saw a movie with my parents. It was a romance movie and I couldn't take it.
- Got the coroner's report.

- Thanksgiving with family.

DECEMBER

- Christmas with my brother and his kids.

- Extended family came over in the evening.

- Friends invited me out for New Year's Eve; I declined.

JANUARY

- A lot of snow.

- Worked from home a lot.

- Lori's dad called.

- Visited a friend in New Mexico.

FEBRUARY

- Remodeling going on in the condo.

- Friend's mom passed away. It brought up a lot of feelings about Lori.

MARCH

- Did my taxes.

- Finished a major project at work.

APRIL

- Went to a concert.

MAY

- Got an attorney.

JUNE

- Estate settled.

JULY

- Mom talked to me about this therapy. I made an appointment.

We began each of our sessions by Johnny telling me about his week and the ways in which grief and other emotions were shifting. After the weekly check-in, I read Johnny's cue sheet over and over, waiting after each cue for him to acknowledge he had the memory in his mind. Once again, I read Johnny's cues to him so the wording made sense to him as the listener. His cue sheet read, "I passed by the casket first. I touched her hand and it was cold…" I read that cue to him as, "You passed by the casket first. Her hand was cold when you touched it, etc." If I had read the cue exactly as it was written, I would confuse Johnny by implying I personally passed by the casket first and touched Lori's cold hand.

At the beginning of the third session Johnny said, "I've been feeling more positive. I think this is working. I've been doing better. I'm still depressed about the money part of it, though. I had a good amount in my savings account before I married Lori, but now it's all gone and I owe money on the condo." After four repetitions of his timeline Johnny had an insight and said, "I actually felt some guilt that Lori's death brought a bit of relief to the medical problems." Like each of the previous Lifespan Integration sessions, Johnny was experiencing the layers of his grief. With each session, and each repetition of the timeline, more facts, insights, and emotions were revealed and integrated.

During the fourth session, Johnny shared that a close friend's mother had recently died. He said, "Talking to him about it—and attending her funeral—brought everything back about losing Lori, but it didn't put me back into the same negative emotional space. It was good but weird."

I asked, "What is coming up these days about Lori and her death?"

Johnny replied, "I realized that I'd been putting all of my needs aside for Lori the same way my mother did for people she loved. I learned this from her." We entered into the timeline phase of our session. Once again I read the cues for the duration of our time together. At the end of the session, Johnny said, "News Flash!

I don't have to be like my mother! I want a woman who is emotionally and financially stable and trustworthy. I've been afraid to be in another relationship because I assumed it would be like my relationship with Lori. It doesn't have to be!" I validated Johnny's new perspective, which arose from the timeline work. Because Johnny reached this revelation on his own without my input, I knew it was internalized and would always be accessible to Johnny in the future.

When asked about his grief at our fifth session Johnny said, "It's almost completely gone. My iPod contains a lot of music that brings up memories associated with Lori. Lately, I've been able to listen to the music anyway. I might get emotional, but I'm not sad all the time. I'm more upbeat, with some depression. Life is regular. I get low points sometimes. After Lori died I wasn't living, I was just existing. Now I've started to take care of myself. I'm still not going out much though due to the leftover money problems."

"How about the guilt?" I asked.

"I haven't thought about that since last week," Johnny answered.

Johnny also offered clarification about the order of some events on his timeline. As is normal with LI, the more we went through the timeline, the more chronologically accurate it became. I adjusted some of the cues based on his corrections and added items he was beginning to remember from the last few months. Getting more accurate recall of events is typical, and indicative of the integration that occurs with LI work. For example, Johnny said, "I thought we had lunch on the way to the cemetery after the funeral, but we actually went to a restaurant when picking out the casket. On the day of the service, we ate at the reception." To finish our session, we proceeded through many repetitions of Johnny's revised timeline.

Johnny started our next session by saying, "I put the condo on the market and it sold in one week. Because of this therapy, I was able to get the remodeling done and list it with an agent. I also took care of Lori's car. I haven't been able to do anything with it in the nine months since she died. It has just been parked in

front of the condo. This week I listed it for sale on the internet."
Johnny was making other positive steps to renew his life. He began
to socialize with co-workers and meet friends after work for dinner. He was developing a deeper friendship with a woman at work.
Johnny said, "I definitely don't feel like I'm depressed, and I'm getting much more interested in women." We proceeded through his
timeline from Lori's death to the present. "Some positive memories
are showing up," Johnny told me when I asked him about the repetitions of his timeline. He even laughed several times during our
session. Johnny concluded by saying, "Wow! I can't believe how
good I feel. Everybody should get counseling."

At our final session four months after we began, Johnny
reported no remaining grief about Lori's death. "She will always
be a part of me, but I'm moving on with my life. I'd like to get
married again and have a family. Now I think I can do it. I talked to
Lori's mom this week and I encouraged her to get counseling. She's
not doing well at all. We are approaching the anniversary of Lori's
death and her mom is totally stuck in her grief. I told her that this
really worked for me and that she should do it. I think everybody
should get counseling," he said.

Since Johnny had mentioned this twice, I asked him to clarify.
"Do you think everybody who goes to counseling does what we
have been doing?"

"Yes. Isn't this what everybody gets when they go to counseling?" Johnny asked.

I laughed and said, "No, this is a relatively new therapy and
not everyone knows about it. If your mother-in-law went for
counseling in the city where she lives, she wouldn't be experiencing Lifespan Integration. This method is the most powerful way
to resolve grief that I know, but counselors are just beginning to
learn about the therapy."

Since Johnny reported no distress about Lori's death, we did
not follow his cue sheet. Instead, we talked about the changes he
experienced during our work and his plans for the future. Johnny

was glad that his work performance had returned to normal and was looking forward to dating again.

"I'm not going to make my whole life about meeting someone else's needs," he offered. "I know a lot more about what I need in a relationship."

The mood for our last session was warm, positive, and encouraging. Johnny reported that his grief about Lori was as close to zero as possible and said, "Now I realize that I loved Lori and I always will, but it's okay to move on. She'd want that for me and I'd want that for her. We had something special between us. In one way it's over, but in another way it's not. She will always be in my heart."

I affirmed Johnny's healthy new perspective and wished him well. We parted ways with a warm handshake.

"I'm going to see if I can get my friend to come see you. He's having trouble after the death of his mom. I know this would help him too," Johnny added.

"I'm sure it would," I agreed.

A few months after our last session, Johnny called to clarify a bookkeeping detail. He expressed his gratitude again for the way LI helped him heal from his grief and reported that he was doing well.

In every case I have seen, trauma and grief resolved for clients through Lifespan Integration. At a recent training, Pace said, "The timelines of LI convince the client's body that the trauma has passed. Their brain may know it, but the body does not. LI shows the body that the trauma is over." Clients' responses affirm this statement. Once the body understands that time has moved on, clients are able to re-enter life with an understanding that their difficult experience had a beginning, middle, and an end. In the cases mentioned here—and in all the PTSD situations I have seen in counseling—it is a tremendous relief for the client's body, soul, and mind to understand that an ending point occurred in the difficult circumstance which the client's body had been holding. Even if aspects of the trauma are ongoing, the client's body generally does not know that the initial shock and impact are not occurring in the present. Logically we can understand that time has moved on, but the nature of trauma appears to create frozen states for clients, which repetitions of the timeline resolve. Other clients make similar comments to Johnny's statement, "Everybody with grief should do this".

I like LI because it doesn't re-traumatize clients by having them tell the story over and over. The integration makes sense to them because they see their story in real time. As they experience it, it begins to make sense and they can manage the emotions in it. Their integration gives them more control and changed behavior.

Candie Warren, LI therapist

8. Relationship Issues

I believe Lifespan Integration is the most effective therapy for relationship problems available to us today. Clients say, "It's unbelievable. I can't believe I have changed like this." Clinicians also find the results remarkable when they begin using Lifespan Integration for relationship issues. When couples contact me for marriage or relationship therapy, I explain how and why we will use LI as the main therapeutic tool. Lifespan Integration works well with struggling couples because couples continually trigger each other's younger-selves. LI reaches the young state that is responsible for the acting out or irrational behavior. When these younger ego states are integrated, the adults in therapy make more appropriate choices about how they will interact with each other.

I generally try to see each person in the couple for individual LI, interspersed with seeing them conjointly as a couple. I understand this is a departure from some trends in marriage therapy. My purpose in counseling the couple this way is to target—in an individual and safe environment—the issues that are getting triggered in the marriage, which can be observed as the couple interacts. It also gives me a behind-the-scenes perspective as I work with one person and then the other. Since the main therapeutic tool is LI rather than my insight or the therapeutic alliance, couples do not find it problematic when I individually meet with each partner. I still have to be conscientious about not appearing overly aligned with one partner or the other, but the pattern of seeing them individually and together works well with Lifespan Integration. Using this format for counseling couples allows issues to be fleshed out more fully than could otherwise occur in individual counseling.

When only one person in the marriage or partnership comes for counseling with Lifespan Integration, it also produces significant change in the relationship. As individual clients change week-by-week, they go back into their relationships and ask for new ways of relating. Generally, clients cannot tolerate inappropriate behavior after LI, even if they had been participating in it for years. This may seem too good to be true, but I have come to expect noticeable and lasting change every time I meet with a client. And, just like dropping a pebble into the center of a pond produces ripples throughout the entire body of water, these changes in the individual—due to LI—work their way into the family system.

Initially, we targeted relationship issues with LI in one of two ways: 1) by focusing on the feelings triggered in one person when the partner acts in a certain way, or 2) through conversation helping partners identify their main behavioral pattern for relating. Once the activated feeling is identified or the problematic strategy a couple is using in their relationship is clarified, the therapist asks the client to find the related feelings in his or her body and guides the client to a source memory by way of the affect bridge. In 2010, a new method for targeting relationship issues emerged and is called the Relationship Pattern protocol. A more detailed description will be given near the end of this chapter.

Targeting Feelings

As stated previously, the reason it will be effective to float back feelings generated inside the relationship is because ego states are being triggered in each of the partners. Clients do not link these triggered feelings to earlier emotional states even though they are reacting directly from them. Even if a client cannot see a direct link between a current problem and its float back target, change will still be produced when the float back target is cleared. For example, if a woman comes to therapy because her husband has an addiction to pornography, in Lifespan Integration we would ask her to point to the place in her body where she personally feels the pain of his behavior and float this body feeling back to an earlier time. In contrast, a traditional talk therapist would guide the same client toward problem solving about her husband's behavior. With LI, we can heal the familiar internal state, which is being aroused inside the female client by the current situation. When previous hurtful and powerless situations are resolved, the client will automatically respond to her husband in adult, empowered ways. A problem-solving conversation between the LI therapist and client may still occur at this point, but it will be a more effective conversation because the client will see her situation in a new light since she is not responding from a younger state.

Targeting a current issue or pattern through feelings is simply done by asking, "What comes up for you when your partner says or does _____? The client notices the internal body sensations and emotions that are generated and follows these to an earlier time through the affect bridge. Sometimes clients will float back to positive memories. These too, need to be integrated in order to produce change. Sally was a young woman I saw for therapy who floated back to a memory of telling her parents she had accidentally broken something in the kitchen while they were away. She feared their harsh reaction and was surprised when they said, "These things happen, the item can be replaced." This appeared to be a positive memory but it held a significant component for helping Sally relieve her current distress. We repeatedly showed the younger ego state the timeline which proved the kitchen situation was over. In the end Sally remarked, "This shows me that people won't always react the way I expect they will. I've been afraid of giving someone important information at work for fear of his reaction. Now I realize I'm not a child anymore. I'm a manager, and I have to let him know the decision I've made." Sally left feeling confident, knowing she could carry out a conversation that she had been avoiding.

Targeting Strategies

Another way to identify LI targets for relationship issues is to identify the methods and behaviors used for operating within relationships. Simply defined, behavioral strategies are the emotional and practical tools we consciously and unconsciously use in relating to others. These strategies—good or bad—are the learned throughout a lifetime and include, but are not limited to, caretaking, hiding from intimacy, controlling others, and initiating closeness.

Melinda was a client who seemed to have an over-developed capacity for tolerating unkind behavior from her husband. She named her strategy as "Tolerating bad behavior." I asked Melinda to focus on the feeling inside the core of her body when she imagined herself tolerating her husband's bad behavior. Melinda recalled herself as a little girl playing quietly alone with her dolls. This behavior does not appear to be inappropriate or problematic and was actually very resourceful behavior for a smart little girl. Yet it turned out that Melinda was playing alone because her older brother was continually mean to her and Melinda's mother told her to ignore her brother's bad behavior. Melinda's mother did not intervene with the older son who was jealous and resentful of his younger sister. Melinda developed a strategy for overlooking her brother's abuse, and consequently ignored her husband's bad behavior toward her the same way she ignored her brother's bad behavior. As an adult, the "tolerating bad behavior" strategy learned in childhood was playing out unconsciously in Melinda's marriage. After we targeted the relationship pattern directly, Melinda made more empowered responses to her husband that led to positive change for both of them.

Justin was another client of mine who benefited from applying

LI to relationship issues. He was in a six-year relationship, which he attempted to end several times. When he tried to separate from his girlfriend who had moved across the country to be with him, she was emotionally devastated and threatened suicide. Rather than face the conflict and its outcomes, Justin acquiesced and kept trying to make things work. Through our conversation, it became apparent that one of Justin's main strategies in relationships was to not be honest with himself or his partner. He had a history of relationships, about which he said, "I knew I was doing the wrong thing but I did it anyway. I wasn't honest with myself and what I knew."

We targeted the strategy that kept Justin participating in dishonesty. This method led Justin back to his childhood: he grew up in an alcoholic family where people pretended things were different than what was actually true. In Justin's family system he learned to ignore his own feelings in order to pretend he had a normal family. Similarly, Justin kept pretending in his current relationship rather than face conflict with his girlfriend. When we showed Justin's younger-self, who used denial to cope with life, that circumstances had dramatically changed and many years had passed, Justin was able to use more honest strategies with his girlfriend in the present.

Justin had previously been in months of traditional couples therapy with his girlfriend. The therapist had repeatedly coached Justin to be more honest with her but he could not bring himself to say the things that were true for him. After this LI session, Justin went home and was compassionate, honest, and unwavering about what he needed. When his girlfriend threatened suicide Justin said, "I don't want anything like that to happen to you, but I can't control what you do just like I can't pretend anymore about how I feel." The couple's therapist was shocked at how well Justin handled speaking the truth to his girlfriend. Eventually, Justin moved out of the apartment he shared with his girlfriend, and she managed the break-up without a suicide attempt.

Steven came for counseling because his wife, Patti, of 15 years was preparing to leave him. He had occasionally used pornography and had been caught entering a sex club while Patti was out of town. Finding out about the sex club incident was the last straw for Patti. Although Steven assured her that nothing serious was taking place and begged her to let the incident pass, Patti could not ignore it. After 15 years of feeling on the outside of Steven's life, Patti was ready to leave her husband. Although the sex club incident was disturbing, what troubled Patti most was his long-term habit of keeping parts of his life secret from her. Steven's style of keeping everything to himself was alienating Patti.

I was curious why Steven was reluctant to share more of himself with his wife. I had met Patti and experienced her as kind and compassionate, one who could be trusted. Steven said that his automatic internal mechanism kept people—including Patti—from knowing the truth about him.

Focusing on the feelings this generated inside him, Steven floated back to the time in his life when he began keeping his personal life a secret. Through this affect bridge, Steven found the ten-year-old younger-self who could not do anything to make life better or safer. Steven was raised in a high profile, wealthy family with an alcoholic father. Horrendous things were happening in his home and the only way Steven could cope in that situation was to be someone else when he was away from the house. As a popular and successful student, Steven mastered the ability to keep his personal life separated from his public life. I coached Steven to tell his younger-self that he was the little boy's grow-up-self and that living with his mom and dad was over. All the difficult things about life in that home were in the past. After a few more comments, I directed Steven through the timeline.

Each time we came back to the memory scene in the boy's home, the younger-self's distress was lessened until, after enough repetitions, he was completely at ease. After several repetitions of his timeline, the adult Steven finally understood that keeping his two lives separate, though once helpful, was severely hurting him now. The little boy understood that he was part of an adult-self who could use more empowered strategies for living his life. The young ego state received compassion and released his need for splitting his emotional worlds and this allowed the younger state to support the adult's desire to create closeness by sharing more of himself with others. This series of timelines and conversations took one standard hour counseling session.

When Steven's younger-self was no longer in distress and believed he was the same person as the client in my office, our target for the session was complete. The adult Steven was able to understand how his behavior was hurting Patti and he had the internal freedom to change it. I gave Steven some principles for relationships that he had not learned through the years since he was dedicated to keeping people out of his life, rather than letting them in. Steven was eager to implement the new tools because he was very lonely, even though he had a supportive wife. Most clients can solve their current problems with little or no help once the root ego state is integrated.

Steven and I met for another ten sessions following the same method of naming the feelings generated in his relationship with Patti and following the affect bridge to an earlier time. We removed the distress from the earlier memories, which left Steven with more adult thinking for his current stressors. After six months in therapy, Steven reported to me that things were going really well for him with Patti. He said, "We have a better relationship than we have had for years." He was able to have more honest conversations with her as I had coached him and they were enjoying each other much more. Steven and Patti were looking forward to the years ahead because they had built a family together which neither wanted to lose. When he initially came to see me, Patti was taking steps to leave him due to his secret life. By targeting this with Lifespan Integration they were able to move closer and continue building a life together.

Relationship Pattern Protocol

Relationship issues get activated in many circumstances, not just in the one-on-one context of couples. We activate our relational strategies at work, in groups, or in much larger social contexts. These too, are relationship issues which can be targeted success-fully with Lifespan Integration. Because our unhealthy relationship patterns operate in the broad context of our lives, it became neces-sary to develop an LI method for treating relationship patterns that emerge repeatedly in various contexts.

I developed the Relationship Pattern protocol from a situation that arose in individual therapy with Susan, a client for whom I had consistently used Lifespan Integration for three years. She first came to therapy to address Posttraumatic Stress Disorder (PTSD) from a burglary at her home where she and her daughter were sleeping alone in the house. After the PTSD was resolved, Susan stayed in therapy and began to work on other issues.

Susan was launching an individual consulting business and often asked for feedback about her work decisions. I contributed my ideas as I felt it was appropriate to do so, while guiding her through the various protocols of Lifespan Integration. At one point in her work journey, Susan became discouraged and said to me with anger, "You're not helping me! You don't get me!" I thought I understood her fairly well after three years of therapy. Susan was an unwanted child from a teen pregnancy who had learn-ing challenges and mixed success in her professional life. When I offered a suggestion that could be useful to her, Susan angrily rejected my idea. "You don't get me," she repeated. "Nobody seems to get me!" There was anguish in her discouragement, as well as frustration with me for not being helpful in the ways that would meet her need. For three weeks Susan and I had strained therapy sessions in which she repeatedly expressed that I "wasn't getting her" and I explained that in fact I understood her to the best of my ability.

The Relationship Pattern protocol was born when I decided to directly target the feelings Susan had in relationship to me. It worked because Susan had enough of a core self into which she could integrate an ineffective relational pattern. Up to this point, therapy with Susan had included many sessions of the Birth-to-Present protocol for self-soothing and the general integration of self-states which strengthened her core consciousness.

At the beginning of our first Relationship Pattern protocol session, I promised Susan that we would save time to talk about our conflict, but I asked her to first engage in timelines about her feelings. I instructed her to notice the place in her body where she felt the frustration of not being understood by me. It was likely that this problem had occurred before and was a recurring pattern in many of her relationships. Even though we had done many sessions of LI, we apparently had not integrated the root of this particular distress and behavior. Susan pointed to her stomach area as the place where she felt the pain of not being understood. Because this pain probably came from more than one incident, I did not rely on an affect bridge to take us to a specific memory for healing. Instead, I asked Susan to focus on the feeling in her gut and used the bodily sensations of "being misunderstood" as our single target for the entire session. In other words, the feeling in Susan's body was our target rather than a memory or a strategy. I was attempting to target a *repeating pattern* in Susan's life which occurred in relationship to others, including me. I knew that if Susan could point to the place in her body where she experienced distress, then the neural networks associated with this relationship distress were also being fired.

Trusting in the miracle of repeated timelines, I asked Susan to notice the feeling in her stomach and imagine the day she was born. I did not know when in her life the distress pattern started so I began the timeline at birth. I believed that the pattern Susan was experiencing would be integrated by repetitions of the timeline no matter where it occurred as long as she could access the body feelings associated with the pattern. *This is not the same as Birth-to-Present protocol.* I did not have Susan envision her birth, nor did I hold a doll to simulate connection to her baby-self. Rather, I had Susan focus on the feeling in her gut and imagine the first day of her life as the start of our timeline.

I guided Susan through infant developmental stages to continue our timeline, such as, "imagine being a baby who can grab at your toes, smiling at people, scooting on the floor and putting things in your mouth." At age five in her timeline, I asked her to focus on her stomach again and notice the feeling there associated with "You're not getting me." We did not talk about this feeling. When Susan nodded that she had reconnected to the body feeling, I continued to age six in her timeline, then age seven, age eight, and so on. At age ten, I asked Susan to pay attention to the body feeling again. Without talking, we continued in her timeline up to her current age of 54. At five to ten year intervals throughout the timeline we paused for Susan to reconnect to the feeling in her body. At age 54, we did not have a younger ego state to bring into the present, so we ended Susan's timeline and I simply asked her to open her eyes. Without much discussion, Susan noticed the feeling in her gut and we began a second timeline from the day she was born. Again, this is not Birth-to-Present protocol, but rather a method for integrating a body feeling which has occurred at many stages in a client's life. Because neither the client nor I could be sure where the feeling started, we began her timeline at birth to include all neural networks and memories that included the feeling tone associated with not being understood.

At the end of one session, with approximately six repetitions of timelines focused solely on the feeling in her stomach, the distress in Susan's body dissipated. Susan was peaceful at the end of the protocol and said, "This is about my mother. She never did understand me. She was 17 years old when I was born, and she never really connected to me. She always told me I was a difficult baby. I can see how I have felt this way my entire life. I get very distressed when people don't understand me." With softness and openness, our conversation shifted to the conflict between the two of us. Compassionately, I said I was trying very hard to understand her. Susan agreed that the distress was internal to her and not about a dynamic between the two of us. "Going through the timelines," she said, "I could see incident after incident where I felt misunderstood. The idea that I'm a difficult person has followed me all of my life."

The method of directly targeting a feeling, which occurred in the session between client and therapist, began the development of the Relationship Pattern protocol. Eventually, a client's relational difficulties emerge in therapy with the counselor. These feelings can be identified in the body and targeted directly and simply with a hybrid method of timelines beginning at birth while focusing solely on the client's body connection to the relationship pattern. This initial method developed into a protocol that can be applied to relationship issues in broader contexts beyond the client-therapist relationship.

Relationship patterns are formed by the experiences and beliefs gathered over a lifetime. Once learned, patterns generally repeat until healed. The Relationship Pattern protocol gives us a way to define relational patterns and target them broadly rather than as specific strategies or activated feelings. The new Relationship Pattern protocol is a way to incorporate strategies, emotions, beliefs, and body sensations into one effective LI method. As mentioned earlier, in order for this protocol to work clients must have a solid core self. Highly dissociated or fragmented clients need Birth-to-Present protocol to help create a stable, integrated core before the Relationship Pattern Protocol method will be effective.

When to Use the Relationship Pattern Protocol

As Lifespan Integration developed, variations on Standard Protocol evolved. As Pace used her new method with clients, it became apparent that early repair work and internal solidification needed to occur for some clients before the methods of Standard Protocol could produce their common results. If clients were too dissociated to integrate a distressing memory into their core consciousness, then many repetitions of the Birth-to-Present protocol were required to strengthen the core self. Evidence also began to suggest that certain protocols of Lifespan Integration could contribute to the repair of clients' attachment styles and consequently their success in relating to others.

The Relationship Pattern protocol of LI follows these other LI protocols and is appropriate for individuals who can identify a troubling pattern in their lives, already demonstrate an ability to regulate their emotions in most situations, can remember their lifetime, and can readily compile a cue list with specific incidents and memories. If a client is not proficient at the above-mentioned tasks, then he or she is considered somewhat dissociated, and is not a good candidate for the Relationship Pattern protocol. The purpose of the Relationship Pattern protocol is to help relatively stable clients discard an outdated relationship pattern they developed earlier in life. With Standard Protocol LI, clients shed outdated defense mechanisms that were initially developed in response to difficult circumstances where they had been powerless. With the Relationship Pattern protocol, clients can do the same with generalized relational patterns. The Relationship Pattern protocol targets ways of relating rather than specific memories or behaviors healed through Standard Protocol. Some patterns in a client's life are the derivative of numerous incidences over many years. The Relationship Pattern protocol appears to resolve a way of thinking or behaving which is present in many situations. It is appropriate for clients with a relatively solid sense of self who are struggling in certain relationship patterns.

Implementing the Relationship Pattern Protocol

Step one: Identifying the pattern. To use the Relationship Pattern protocol, a therapist helps a client identify the main components of the pattern the client would like to address. The pattern can be evident in virtually any context, including therapy, work, social, and family settings. Together, the client and counselor break the pattern into simple steps. It can follow a general A, B, C pattern such as "Whenever I'm in a meeting at work, I get really quiet and hope no one asks for my opinion. I'm scared to say what I think." This is a relational pattern comprised of: A) When I have to perform, B) I feel afraid, and C) I can't think of anything to say. Therapists need to keep asking the client questions until the relational pattern seems well understood and clarified. The goal of this step is to accurately name the pattern.

Naming the pattern can also be as simple as the therapist or client pointing it out in a session. Susan helped me understand the importance of this by repeatedly telling me, "You're not getting me!" Her experience of our therapeutic relationship represented a long-standing relationship pattern for her. By identifying the dynamic between us, we were able to target Susan's pattern with the Relationship Pattern protocol of LI.

In a broader social context, clients are usually able to describe recurring relational themes from their lives. The Relationship Pattern protocol provides a way to target a general pattern, which is present in more than one setting and has occurred over a period of time. Examples of these patterns include:

- "I try to be really good by being focused on the other person. Then I get blind-sided because I don't see what's coming. I change myself to take the criticism so I don't repeat this experience. But it keeps happening over and over."

- "I'm weary about having to be the strong one in my relationship. I'm angry at my partner's rigidity and I'm tired of having to run interference with people because of the way he acts."

- "When I don't know what to do in a situation, I end up feeling powerless. I hate that feeling so I tune out what's in the environment. I get social confidence by ignoring things."

- "I don't deserve the good friends I have. Because I don't react the way I think I should, I feel guilty. I don't deserve good relationships."

These examples speak to the variety of patterns clients have developed. The patterns seem to be "wired" into their brains and repeat without the client's choice or control. Naming the relational pattern is the first step to implementing the Relationship Pattern protocol.

Step two: Pointing to the body sensation. Once the pattern has been identified, the client is asked to point to the place in the core of his or her body where physical sensations get activated when talking about or remembering the pattern. This can be more than one place in the client's trunk. As therapists have used the Relationship Pattern method, they notice that the feelings associated with a relational pattern generally start in the stomach area and move up to the heart and throat areas before finally clearing. Clients do not talk about the feelings in the body. Once the area has been identified, the therapist moves into the timeline phase of the protocol. The body feelings are the single target for the entire protocol.

Step three: Repetitions of the timeline. The timeline used in the Relationship Pattern protocol is the simplest version of a timeline used in Lifespan Integration. It starts at birth and ends in present time without bringing a younger-self into the present. As mentioned previously, the Relationship Pattern protocol is not Birth-to-Present protocol because it does not include all the steps of BP. The Relationship Pattern protocol excludes seeing the baby born, bathing and swaddling the baby, taking the baby to a peaceful place, and so on. Instead, the Relationship Pattern protocol is simply a timeline that begins on the first day of life, followed by the infant developmental stages, on through the written memory cue sheet, and ending in the present. There is no step at the end of the timeline other than taking a break if needed or beginning another repetition of the timeline after noticing the body feeling again. It is a very simplified form of the timeline. At the point where a client would be reminded to "check on the younger-self and make sure he or she is still with you," the therapist asks the client to only notice the feeling in his or her body associated with the relationship pattern. Once the client acknowledges the sensation, the timeline continues.

We start the Relationship Pattern protocol at birth because we do not know when the client began the relationship pattern. Since the method is exclusively body-based, we are safe to begin at birth knowing that the neural networks associated with the relationship pattern will be fired at points along the timeline, including before age two when concrete memory begins. Just like other forms of the timeline that begin before the client has memories on the cue sheet, the therapist mentions developmental stages up to the actual age where memories appear on the written timeline sheet. Timelines are repeated until body distress associated with the relational pattern is clear. Clinicians know the target for a session is complete when the central core of the client's body is free from distressful activation when thinking about the relationship pattern.

As is common with all repetitions of the timeline, clients will begin to fire other neural networks associated with the target feeling. They often comment, "I can see where this happened many times in my life," or "Wow, this pattern is not very effective anymore!" In some cases, clients may cite a specific time or incident where the pattern began. When this happens, the therapist can shift the start of the timeline to the age indicated by the client. Such a scenario could play out in the following way: After three repetitions from birth, a client might say, "I began doing this at age five when my brother died." If so, rather than starting at birth, the therapist can begin the timeline at age five and guide the client up to his or her current age.

More than One Session with the Same Relationship Pattern

Because the Relationship Pattern protocol addresses a problematic pattern that occurs repeatedly over time, it is typical to target the same pattern and body sensation in follow-up sessions. It is possible to resolve a relational pattern in a single session, but it is more common to readdress the pattern in successive sessions until the pattern is fully resolved. Two to four counseling sessions for the same target pattern is typical. With each session, the body distress associated with the pattern will be reduced or move upward through the core. During this time, the client will gain understanding about how the pattern has operated in his or her life. After a few sessions of the Relationship Pattern protocol, a solid client will probably observe that the pattern does not operate in his or her life anymore and the body distress associated with it is gone.

Dana's Story

Dana initially sought counseling around a relationship pattern with coworkers. Our work together concluded after four sessions of the Relationship Pattern protocol. Dana was a successful and high achieving professional with a relatively solid core self. She was smart, self-aware, and was able to complete her written timeline of memories rather easily because she had good recall from her childhood. If Dana had not been able to complete her timeline so easily, we would have begun our work together with the Birth-to-Present protocol. Dana presented with a specific issue to target and described the place where she held it in her body quite quickly, which informed me that we could begin focusing on the topic directly. Her single focus for therapy fit criteria for the Relationship Pattern model so we began our work with this method. In her words, Dana wanted to be "included, accepted, liked, smart, and connected at work." Instead, Dana reported hiding behind a shell with a heavy, hard exterior. She said, "The shell is predominately cold on the outside of me. I have a protective barrier to protect me from being sad." This shell represented Dana's self-protective way of relating and was a symbol for the relationship pattern. When asked where she felt this in her body, Dana pointed to her stomach and said, "It's in my gut and feels a little nauseous, like a deep pit."

We began timelines addressing the "hard shell protecting her from sadness." Dana focused solely on the feeling in her gut while I asked her to imagine the day she was born. We proceeded to an image of her at six weeks old in the crib grabbing her toes and smiling at people when they looked at her. We continued through Dana's developmental stages and through the written cue sheet up to her current age of 37 years old. During the break after the third timeline, Dana noted, "I felt a lot of sadness early on. There was sadness and confusion in my younger years. I was lonely for most of it. I knew right away that my younger-self wanted more of her mom's unconditional love. Mom was busy and distracted. The baby never felt satisfied or filled. The shell came from the fear of reaching out and not getting relationship back. It was a way to eliminate vulnerability."

At the beginning of the next session, Dana remarked, "During the past two weeks I was more interested into doing things. I wanted to get out. I was more open to connecting with others and was a lot more present with my kids. I had an unusually good conversation with my sister. Even my desire for wine decreased."

I asked Dana to focus on the shell again. She replied, "I can see it and feel the weight of it in my gut." We proceeded through a timeline focused on the feeling in her body. At the end of the first repetition Dana reported, "I was cold and alone." We continued with several more timelines throughout the second session.

Dana began our third session by saying, "I was able to handle stress a lot better since our last session. For the past couple of years, my brain was not connecting in personal conversations.

Face-to-face conversations were harder for me than email. There has been a huge change in this." She continued by reporting, "85 percent of the time I don't react the same way anymore. I've stepped out of a very young girl's body. I'm less dependent on my boss."

"What about the shell?" I inquired.

"It's only a thin veil. Most days I don't think about it anymore. It was a barrier between feeling and thinking," Dana answered. When asked to identify the shell in her body, Dana pointed to her gut again and said, "There is an empty space in here. There's also something in my face and throat." We proceeded through repetitions of the timeline focused on her body until our session was finished.

The fourth Relationship Pattern protocol session occurred two months after the first session. "I was able to feel during this break between sessions!" Dana exuberantly began. "I was caught off guard two times when tears and words I didn't plan on saying came out. They were better than what I planned to say. A protective child inside me is not taking over anymore."

Guiding Dana back to the relationship pattern, I asked her to check her gut. "There's still something in that area," Dana answered. As we moved through the timelines, she remarked, "I spent the first 14 years of life in anxiety. I had to keep myself moving." Checking on her body after the fifth timeline, she peacefully said, "It's like there is a butterfly in here (pointing to her stomach) and it's flying away. It's saying goodbye to Mom and Dad."

From that point forward, Dana indicated that the "protective shell of hardness" was completely gone. She said, "I'm so different at work sometimes I can't believe it's me." A year after our work together, Dana reported that she had experienced no recurrence of the relationship pattern we targeted in four sessions. She laughingly added, "Can you put a little of the stress back in? I'm so low key at work now I can't get excited about some of the things that used to drive me. I don't know if my boss notices, but I'm a lot less driven at work."

"Sorry," I replied with a smile. "When we do this kind of healing it lasts."

The Relationship Pattern protocol of Lifespan Integration is a new addition to the variety of techniques available to trained LI clinicians. When an overall pattern of relating needs to be treated in therapy, the Relationship Pattern protocol provides a way to integrate the many occurrences in a person's life of a repeating pattern. Simply targeting the sensations in the client's body related to the pattern will provide significant change for most clients who have a solid core self. When clients lack a solid core, therapists should use other LI protocols to help clients with their relationships.

9. Depression Protocol

 Depression is a problem with many facets. It is a biochemical, emotional, mental, and spiritual problem with serious implications. Although people suffering from depression long for relief, they often live many years struggling with the ramifications of depression. Mike's case represents such a story. He had tried every medication available for depression as well as counseling with many therapists over the years, but Mike had not been able to get freedom from the devastating grip of depression. When I began working with him, I did not have the tools in hand that are available now for clearing depression with Lifespan Integration. Mike's treatment was a learning experience for me and a miracle for Mike. Thanks to help from Peggy Pace, Mike's situation was my first experience seeing a client's depression disappear week by week.

I have included a section at the end of this chapter titled *What I Learned About Depression* where I discuss some basic components of this malady—low sense of value, poor connection, performance-orientation and hopelessness. But first, a summary follows on two case studies which exemplify the main components found in virtually all depression. Each case of depression is unique to the individual, but after working with many clients using Lifespan Integration, I have found straightforward, simple methods for diagnosing and treating this condition. Although depression is a malaise for clients, for the therapist it can be straightforward and fixable if the right tools are implemented. Lifespan Integration, with a few adaptations, is proving to be the most effective treatment for depression that I have seen to date. Since my work with Mike, and due to input from Pace, I have accumulated a set of working tools that have proved to be effective with essentially every client who has presented with depression.

Mike's Story

At our intake session, Mike said, "If this therapy doesn't work, I'm going to commit suicide." Unfortunately, he meant it. A reputable psychologist had worked with Mike for six months and referred him to my office after a colleague told her about Lifespan Integration. The psychologist was at the end of her resources for ways to help him. Mike was also seeing a psychiatrist at least three times a month. He was currently on four medications and said, "None of them are working." I ascertained that Mike was under contract with his psychiatrist to not commit suicide. Mike suspected that depression was a hereditary condition. His sister was currently hospitalized for severe depression and Mike felt that he had tried every avenue available to get relief from his own depression. He hoped to avoid hospitalization himself. I assured Mike I could help with the anxiety he was experiencing, but I declined to offer him a miracle cure for his depression. He was eager to begin working with me, hoping something would change his miserable state.

Mike described his family of origin and told me about his childhood years. He was a lonely child who often felt isolated from his peers. When Mike changed schools in third grade he was ostracized for being racially different. He became the classroom target for teasing and was seldom invited to birthday parties in his upper class community. For Mike's tenth birthday party, only one or two friends came out of the several who were invited. Growing up, Mike remembers his father as successful, domineering, and critical.

Mike never felt close to his dad even though he actively tried to please him. When Mike or his siblings made mistakes, their father raged and demeaned them for being stupid. This was especially true for Mike, the only boy. The first time Mike remembered being well connected to others was in late high school when he joined the basketball team. After the high school and college years passed, Mike longed for the re-connection he felt to his fellow athletes during their basketball seasons.

Although the adult years of Mike's life looked more successful, they felt the same way as his childhood years. In the same way that Mike had few or no friends as a boy, Mike did not have any social groups where he felt closely connected as an adult. He had a job that paid well, but he did not enjoy his work and felt ostracized by coworkers. Mike was hired to make changes and he paid the social price for being the hatchet man. Once again, his peer community avoided him and complained about him to upper management. Mike feared that he might be fired and considered changing jobs but did not have the energy to look for another position.

I felt compassion for him and explained the rings of the tree analogy to him. I told him that people—like trees—are cumulative, so the little boy of his childhood was still inside him. Mike easily understood my description and longed for some method to make things different for the adult or the child. I explained that feeling states repeat throughout a lifetime until they are healed. Mike's loneliness and isolation were evident in his relationship to his father, childhood schoolmates, and colleagues at work. His child-self from the early "rings" of his life needed to be healed in order to bring new direction and connections into his adult life.

In our beginning use of Lifespan Integration, we targeted the feelings Mike was experiencing in the present and floated these back to childhood memories. Mike was an eager and dedicated client and worked hard to be successful. He compiled his list of memories at home with ease and he cleared distress from the memory scenes successfully.

After two months of therapy, though, Mike was still deeply depressed. Because he was seriously considering suicide, his psychiatrist recommended that he commit himself to a hospital. Mike went to the hospital and sat eight hours in the waiting room to be admitted. As evening approached, Mike went home to his wife and children in despair because a bed had not became available for him.

In my office a few days later, I arranged for Mike to see a naturopathic doctor who had successfully treated depression for some of my other clients. Mike was open to this idea since the standard medical treatment—which brings relief to many people—had not brought significant change for his condition. Mike agreed to continue his medication prescribed by the psychiatrist. The naturopath also encouraged him to stay on his medication, augmenting it with treatments of his own. I knew if LI was going to work, I would also have to modify my treatment plan for Mike. I sought out Pace's advice and she told me that depression is always about a personal, low sense of value and poor social connection. In using LI for depression, it is imperative to have the adult client re-parent his or herself with imaginary activities that communicate value and belonging to the isolated child ego state within. It was not sufficient to simply clear the client's memories of their distress.

Re-parenting is accomplished by directing the adult to go into an imaginary basement and find his or her child-self. Once found, the adult leads the child through activities of the child's choosing while the adult-self shows attentive and loving actions. The goal of this intervention is to create attachment and the sense of value that was missing in the client's growing up years. This tool is more than conjuring up make-believe stories for a placebo effect. The internal child is longing for connection and will bond with the adult-self—rather than be a lonely, unattached child—when given the opportunity through these imaginary exercises. After the child feels valued and connected in the internal world, the adult can create a life in the present to match this sense of self. The imaginary re-parenting process for depression is described in further detail in Pace's mnaual, *Lifespan Integration* (2012).

Mike was eager to try anything that would dispel his depression and I was ready to make any adaptations that would create positive change for him. Following the instruction provided by Pace, I asked Mike to close his eyes while I counted from nine to one and imagine himself walking down into a basement. When Mike was at the bottom of the stairs, I asked him to find his child-self who was lonely and wanted connection. Mike could not clearly see a child in his imagination, but he sensed himself in the basement as a young boy wearing a tennis sweater and saddle shoes. He described the child as, "not very alive, more like a picture." This indicated to me that he was quite dissociated from his younger-self. We invited the child to enter into an activity of his choosing with Mike's adult-self. The child wanted to play ping-pong.

"Take him somewhere you can play," I suggested.

"We have a table in our basement; I'll play with him there," Mike said.

I watched Mike who sat quietly in front of me. Internally, through his imagination, Mike played ping-pong with the little boy. This took several minutes during which I waited and watched. "Now he wants to go buy baseball cards, the big kind. Not like the ones you get today. These were bigger ones. I love that kind," Mike said, smiling and agreeing with his child-self.

"Take him somewhere to buy baseball cards," I kindly directed.

"I'll take him to Woolworth's," Mike replied. "I loved going to Woolworth's. My grandfather used to take me there and buy me baseball cards—the big ones." Once again I quietly waited and let Mike lead his younger-self on their outing. After a few minutes Mike said, "Now I'm going to buy him something at the Woolworth's fountain, a chocolate sundae." I encouraged Mike to sit with the little boy, talk with him, and give him undivided attention.

"Tell him there's no one else you would rather be with today.

Tell him he's the most important little boy in the whole world to you," I said.

"He likes that. He's talking to me about the cards. We open them and find out what's inside. We talk about the players on the cards. He really likes that I'm doing this with him," Mike explained. As I watched, a positive connection was taking place between the adult Mike and his younger-self.

"Now ask him to watch these pictures," I guided. "This is the story of how he grew up to be you." I led Mike through the memories on his cue sheet, beginning at age ten, which was one year older than the internal little boy at the Woolworth's lunch counter. When we finished with one timeline I told Mike, "Now go back and find that little boy again." The little boy was still with him at the Woolworth's counter. "What would he like to do now?" I asked.

"He wants to go collect rocks at the shore," Mike told me.

"Take him there," I said. Mike, in his imagination, took the little boy to the shore. They gathered rocks and talked about what they found. Mike's adult-self was attentive, loving, and responsive to the little boy. I gave Mike lots of time for his seashore adventure, occasionally checking in with him to see what they were doing. When we were almost out of time for the session, I guided Mike through one more repetition of the timeline.

Back in real-time in my office, Mike said warmly, "It's like I'm his dad. I can do the things for him my dad never did for me." Mike was surprised to find that 40 minutes had passed while he was doing the imaginary exercise. He was so engaged in the experience of re-parenting his internal child that he was completely unaware of time.

The following session, which was two weeks after his visit to the naturopath, Mike came in and reported, "I've been sleeping really well lately. This is a significant contrast to my usual pattern. My energy level is terrific and I feel more relaxed about things." As for issues which needed to be addressed, Mike identified that he was feeling cut-off at work and recognized a similar pattern in his relationship with his dad. He was more than willing to engage in the imaginary exercise he had experienced the week before. Taking my direction from his current report, I asked Mike to go into the imaginary basement and find the little boy who felt cut-off and lonely. Going into the basement, he once again found the little boy wearing a tennis sweater and saddle shoes. I invited Mike to engage with the little boy in whatever activity he would like. Mike told me, "He's very insecure and he doesn't want to be alone. He wants to hold my hand and be close to me."

"Do whatever he would like to give him the feeling of closeness," I said.

"He wants me just to hold him," Mike replied. I sensed the sadness in the little boy, which was coming through the adult. I waited while Mike held his child-self. After several minutes Mike said, "I'm going to read to him like I do with my own son," and proceeded to share a storybook with his child-self as they sat in a chair. After the imaginary story reading, I led Mike through one timeline and coached him to find the little boy again. "He's still holding my hand," Mike reported. "He won't let go of me. He's afraid of dying because my life has been so messed up." I speculated that he younger ego state was referring to Mike's serious, chronic depression and ideations about suicide.

"Tell him you're getting help now and you don't want to die. Reassure him that he's very important to you and that you are a grown-up who can provide what he did not get before. Let him know that you love him and will always be connected to him." After Mike shared these comments and held the little boy, we proceeded through the timeline. Once again, Mike was surprised that this imaginary activity had taken more than 40 minutes.

Interestingly, Mike experienced the same type of warm attention from someone in his adult life that week which Mike had given to his child-self in our previous session's imaginary work. To my surprise and delight, this pattern repeated every week. The positive intervention Mike supplied to his younger-self manifested in his adult life following each session. For example, Mike was scheduled for a job interview in a community where he had been previously established. He flew to the interview and was greeted by a former colleague in the parking lot. "Mike, I hear you're interviewing for a job. It would be great to have you back here," the friend said enthusiastically. Throughout the series of interviews, Mike encountered associates and friends with whom he had previously worked. In contrast to his current job where he felt isolated from his colleagues, his former coworkers were eager to reconnect.

At the next session, Mike reported that he thought the job interviews had gone well. Because Mike had been in situations before where things had appeared positive and then not turned out as he hoped, Mike was trying to maintain a neutral position.

He agreed to engage in the imaginary activity again of building positive experiences for his internal child. I asked Mike to go into the imaginary basement. He found the same little boy, except this time Mike described him as "way more alive." When asked what the little boy wanted to do, Mike said, "He wants to hold my hand and go get baseball cards. We're doing that now." I waited while the two of them went to Woolworth's, bought cards, and talked. I occasionally checked in with Mike to make sure he was staying focused on the internal little boy and giving him undivided, loving attention. Mike was already doing this and more. He was in a natural rhythm, responding to the little boy's needs. Mike was demonstrating intuitive attunement to his internal child—one component of good parenting. When they were finished at Woolworth's, I led Mike through one timeline.

After the timeline, the internal little boy wanted to go to his favorite neighborhood deli for lunch. Mike described it to me briefly and I could tell this was an important childhood touchstone. The little boy and Mike enjoyed their favorite sandwich and soda. "He's got a big smile on his face," Mike reported.

After lunch the little boy wanted to walk around a favorite part of his childhood city. Holding hands, Mike and the little boy looked at shops and talked about the things they saw there. As an observer, I sensed this was a positive experience for the adult and the child. Before our session ended, I guided Mike through two repetitions of the timeline, which he showed to his internal child-self.

At our next session, Mike talked about waiting to hear about the outcome of his job interview and reflected on his desire to be wanted. He was hoping that his potential company would be eager to hire him and described how much he wanted to be sought after and chosen. "Being sought out" was a missing part of Mike's childhood which he longed to repair. I suggested that we could heal this missing emotional piece and increase Mike's chances of having a positive experience of being wanted in the present by using imagination to create that feeling state for his internal child. Mike was happy to do this, but most of the work for creating the experience fell on me. When I led Mike to imagine himself going into the basement and finding the little boy who "wanted to be wanted," he once again found the same little fellow. This time he was lively and ready to interact with the adult, indicating to me that Mike was less dissociated. I told him to ask the child, "What would make you feel special and wanted?"

"I don't know," Mike replied.

"What about you as the adult?" I asked Mike.

"I don't know either," he answered. The adult part of Mike could not generate an idea that would meet the child's need for being wanted. Clearly, "being wanted" was a significant missing emotional piece for Mike, one that Mike was going to have trouble replacing by himself. I began thinking of ways to create the feeling in a child of "being wanted" and made some suggestions. Just as the internal dialogue between adult and child most often needs to be coached by the therapist, it was evident that I needed to help invent and coach this imaginary exercise. It was important to create the feeling of being wanted primarily between Mike's adult-self and his child-self, although peers could be invited to enhance the process. When working with depression and re-creating emotional experiences clients did not receive in their childhoods, it is important for the therapist to step in and direct appropriate, loving interactions as needed.

To create the feeling of "being wanted," I suggested that Mike imagine taking his younger-self on a field trip with classmates. As he climbed on the bus with the adult-self as the chaperone, Mike imagined kids shouting, "Sit with me! Sit with me! Mike, come sit here!" As the little boy chose one of the many seats offered by his friends, the adult-self looked on with validation and respect. I prompted him to gain eye contact with the child and silently communicate, *Of course all these friends want to sit with you. You're valuable and special. I feel the same way about you, too.* The field trip continued, and as it did, I interjected opportunities for the younger Mike to be wanted and sought after by his peers, while the adult-self offered a peaceful and available connection. At my suggestion, Mike imagined that one little boy asked to be his partner for a tour; other children asked if they could eat lunch with Mike. I coached Mike to tell his younger-self how happy he was to be with him and how much he enjoyed and looked forward to their times together, just as the boy's friends on the bus enjoyed his company. At the end of the field trip, I directed Mike to show his younger-self the timeline, which proved to the young ego state that he had grown up to be the adult Mike.

With time remaining in the session, Mike went again to the little boy in the basement. Still targeting the need to be wanted, I suggested to Mike that he arrange a wonderful birthday party for his younger-self. Of course, the younger-self was the focal point of friends who wanted to be there and celebrate with him on his special day. Mike said, "I see the hats, cake, and presents. All the kids have smiles on their faces." I let this scene play out, while occasionally asking Mike to describe what was happening. Confident that Mike was creating the feeling of being wanted in his younger-self, I waited quietly until the party was over. As Mike put his younger-self in bed at the end of an enjoyable day, I coached him to tell his younger-self how much he was wanted, loved, and respected. We concluded with two repetitions of the timeline.

The following week, Mike came in and said, "I feel so much better and it's not because one external circumstance of my life has changed. Everything is the same, except that I feel good now." Mike went on to describe how he was connecting with a social group, was able to exercise daily by running, and was doing well at work having direct and productive conversations with his boss and coworkers. He was not reporting any of the depression from the previous months. Yet Mike was feeling insecure and vulnerable because he was still waiting for a job offer. He said, "I always felt vulnerable to my dad's anger. His anger really scared me."

Taking a cue from the presenting issue, we set up another imaginary exercise in which Mike guided his younger-self through a series of created memories. The child was allowed to make mistakes and receive compassion, love, and age-appropriate consequences instead of rage from the adult. In this created memory it was important for Mike to be a firm and loving parent. In the imaginary process, it is not necessary for young ego states to always have their way or be allowed to misbehave. Creating boundaries for them with love and support is the goal. I guided Mike through three repetitions of the timeline during this session, showing the younger ego state Mike's life in the present. "Wow! Nothing like this ever happened in my home as a boy," Mike said, referring to the positive, new experience of his internal child. "Also, my family now is really different from the one I grew up in. My younger-self definitely wants to stay in the present with me," he spontaneously added.

The next week Mike came in and reported that he' had been offered the new job. The new company was eager for him to start immediately and colleagues he had known previously were excited that he was coming back to their state. Mike's external adult world perfectly matched the imaginary experience of his internal child from the previous week. The CEO at the new job arranged to meet all of Mike's financial requests. Having lived there before, Mike knew that the location and climate would be a better match for his temperament. He was looking forward to the move, while still being realistic about the challenges ahead.

Things were continuing to go well for Mike emotionally. We hoped to meet together one more time before his move, but the time pressures of starting a new job and transitioning out of an old one made it too difficult for Mike to come to his last appointment. Apart from the new job, all other aspects of his life were the same, yet Mike reported no depression. He had remarkable changes through the Lifespan Integration protocol for depression, the addition of a naturopath's medication, and the continued treatment from his psychiatrist. In addition to his diligence to find a workable anti-depressant, the psychiatrist told Mike that he needed to develop the spiritual part of his life, connect with a community, and possibly get a pet. Mike faithfully worked towards these goals.

Mike was the first patient with whom I regularly used the LI Depression Protocol. Week-by-week, I saw remarkable changes in his outer life which matched the emotional target for that particular week's session. Mike found the work so interesting and helpful that I never had to persuade him to use it in our therapy. He came to each session wanting to create new experiences for his younger child-self. Other clients with whom I have used the Depression Protocol responded as Mike did. Week-by-week their real-life changes corresponded to the target we used for the interactive internal process.

Dominic's Story

Dominic, a man in his 40s, came to his first session saying, "I'm serious about suicide. I wake up in the morning with three choices: go to work, lie in bed all day, or commit suicide. All of them seem like bad choices." I agreed those were very difficult choices to begin the day. Dominic was under the care of a psychiatrist who was working diligently to find appropriate medications to relieve his depression.

They were meeting weekly for talk therapy and medicine management. The psychiatrist was aware Dominic was meeting with me. Our therapeutic approaches were different, but complimentary.

At our intake session, Dominic spoke about his family of origin and I interviewed him with questions from my basic depression format. When asked about his personal sense of value he said, "It is very low. I don't want people to know me very well because they won't like what they find. I wish I were dead. I have hated myself since my late 20's." As for connection, Dominic said, "It takes a lot of energy to be around people. I isolate on the weekends. I'm not having sex with my wife. We are living separate lives." When asked about his performance-orientation Dominic said, "Gaining other's approval is very important to me. With the work I'm doing now, I get less approval from my managers. I was better suited to the work I was doing before my promotion. I got a more positive response from my superiors when I was in that other position."

When we met together for the second time, I introduced Dominic to the LI Depression Protocol. He named approval seeking as the most pressing component of his depression. His father had been hard to please and left the family when Dominic was a boy. In his childhood, Dominic remembers striving to gain his father's love and attention when he stayed at his dad's apartment on the weekends. Dominic's dad was preoccupied with television or adult friends during visits and Dominic was expected to entertain himself.

To begin the Depression Protocol centered on the need for approval, I asked Dominic to close his eyes. I counted from nine to one, while Dominic imagined himself going down a set of stairs into a basement. At the bottom of the imaginary stairs, I coached him to find the little boy Dominic who also longed for approval. On finding a little boy about four years old, Dominic reported, "He has really low self-esteem." Spontaneously, Dominic told the child he loved him very much. When asked where Dominic would like to take his child-self, the adult replied, "To an amusement park."

With eyes closed, Dominic imagined that he and the younger child rode on a roller coaster; the adult carried the child on his shoulders; they enjoyed cool drinks together; and ended the day on a spinning ride. Throughout the exercise, Dominic repeatedly communicated approval of the little boy and told him specifically, "No matter how you do in school I love you and approve of you." They spontaneously hugged each other. Throughout the session, at natural breaking points I guided Dominic through a timeline starting at age five, which was one year older than the child ego state he found in the basement. At the end of the session, I coached Dominic to take the little boy to his current home. They rode together in Dominic's truck, he introduced the little boy to his current family, and they played with the dog. Dominic closed by saying, "I tell my children how important they are to me. I'm telling him the same thing."

The following session, Dominic was still depressed and discouraged. "I won't commit suicide but I wish God would take me," he said. Hopelessness pervaded his worldview. We talked more about his relationship with his father. Dominic said his father was primarily absent from his life. "He spent very little time with me as I was growing up," he commented. "I had to figure everything out myself. With this depression I have to figure it out on my own, too. At work, I hate to ask questions. I should be able to sit down and figure stuff out by myself."

"Have you ever had the experience of being led? Or has someone ever shown you how to do something and then encouraged you through the process?" I asked.

"Not really," Dominic answered. "My dad never did that for me and neither did my stepdad. I was pretty much on my own."

I used this conversation as a segue to explain to Dominic about an important requirement for working with clients who are depressed. I told Dominic that I would lead the process of getting him out of depression. Together we would determine the right targets for LI. He would have to do the brainwork of following the timelines, but it was my job to guide the process. I was not responsible for Dominic's depression, but I was taking responsibility for setting the course for his treatment. It is imperative for depressed clients to hear that someone beside themselves knows the path out of their hopelessness, despair and self-hatred. Fortunately, with medication and LI, every depressed client I have worked with has had significant improvement. I felt confident taking leadership for his healing.

Clients in depression are lost and cannot find their way out of the malaise in which they are living. As children grow, they make mental maps out of their life experience about how to live in the world. When people are in depression, their mental maps have led them into dark places. The same map that led them into depressing conclusions about themselves cannot be trusted to move them forward in life. Another individual, such as a counselor, has a different mental compass and can serve as a guide for the person stuck in depression. Repeatedly, clients tell me that my reassurance to lead the process gave them hope and relief at a time when they could not imagine living another day.

A faulty mental map can be compared to the often-repeated saying in Alcoholic Anonymous (AA), "My best thinking got me here." Alcoholics are intelligent people who damage their lives with alcoholism. When their best thinking leads to embarrassment, financial crisis, jail time, failed marriages, or other significant losses, alcoholics receive help from others who can guide the way.

The same is true for depression. Depressed clients with ineffective mental maps need help from someone else to find their way to safety and well-being. Assuring these clients that the therapist will take the lead offers them a much-needed safety net. Clients with depression might not believe it's possible to get well, but they are relieved to discover they will be assisted by someone else. That is the role I offered to Dominic as well as to other clients I have seen for depression.

When working with Dominic, it was clear that the younger-self inside Dominic also needed reassurance from an important adult that help and guidance was going to be provided. In our third session, it became apparent that Dominic needed the experience of being cared for, guided, and mentored by someone else. The pressure to figure everything out alone was contributing to his depression. Through the LI Depression Protocol, the adult Dominic could begin healing this same need for his younger-self. Once again, I asked Dominic to close his eyes, imagine going down into a basement, and find the younger Dominic who needed someone to take the lead in his life. Dominic found his younger-self at the bottom of the stairs. "What would you like to do with him? What could you do together to mentor him and lead the way?" I asked.

"I could teach him how to throw a baseball. No one really worked on that with me," Dominic replied.

"Okay. Can you take him to a place where you can teach him how to throw a ball?"

Dominic took his younger-self to a ball field from his childhood. The adult carried a bucket of balls and set them down at a proper distance in front of a fence. The adult went to the fence and drew a circle in the middle of the fence.

"What you want to do," he said kindly, "is throw most of the balls in this circle. It's okay if they don't hit inside the circle. This is just practice. You're not going to get every ball in. Some will go over the fence and some will hit the dirt in front of the fence. That's okay. We're here to practice. It's going to take a while to get this right." Next, Dominic instructed his younger-self on the right way to hold and pitch the ball. When the child started throwing the balls, many hit the ground or went over the fence. "That's just fine," the adult-self said. "Pitching takes a lot of practice. It's no big deal to make mistakes. You don't have to get it right today. We're going to do this again." With warmth and patience, Dominic led his younger-self through the pitching exercise. Increasingly more balls hit inside the target and the younger Dominic was pleased with his success. He radiated in the attention and care his older-self was giving him. "You don't have to do everything perfectly," the adult said. "Do the best job you can." At the close of their pitching practice, the adult hugged the child and said, "Good effort. I love you no matter what." Throughout the session, I guided Dominic through several timelines at appropriate breaks.

One week later, at our fourth session, Dominic indicated his depression level was about the same. "Maybe it's a little less intense, but I still wish I could just die. I don't want to live anymore." I inquired about the topic of receiving guidance from the previous week. "It'd make things easier if I didn't have to do everything myself. I wish a magic chalkboard would come down with the directions on it," Dominic said. The adult's main need in depression is also an indicator of the child's unmet need. Our conversation made it clear Dominic needed to continue healing the younger-self who longed for parenting and guidance. I coached him to find his younger-self in the basement. We once again focused on repairing the missing piece of needing an older adult to be interested and provide leadership for the child-self. Dominic reported, "My younger-self wants to know why his dad isn't around very much."

"Does he have an answer?" I asked. I was curious to see how the younger-self had interpreted his dad's absence. Usually children internalize the lack of a parent's attention by believing they are bad.

"No. It makes me sad." Dominic replied.

We entered into the imaginary exercises again in which Dominic's adult-self gave undivided attention and leadership to his younger-self. The child wanted to climb a tree and the adult boosted him up into the branches. Later they heard the Popsicle truck coming and the adult bought them treats. At natural breaks between the imaginary activities, I guided Dominic through timelines. When we closed our session with the younger-self in Dominic's present home, I asked if the younger-self believed he was the same person as the adult Dominic. "I'm not sure," Dominic replied.

The next time we met, Dominic indicated that his depression

had lessened. He was still sleeping a lot, but he had not thought about suicide during the week. He commented that he had good days and bad days. When asked about the worst part of his depression in the present Dominic said, "I can't have the relationship I want with someone I love." Dominic's marriage had turned into an arrangement with virtually no intimacy. His remarks reminded me of the little boy whose father showed no interest in him. Children love their parents unconditionally. Dominic carried around his child-self's unrequited love for his father. Dominic's marriage had similar overtones. It was not surprising that we were focusing again on the younger child's relationship to his father. The relationship had been an unfulfilling one, which contributed to Dominic's depression. Each time we focused on the child's relationship to his father, aspects of it were healed and the timelines from each session decreased Dominic's dissociation. As his dissociation decreased, Dominic's awareness of his current emotional needs increased and he was able to clarify how the angst about his marriage affected his mood. As LI therapy progressed, Dominic, like all clients, was able to more clearly articulate the components that made up his depression.

During the session, the adult Dominic created imaginary scenarios in which his younger-self felt loved and valued by his adult-self. These were followed by timelines. It is important to note that we did not ever use Dominic's real father in the imaginary scenes. In the LI Depression Protocol, the goal is to create healing between the adult-self and the child-self in all cases. We do not change the reality of what happened in the past. The protocol does not alter what Dominic's father said and did; it changes the feeling states within the child by giving him what he needed through his adult-self. This is a very important distinction for the Depression Protocol. When the adult-self has created the emotional repair, the new feeling state is integrated through the timeline and remains as an internal resource for the whole self-system. At the end of the session, Dominic's younger-self felt quite a bit better and started to believe that he was part of the adult-self. Before I saw him again, Dominic had arranged for marriage counseling.

It was appropriate for Dominic and his wife to begin counseling, but I also knew that something inside of Dominic was drawn to marry a woman who would not be able to give him the emotional intimacy he needed. Couples dance a mirroring relationship dance. When one partner consistently does not give what is needed, the other partner also tends to be poor at receiving the element they long for. It was clear that a lack of intimacy with his wife was a contributor to Dominic's depression. Yet, given his history, it appeared that he had poor receptors for emotional intimacy. I directed our LI session towards increasing Dominic's capacity to receive emotional nurturing, knowing it would aid in the decrease of his depression and improve the outcomes in his marriage counseling.

To better understand Dominic's attachment style, I asked about the early weeks and months after his birth. The conditions around his birth were difficult. Dominic had two siblings at home when he was born and his father was an alcoholic who often raged at his mother and the children. Dominic's mother was frightened most of the time and very unsure of herself as a parent. Dominic entered a chaotic household where fear, not love, was the predominant feeling. Knowing we needed to repair Dominic's early experience of receiving love, I guided him to imagine himself as a baby less than two weeks old. He imagined finding his brand-new baby-self and picked him up. "I love him," Dominic spontaneously told me. "He put his head next to my chest. I feel nurturing."

"As you're holding him," I coached, "Let him feel that in your arms he can just *be*. You, as the adult, will meet his needs and he doesn't have to produce anything to get what he needs."

Dominic opened his eyes wide and said with shock, "I never heard this growing up! In my family, you'd better do what you're supposed to do or you're not going to get what you need."

"It's different now," I responded. "Because you're his adult-self, he can relax in the arms of someone who loves him and have all of his needs met." I guided Dominic through a timeline, asking him to reassure his baby-self that he was indeed living with an adult who could take of him.

Returning to the image of the baby, Dominic said, "He's opening up and letting the warmth in." We focused solely on the adult-self nurturing the baby followed by timelines for the entirety of the session.

Finding value through performance is one of the four main characteristics of depression. Rarely is someone depressed without this feature. Dominic's childhood, as he interpreted it, confirmed his belief that he had to do many things to be loved. He was shocked when I suggested it was possible to receive love by just being in the world. Dominic's experience in his childhood home was similar to the relationship with his wife. Dominic was dutiful toward his family by providing a paycheck, a good home, and other resources, but he could not get his emotional needs met by simply being a member of the family. People get depressed when their strategies for living stop working. Dominic was a superior performer but it was not returning to him what he needed most—emotional intimacy.

After the session where we focused on simply nurturing his baby-self, Dominic had more clarity about his performance orientation. He said, "I'm mad at home. I have all the responsibilities of a husband and none of the benefits. I don't get any recognition at home. At work, I never get enough recognition either. Things are constantly changing. It's never enough." To start our tenth session, I drew an upright rectangle on my notepad and asked Dominic to mark his current level of depression. Assuming that it was at the top of the rectangle when we started our work together, I asked him to indicate conceptually how much depression remained. Dominic drew a line about halfway through the rectangle. "If I had to give it a number, I would say about 5.5 out of 10," Dominic told me.

To get our bearings for the second half of therapy, I inquired about the general components of depression—sense of value, connection, performance-orientation and hopelessness. Dominic said his sense of value was improving. It was much better than when he started working with me. He also noted that approval-seeking through performance had improved a great deal. He reported, "I'm not striving for anything material or wanting much approval from others." Regarding hopelessness, he said, "I can't see anything that would make me want to stay on earth, but I don't think of suicide at all. It isn't part of my thinking anymore." As for connection, Dominic said it had not improved.

We focused on Dominic's need for connection in the following two sessions and used the LI Depression Protocol to repair the main aspects of his early failed attempts to get others to connect with him. A raging father and a frightened, overwhelmed mother were not capable of giving Dominic the message that he was a valuable individual with whom they wanted to connect.

By our thirteenth session, Dominic had been seeing me for four months and marked his depression near the bottom of the rectangle. Inadvertently, I had drawn the rectangle twelve lines high on my notepad, and Dominic marked his depression at the second line from the bottom. He said, "Life is good! This is my second week of feeling good." We talked about the changes in his life and he said, "Work continues to go well. The main thing still bothering me is my marriage. I don't think I can go on living like this." Dominic reported that he and his wife were continuing to see the marriage counselor, but he surmised that she really did not want to change. "She likes the relationship the way it is," Dominic said. I inquired whether he felt hopeless about getting his needs met in the marriage and Dominic replied, "My wife is giving me a little bit more of what I want at home—not as much as I need, but it's an improvement. I have a choice, though. I'm not trapped. I've given myself permission to leave. I'm not worried about a year from now. I don't want to leave, but I don't want things to stay the way they are with my wife." Although Dominic was discouraged about his marriage, he felt a high degree of commitment to his children. Later, his wife decided to discontinue marriage counseling. Dominic felt frustrated by his predicament, but he approached the challenge as an adult and not like a helpless child. He had a realistic appraisal of his marriage.

As we debriefed our work together, Dominic said, "When you told me in the beginning that depression could be healed, I didn't believe you. I thought it was impossible to ever get out from under the way I was feeling. I was afraid nothing with my wife or work would change. Now I see it very differently. Work is a lot better and I know I have choices with my wife. I used to have a high level of unhappiness about my job, but since I've made changes in my work situation, I now have job satisfaction. This has been really helpful," he continued. "Life looks really different now compared to when we began. And truthfully, not a lot has changed externally. Thank you."

Overall, Dominic reported his depression as very low. We continued to meet once a month to address issues as they arose. Six months after our intense weekly sessions, Dominic reported that his depression was still very low. "The only thing I'm depressed about is my marriage. I'm not willing to move out because of the children, but I'm still frustrated with my wife. I can handle it, though," Dominic said.

Dominic continued his medication for depression throughout our therapy and beyond. Medication is a critical component for people facing depression. I also believe the work he did using the LI Depression Protocol contributed greatly to the turn-around Dominic had after four months therapy. His thinking was drastically different about himself, his work, and possibilities regarding his marriage. I cannot filter out which part of Dominic's healing was the medication and therapy with his psychiatrist or the Lifespan Integration Depression Protocol, but I do know that earlier life experiences which caused Dominic to feel hopeless and badly about himself were healed through LI. I believe these changes will have ongoing, lifetime effects.

The outcomes Mike and Dominic experienced from the LI Depression Protocol are typical. Most clients experience the kind of change these men reported regarding their depression. In order to use the LI Depression Protocol, it is useful to help clients identify the components that make up their depression, and heal those components with imaginary, reparative experiences. Mike and Dominic are only two of the many clients who have had their depression healed, in part, with Lifespan Integration. Since my work with these two men, every client I have seen for depression has had significant improvement in his or her condition, and most have declared their depression gone. I propose that in combination with the right medication, Lifespan Integration offers an effective treatment modality for not only healing the symptoms of depression but its origins as well. One might argue that medication alone caused these clients to heal from depression. Maybe that is true. Medication has been a lifesaver for many. Clients should seek out medical treatment for their depression. But, it is equally important to address a client's underlying thinking, which contributes to his or her depression. That is the work of Lifespan Integration. Younger ego states within a client think and feel based on their experience in life. These collective beliefs are a major contributor to a client's depression. To heal the depression, we must heal the thinking and feeling of the ego states within the client. Telling them that "all is well" today, does not repair the discouragement and loneliness a client may have experienced as a child. A child's connection to others and the way in which he or she found value are the key ingredients that affect depression. Through the tools of LI, we can heal these formative beliefs and give clients an opportunity to think differently in their present lives. Changed thinking changes depression.

What I Learned About Depression
Four Components

After Pace pointed out that depression is comprised of two main components, I developed sub-points under her categories. As stated previously, Pace identified a low sense of value and poor connection as the causes of depression. As I began to use the Depression Protocol more regularly, I found that a low sense of value included a performance-oriented way of finding worth. Performance-orientation is a sub-point under a low sense of personal value.

Performance-orientation can be defined as seeking out accomplishments and success as a method to find personal value. It is self-esteem based on a mindset of *I'm good when I perform well.* Not surprisingly, the alternative is also true: *I'm bad when I perform moderately or fail.* To keep the performance-orientation system working, one must always find new avenues for succeeding. When one cannot find enough success or another achievement, the performance-oriented system breaks down. Eventually performance-oriented people own enough stuff, earn enough money, or have received enough awards that new successes do not offer them the hit of self-worth they crave. In all cases, the performance-oriented system eventually breaks down and no longer serves as a way for clients to feel good about themselves.

Performance-orientation is a method for finding value. Accepting one's entire self with flaws, weaknesses, strengths, and failures is a much better way to feel valuable and worthwhile. Being in relationship with others who love us with this type of acceptance affirms our worth, while seeking recognition through accomplishments inevitably leads to depression. Depression is the difference between expectation and reality.

Under Pace's category of poor connection as a cause for depression, I added the sub-point of a client's hopelessness to get his or her needs met. Hopelessness is the belief, *I can never get what I long for or need.* When the systems clients use to gain value or connection stop working, hopelessness sets in. The feeling of hopelessness is present to some degree in all depression, although it can manifest in many different ways. Hopelessness in depression can relate to money, relationships, work, health, family, aging, death, religion, and many other topics. Underlying all these areas is the belief that without the sought-after object, the client cannot have a satisfying degree of personal value and connection. Outsiders might be able to see ways in which a client can make life better for him or herself, but the client's inability to see this on his or her own creates hopelessness and despair.

In summary, depression, as I have observed it, is comprised of four main elements. They are: 1) a low sense of personal value, 2) lack of—or poor—connection to others, 3) finding value through performance, and 4) believing it is hopeless to get one's needs met. By using the tools of Lifespan Integration, we can identify which of these four components are contributing to a client's depression and help him or her reverse their effects through imaginary scenes and LI timelines.

The most direct way to find the component most predominate in a client's depression is for the therapist to ask the client, "Where are you feeling trapped and powerless?" The area where the client feels completely unable to generate empowered solutions for him or herself will most likely fall into one of the four areas mentioned above. Naming this area, and using the tools of the Depression Protocol to heal the identified area, will create a direct pathway for healing the patient's depression.

Referring back to the rings of the tree analogy, clients who experience the four components of depression have spent a lifetime loading these beliefs into their hearts and minds. A client who spent many hours alone as a child would have a lack-of-connection experience in many 'rings' of his or her internal self. As an adult, it is likely that this client would have difficulty connecting with others and would create a life consistent with his or her internal belief system. Talk therapy sessions 30 years later would not replace all the ways in which loneliness and lack of connection were contained in the client's neural networks. If this client sought out counseling for depression, therapy would need to address the mental perceptions about connection loaded into his or her brain over many years.

Mike inadvertently taught me that depression is healed in layers. With help from the therapist, a client can identify the layers of depression as they unfold each week. Clients can name the most troubling aspect of their depression for each session, and the most troubling aspect will be different—or less intense—each time the counselor and client meet. Of the four main components of depression mentioned, one of them will be present at every session. By asking, "What seems to be the main part of your depression right now?" or "Where are you feeling powerless?" the client and therapist can create an imaginary intervention to heal the same issue for the internal child. In Mike's case, he named the component of his depression which was troubling him the most each week, we created a memory scene between his adult-self and younger-self specifically to meet the need, and then a matching external experience naturally showed up in Mike's adult life the following week. Since working with Mike, I have developed a simple system to name and track the client's layers of depression for each session.

Gauging the Client's Level of Depression

After a few sessions with clients in depression, I draw a blank bar graph on a piece of paper and ask clients to draw a line across the bar graph to indicate their current level of depression. Pointing to the top of the graph I ask, "If this was your depression when we began, where would you say it is now?" I stress that it is possible for the depression level to go up or down and I reassure them we can heal the specific components of their depression.

Once clients have marked the bar graph, I ask them to name the main aspect of their current depression level. If they cannot name the primary component for the current session, I review the four categories with them and ask them to pick out the top priority from the list. By breaking the task into a multiple-choice exercise, clients can find the element of depression that resonates with their current circumstance.

Once the main component of depression has been identified, the counselor guides the client to find the younger-self who felt the same difficulty the adult currently feels, and the client engages the younger-self in an imaginative, reparative activity followed by timelines. If a client says, "I don't have any friends at work; I'm disconnected," the therapist would guide the client to find the younger-self who feels disconnected. Obviously, the younger-self did not go to work each day, but the feeling of disconnection will be present at some place in the client's earlier years or it would not have presented as a factor in the adult's depression.

In Mike's story, much of our work on his depression each week focused around the issue of connection. In describing his work and childhood, Mike used phrases like "I want to be wanted," or "I was afraid of my father's anger." Mike's fear about his father's anger prevented Mike and his father from forming a safe relationship. Therefore, we created internal experiences for Mike's child-self to be safely connected to his adult-self when the child did something that would make an adult angry. Mike started a fire in the basement by playing with matches when he was five years old. His father raged at him and beat him. I guided Mike to imagine an identical scenario for his internal five-year-old self in which the adult Mike responded with strength, appropriate consequences, love, and connection to his younger-self. Wrong-doing does not have to be met with separation and abandonment. Misbehavior can be corrected through appropriate consequences, love, and hope.

The Therapist's Role

A therapist directing the process is especially important when using the Depression Protocol. It would have been difficult for Mike to generate the appropriate response to his younger-self who started a fire without guidance from an external source. Where would Mike have found the resource to be strong, appropriate, and loving after a childhood that taught him that he was barely acceptable as a human being and was especially despicable when he endangered the family with misbehavior? Mike needed an outside source to guide the reparative exercise. If left to create the imaginary response to his younger-self, Mike probably would have been as rejecting and self-hating as his father had been. It is imperative that the therapist monitor or guide the imaginary, internal experience in a way that is safe, loving, and appropriate while focusing on the main component of the client's depression.

For every imaginary re-creation, the counselor needs to keep in mind the focus for the reparative scene. Is it about connection, value, performance-orientation, or hopelessness? The nature of the repair will be shaped by the focus of the session for the week. The behaviors, guided by the therapist, in the re-enactment will differ depending on the purpose of the healing. The therapist structures the imaginary experience according to the specific component of depression the client identified at the beginning of the session.

Summary

The LI Depression Protocol is outlined by Pace (2012). I have developed a method for applying her protocol with three basic steps:

1) At an intake session, I share the four basic components of depression—low sense of personal value, performance-orientation, poor connection to others, and hopelessness to get one's needs met—and invite clients to describe to what degree these elements make up their depression.

2) In subsequent sessions, clients mark a rectangle as a quantitative gauge for their depression and name the main aspect of their depression for the current session.

3) The client finds the younger-self who has the same problem as identified in step two. The adult-self takes

the younger-self through positive, imagined experiences that repair the specific component of depression the client named at the beginning of the session. Throughout the session, the imaginary interventions are followed by the LI timeline and end with the younger child in the adult's home.

An important point about Depression Protocol needs to be emphasized: *The healing occurs primarily between the adult-self and child-self.* For example, if a client seeks to heal the need for connection, the feeling state of increased connection is created between the adult-self and the internal child—not between the child and his or her real parents or peers. We do not magically transform what others did in the past. We do not let clients pretend that abusive parents have become loving and kind. Instead, we show clients that their adult-self can be loving and kind and the child's need for authentic connection is satisfied within the adult-child relationship. This way, the created positive feeling state is *within* the client and not dependent on outsiders. The goal of the Depression Protocol is to create a healed internal state between the adult-self and child-self. An inner child seeking more connection will be satisfied with the adult's response to him or her. The adult can follow up by developing more externally connected relationships once new neural networks for connection have been created in the client's mind and body.

In his therapy, when Mike focused on his desire to be wanted, he was coached to imagine his adult-self wanting and enjoying the relationship with the younger Mike. For this reason, I suggested that the adult Mike chaperone an imaginary fieldtrip. Children look to significant adults first to validate their worth. Once they feel loved and appreciated by their important caregivers, children can venture into the world knowing they have the support of their caregivers. The other children present in Mike's imaginary field trip expressed interest in his younger-self, but the primary and lasting repair was between Mike's child-self and adult-self, evidenced by adult Mike's loving eye contact, a closeness Mike expressed without words, and his obvious interest in his younger-self.

Growing up, we develop ways to attach to parents and others in our social circles according to their personalities. As children, to get connection we develop internal styles in response to our parents' styles of relating to us. Even though we move beyond our childhood relationships, we still carry our internal way of attachment with us into the world. Not surprisingly, our ways of attaching to others in the adult world perfectly matches our pre-formed attachment style from childhood. In order to have a new experience, we must change our internal, neural networks about attachment. In a rich way, the Depression Protocol of Lifespan Integration appears to accomplish this.

10. Bipolar Disorder

Bipolar Disorder is the diagnosis for a condition in which a client's mood swings from a very high, active state of mania to the low state of depression. The manic stage brings uncontrolled, impulsive behaviors and the depressive state can lead to feelings of suicide and depression so debilitating that the client cannot function in normal life. The time frame for the swing can be months, days, or hours. At the manic end of the disorder, clients gamble, spend compulsively, and engage in risky and excessive behaviors. Clients think they have unlimited ability to perform certain tasks, such as writing a symphony overnight or moving out of their apartments before morning. They have the feeling they can accomplish almost anything and the motor inside them says, *Go, go, go!* In the manic phase, Bipolar clients often go many days without sleeping. They do not feel the need for sleep, nor could they sleep if they forced themselves to bed. If it is not too excessive, Bipolar clients may like the feelings of the manic phase. They can be extremely productive during manic episodes and feel giddy and high. Unfortunately, Bipolar clients also lack judgment in this phase. At its extreme, the manic phase can go as far as psychotic episodes and require hospitalization. Bipolar clients are often highly creative, very intelligent, and gifted in the arts. Partners and friends can challenge the behavior of people in the manic stage, but seldom can a Bipolar client change his or her behavior by choice.

The low side of Bipolar Disorder is equally impactful. At the extreme low end, clients want to die and may take steps to do so. They cannot get out of bed in order to continue their normal routine of work and daily life. Again, the loved ones near them cannot influence the Bipolar client's mood or successfully challenge them to be different. They see themselves alone, disconnected, and hopeless. This depressive state can last for many weeks. Depending on the client, either end of the Bipolar Disorder spectrum can be the predominant aspect presenting in this disorder.

Bipolar Disorder is primarily treated with a combination of medications, including lithium and other mood stabilizers. Hospitalization is also used for stabilization. Once Bipolar Disorder is diagnosed, there is very little expectation that the condition will abate. It often first appears in adolescence and the treatment is primarily related to managing symptoms and mood swings through medication.

Throughout the years in which clinicians have been using LI, we have anecdotal evidence that Lifespan Integration is highly successful for non-psychotic Bipolar clients. On a continuum of successful applications of LI, Bipolar Disorder is at the high end for positive outcomes. Therapists consistently report successful results using LI with Bipolar clients. Clients diagnosed with Bipolar Disorder that experience LI report that their mood-swings significantly decrease and their lives are easier to manage. They gain the capacity to regulate their behaviors and the high-risk, excessive compulsions become less of a problem. One client told me the condition he described as "physical Bipolar pain" disappeared after our work together.

Maria

Maria, one of the first clients with whom I used Lifespan Integration, came to therapy because her treating physician felt the need to increase her medication for Bipolar Disorder. "I don't want to increase my medication anymore," Maria said. When I asked her to name her goal for therapy Maria added, "I want to deal with the stuff in my childhood and not raise my medication again. I get side effects from the medicine and I don't want them to get any worse." We began targeting difficult memories from her childhood with Standard Protocol LI.

Two months after our first session, Maria's physician told her at a follow-up doctor's appointment, "I have never seen your mental status better. You are doing really well. There is no need to raise your medication." Maria's blood pressure was lower, other vital signs had improved, and Maria reported to her physician that she was doing really well. Previously, the physician had treated Maria's emotionality and family distress with medication. After LI, the physician was impressed with how well Maria was managing her life and emotional mood. The only difference in Maria's life was two months of weekly Lifespan Integration. Her work, family, and social life had not changed, but Maria's ability to function within these contexts had improved significantly.

Over the following three years, I treated Maria with approximately twelve sessions of LI each year. When she returned for her sessions during the third year, I noticed there appeared to be some swing in her mood and in 2 of our 12 sessions she had a bit of rapid speech, which is an indicator of Bipolar Disorder. When I inquired about her medication, Maria replied, "Oh, I stopped taking it eighteen months ago. The little bit of swing I still notice is manageable and lots better than the side effects of the medication." *I always direct clients to keep taking their medication unless otherwise directed by a physician.* I have noticed that all the Bipolar clients with whom I have used LI have been able to reduce their level of Bipolar medication per a physician's direction. My clinical sample represents the work of only one therapist, but other therapists in the Lifespan Integration network also report consistent and positive outcomes using LI for clients with Bipolar Disorder.

Antonio

On the intake form, Antonio indicated his reason for coming to therapy as "being very unhappy and hurting, Bipolar pain." He was taking the highest allowed dose of lithium in addition to three or four other medications for Bipolar Disorder. During our initial conversation, Antonio said he was diagnosed with rapid cycling Bipolar Disorder and "never really felt that great." A few years before I began seeing Antonio, he attempted suicide by stepping in front of a car. "I don't want to give up on my life and I want to get rid of the negative thinking," he said.

Antonio's professional life took him around the world as a vice president for an international company. He said, "I'm a high performer at work, but a disaster at home. I've failed in all my relationships. Currently, I'm not suicidal but I have anxiety about attachment. My default is Bipolar. I have a lot of trauma, but I can't feel anything. I cry, but I have no feelings. I seek out people I can cling to because I need validation. I want to be stronger and more independent." Returning to the topic of vocation, Antonio said, "I love my work and am really good at it. I supervise a lot of people."

Antonio described his childhood, connection to his parents, and various traumas he had experienced in his lifetime. He had many areas of concern for therapy. After our initial session, I surmised that we would need to work on his Bipolar Disorder with many sessions of Birth-to-Present protocol, resolve trauma with the PTSD protocol, improve his attachment to others with the Attachment Repair method, and probably include some Depression Protocol.

I engage clients in prioritizing what feels most important to them as we begin our work together. By doing so, I believe I am helping clients get what they desire out of therapy. Generally, we start with the issue clients name as the most pressing one for them. For Antonio, it was the resolution of childhood trauma. "Even though I feel depressed about my marriage, this week I had a dream about my trauma which was very vivid. It was so real to me; the dream kept coming back throughout the day. It's hard to manage a division of people when I keep remembering being raped as a boy."

Some clinicians always begin LI with Birth-to-Present protocol. I knew that at some point we would need to include BP in our work, but Antonio's distress about the childhood rape was high so we chose it as our first target. I used a combination of Standard Protocol, in which Antonio imagined his adult-self protecting his child-self, and the timeline from the PTSD protocol to prove the rape was over. We compiled many cues close to the time of Antonio's trauma and I read them after the interventions in the memory scene with his younger-self. At the end of our first session Antonio said, "I don't think I've ever felt this calm. I feel a lot safer now."

At the beginning of our fourth session, Antonio said, "I definitely feel better. I'm staying on my Lithium, though." I strongly encouraged him to do so, and we targeted another trauma from his childhood.

Antonio began the fifth session with insight about his contributions to the difficulties in his marriage. Increasing awareness is a by-product of LI timelines, and Antonio's new perspectives impressed me. After the trauma work from the previous two weeks, he was beginning to see himself as less of a victim in his marriage and more of a contributor to the challenges he and his wife were facing.

One month after our intake session, Antonio began swinging to the low side of the Bipolar spectrum. "Now I feel very suicidal," he expressed. "I feel like bolting. I have no hope. I want to run back to Spain where I was born. I feel hopeless to get the love and connection I need." I guided him through the Birth-to-Present protocol and had him imagine the lovable and valuable nature of his baby-self. I held a doll as a representation of love and nurture for his infant-self. I told Antonio that together we were imagining the doll was his baby-self. He had done nothing wrong, he could receive love by just being alive, and he did not need to perform in any way. The entire session was dedicated to repetitions of Antonio's timeline from his birth to the present. At the end of the session, Antonio said, "I feel stronger and calmer." He also reflected that he noticed a change in his leadership style at work. "I'm doing more teaching when I speak," he added. I surmised that Antonio's comment meant that he was becoming more connected to his internal self and his natural gifts were emerging. As we lowered his trauma level and created greater integration, more of his natural strengths became evident in his adult life.

The following session Antonio reported, "I'm still cycling this week. At work I'm up, but when I get tired, I get very, very tired and I can't think. Fortunately, just one day I felt and thought suicidal. But I have Bipolar pain." Antonio described the physical pain that accompanied his cycling. It was deep inside his tissues and very uncomfortable. "Other people have it, too," he said.

For the entire session, I guided Antonio using the BP method while holding the baby doll again. Over the session he said, "I didn't feel love for my mother. Only once did I feel it. I feel hopeless about getting the love I need now. I can't feel love. No wonder my marriage is failing."

One week later, Antonio said, "I had a terrible time this week. It was really, really bad. I was suicidal, especially on the weekend. I'm looking for affection and if I'm not careful I'll end up in an affair." Again, we spent the session using the Birth-to-Present protocol.

The Christmas holiday followed and I did not see Antonio for three weeks. He reported the Christmas vacation with his family was really good. He continued, "I relaxed. My wife's family came over and I enjoyed being with other people. I felt suicidal only three days during the holidays." Antonio assured me that he had no intentions or plans of actually killing himself. His only attempt had been many years ago. Since then Antonio's responsibilities kept him from attempting to take his life, but he did think of suicide as an alternative to the mental and physical Bipolar pain. He also reported another positive change that was evident during the holidays: The relationship with his oldest son was changing. "He's starting to talk to me and has been opening up to me consistently," Antonio shared.

We used the Birth-to-Present protocol again for the duration of the session. During one of our breaks between repetitions I said, "What would make the baby happy?"

He answered, "To be loved—a relationship with a woman. I know it's not as simple as that. I could be married over and over and still be in the same place wanting love." As per the guidelines for an imaginary repair in LI, I did not let Antonio imagine that he received the love he craved from a lover, but rather I guided him to experience the value and love communicated to his infant-self right after birth as I held the doll in my arms again. The internal relationship between Antonio's adult and baby-self is permanent. Therefore, if he could build the deep love internally, it would always be a resource to him. His baby-self would be satisfied and peaceful while the adult went about his daily life. Antonio would not need to seek out extra-marital affairs as an attempt to gain female love for his child infant-self. I knew the early pieces of Antonio's life would fit together like a puzzle when he nurtured and loved the child-self within.

Like most Bipolar clients, Antonio was smart and made connections quickly. As we progressed through repetitions of BP, he began to see truths about himself. He said, "God has made me a leader and I want to be a leader in the world. I've been given specific talents to bring people together. The baby and adult understand the mission." Antonio's comments reflected an internal integration. The repetitions of the LI timeline were highlighting strengths and challenges that were present throughout his entire life. "I can work with different kinds of people. I can bring them together when things are fractionalized. I have to be a leader. The low self-esteem, low self-worth, and shame have stopped me in my tracks. I have misspent opportunities. I've let other people hurt me trying to be a peacemaker," Antonio reported.

At the end of our session Antonio glowed and said, "I feel good about the baby for the first time in my life. I'm sensing three things: 1) This is the first time I've felt okay about the baby. He had a lot of emotions over the years, 2) things can change, and 3) there is something ahead. I'm not living to die. For seven years I've been living to die, but now I realize there is something ahead. I have a sense of purpose."

Even though the previous session ended positively, Antonio returned in a very low mood. "I feel really bad," he began, "very depressed and confused. On Sunday I couldn't function. I felt very fragmented—like a plate smashed on the ground. I was looking at the pieces and it was tough. I felt hopeless. But," he added brightly, "I felt okay about one hour before this appointment."

I told him about the components of depression: low sense of value, lack of connection, performance-orientation, and hopelessness to get one's needs met. Antonio told me that performance-orientation—trying to achieve value through accomplishments—was the dominant component of his depression. Although it would have also been helpful to continue with BP, I decided to briefly address the most pressing aspect of his depression—performance-orientation. We had many items to address before our work would be finished, and I sensed enough stability in Antonio from the previous BP sessions to make a temporary departure from BP to deal with his acute depression.

Using the steps of the Depression Protocol, I guided Antonio to find the little boy who tried to acquire love and value through performance. He found his younger-self and reassured him through words and imaginary activities that he as the adult could love the younger-self for simply being Antonio. No more awards or achievements were required for him to get the attention he needed. Each of these imaginary scenes was followed by a repetition of Antonio's timeline. In the middle of the session Antonio cried and said, "I have horrible grief over letting go of performance-orientation." As he cried, I felt encouraged about the inroads we were making. I knew that Antonio would never be content within himself as long as he used performance-orientation as a way to justify his presence in the world and his grief at letting it go told me that he was shifting a deep internal belief. As is common for LI, the intense emotion peaked about the middle of the session and subsided as we continued with imaginary interventions and repetitions of the timeline.

After three months of therapy, Antonio was able to describe a pattern he experienced after our sessions. He said, "I feel bad for the day following our sessions." In the beginning of our work—due to the dysregulation and rewiring that appeared to be taking place—Antonio felt badly after each session. "Walking about 45 minutes everyday makes me feel better. I intend to work on my marriage. My wife and I have started seeing a marriage counselor," he said.

Antonio was experiencing "Bipolar pain" at the beginning of his next session and described it to me. He said, "It's a physical, shimmering thing. It's emotional pain with desperation and it includes the thought that dying is better than this. It gets very dark and very alone. There's no hope. I want to die so I won't have the pain." We returned to the Birth-to-Present protocol, but I opted to start Antonio's timelines before birth, when the baby was in utero. During our breaks, when his baby-self was in the present, Antonio made remarks like, "The baby is self-conscious but wants to live. The decision has been made to live but the baby is lonely. The baby has determination to live no matter what." After two repetitions, Antonio said, "My Bipolar pain is born from anxiety. Its sidekick is shame and embarrassment." After two more repetitions of the timeline, he said, "My Bipolar pain is gone. I feel like I have a purpose for living."

Three and a half months into therapy at our 14th session Antonio gave a surprising report from his physician. Because his mood was more stable and his blood report was good, Antonio's physician lowered his lithium dosage by 900mg. Before our work, the physician said Antonio was on the highest dosage of lithium allowed, which still was not adequate to stabilize his mood swings. Antonio's blood pressure had dropped to 107 over 85—down from 139 over 110—and his blood sugar level was down to 84 from 168. Antonio's previous exam had been six months earlier. The only changes in his life during the previous six months were fourteen weeks of Lifespan Integration.

Reviewing some other aspects of his life, Antonio said, "I got some Bipolar pain today. It comes with a suicidal fantasy, like I want to die, but actually I'm not feeling very depressed. I feel safer, and more secure." I sensed a progression from the emotional, dark desire to commit suicide previously expressed to a more factual nature to his suicidal thoughts. He continued his review, "My life was like a terrible car crash. The only option was to die. I've let everything happen to me. I don't plan anything. I don't even know what I'm capable of doing. Why don't I try? I want to start planning." Antonio's next statement surprised me. He said, "I feel really close to my wife. I'm much more secure in our relationship."

I asked Antonio what he wanted the focus to be for our current session. He said, "I've got too much blowing in the wind. I need self-confidence. I'm immature. I need to build maturity. Where is the core getting built? Who is that man that is going to take a stand for others?" Antonio's thinking represented a significant increase in self-awareness over fourteen weeks. We proceeded through three repetitions of the Birth-to-Present protocol. At the end, Antonio offered, "I like the baby." This was about the midpoint in Antonio's therapy and a lot had changed for him. Antonio still experienced swings in his Bipolar episodes, but they were not as extreme or devastating as they had been previously. He vacillated between closeness and rejection with his wife, but overall Antonio had settled into a friendship with her that was comfortable and stable. We continued to meet weekly for another three months, and then began meeting twice a month.

At the beginning of the fourth month of therapy, Antonio began the session saying, "I feel fuzzy today. I feel Bipolar pain."

When asked about the week, he replied, "I felt fairly balanced. I didn't crash at all."

I challenged his fuzzy thinking and asked, "What are you avoiding by being fuzzy?"

After a moment of silence Antonio offered, "For the first time in 20 years I'm asking if my wife loves me. Before it's been, 'Do I love my wife?' Our friendship is pretty strong but our intimate life is not." Antonio's statement reflected a rather significant shift which I believe is a result of the many BP repetitions we completed. Antonio's question for the past 20 years of "Do I love my wife?" is ego-centered and narcissistic. It reflects the baby perspective of "Who am I and what do I want?" Shifting to the question, "Does my wife love me?" means there is another adult in the relationship—separate from Antonio—who has thoughts, feelings, and needs, which are separate from Antonio's. These are subtle indicators of a deeper work that was happening inside Antonio.

We shifted into Attachment Repair to heal the early disruptions in Antonio's childhood. After many sessions of Birth-to-Present protocol, I sensed the need to directly rebuild Antonio's attachment style to others. I asked him to imagine himself around two months old. Finding his younger-self, Antonio expressed, "He is embarrassed and feels shame. There is no closeness to my mother and father." I guided him to make the appropriate, relational repairs and took him through a timeline. At the end of the first timeline, Antonio said, "I feel revulsion for the mistakes I've made over a lifetime." The next time Antonio returned to the young child he said, "I don't fully accept him. I feel worthless." Again, I gave Antonio specific directions on ways to love his child-self as a good parent would love him, followed by the timeline. At the end of the session, he said, "He is saved. What's ahead of me I'm going to do. He is special to God. He saved me for a purpose." These thoughts and feelings were totally spontaneous as Antonio progressed through the timelines.

The deep shifts were evident at the following session. Though

Antonio's mood was low, there was a connection to his child-self that seemed directly related to our work the previous week. Antonio was creative and he wrote a poem during the week about longing for love. He shared that he had grieved for ten years after the break-up of his first marriage. He also said, "I feel angry. Now I realize I was neglected—intentional neglect. Is something so wrong, or so ugly, about me? Was I a mistake? My first wife didn't know me, and my current wife is withholding love." These remarks told me that Antonio had tapped a vein of loneliness and neglect from his baby-hood. His words were a mix of the past and present and was the expression of his younger-self being spoken through the adult. As is typical with LI, Antonio made connections from this past neglect to his behaviors as an adult. He said, "Who have I neglected?" and went on to answer his own question. "I neglected my first wife and my second wife by traveling and being emotionally distant, and I've neglected my sons. I have to take responsibility for this," Antonio concluded. This is the miracle of Lifespan Integration. Antonio accessed the deep pain from his baby-self, saw the patterns in his life through the timelines, and took responsibility for his part in neglecting others as an adult. Taking responsibility meant changing his behavior for the future. The power of brain connectivity was evident in his self-awareness and planning. Antonio also said, "It's been a bad week for me and I never got relief. But I don't care. I've been doing real grieving. I have a responsibility to my wife and kids." Even though Antonio's mood was low, there was an aspect of an empowered adult perspective in it—rather than the powerless, self-pity he had expressed before. We continued with Attachment Repair during the session.

As an indicator that this process takes time, the next few weeks were difficult for Antonio. It appeared that every time we accessed a new neural network, we had to work it through for a few sessions before Antonio got relief and healing. Antonio began therapy in November and by the middle of April, at our twentieth session, he said, "I'm very, very unpredictable. I think it's the Bipolar. It guides a lot of things I do." Antonio was primarily speaking about his home life and relationships, because things at work were going quite well. He was being considered for another promotion and his performance at work was excellent. To prove to me how problematic his Bipolar condition was, Antonio shared for the first time comments from his previous counselor. "She told me I'm one of the sickest people she's ever met. And she was a specialist in Bipolar." To add to his miserable week, he added, "Our marriage counseling session this week ended up in disaster. I feel so bad about myself. I feel really, really lost."

I asked about the main feeling underlying his life and he said, "Being alone."

"Where does the feeling of being alone start?" I asked.

"Day one," came Antonio's dry reply. Again we used the Birth-to-Present protocol to create a sense of value and connection between Antonio and his baby-self, followed by timelines. At the end of the session, Antonio quietly said, "It all fits right now."

Even though Antonio still felt loneliness, by the next session it seemed to me that our previous LI work was filtering insight and self-awareness into Antonio's self-system. He said, "I can't remember it ever being any different. I have huge expectations for women that they will take my pain away. In a first conversation, I'm very open. I could date 100 women to suck out as much love as possible before they are sick of me. My poor wife has had to field this. She's stable and functional, but she doesn't like this kind of talk. I believe women are going to betray me." I sensed Antonio was expressing the true, deep need of his infant-self. I believe that the role of a good mother is to meet the deepest needs of her child as much as possible. That includes nurture, love, attention, and attunement to the specific personality of the child. Antonio appeared to lack this connection with his mother, so he was endlessly seeking it in others.

Not surprisingly, Antonio had another shift in the week following our session. He said, "I had a dream unlike anything I've dreamt before. When I woke up I was thinking I could be happy in a marriage. It's possible, so unique. I've never felt this in my lifetime." He briefly described the dream. Antonio said, "I was with a woman and loved being with her. We were meant to be together and there was fresh air throughout the house. I actually felt happy in my marriage. It was much better than being lonely. We wanted to be with each other." Although we did not discuss the dream in depth, I believe Antonio's unconscious was providing him with prospects for the future. Once again, LI was producing awareness about the past, responsibility for self, and possibilities for the future. One of the observed outcomes from Lifespan Integration is a client's increasing awareness of self across time and space. This capacity is said to be a marker of mental health. Although he was still in pain, Antonio's capacity to see himself, and take responsibility for himself across time and into the future, was increasing.

During the current session, I guided Antonio through three repetitions of the Birth-to-Present protocol. At the end of the first timeline he remarked, "Nothing is really coming up inside me. I don't hate the baby the way I used to. I feel calm toward the baby." After the third timeline Antonio said, "There is calmness. I feel peaceful toward the baby."

In the middle of May, Antonio reported, "I'm saying what I think now. I'm more outspoken. I can talk and think faster. I can talk about concepts faster. My Bipolar is average. I swing and I'm never stable. It dominates a lot of behaviors. The manic aspect has been a lot stronger in the last two months, but the Bipolar is different. I'm not feeling down anymore. The Bipolar is changing in nature because the depression is going away. I've lived for 51 years without a good day. I feel hope here. I'm now in the game."

During a follow-up session, Antonio reported, "I felt happy when I go through the timeline. I'm excited about having direction. I'm just getting to the starting line." Before our session closed, Antonio expanded on the changes in the Bipolar swings. He said, while drawing a line across a blank piece of paper, "Previously, my swings would mostly be below the line into depression. When I did swing toward manic it would barely be above the line. Now there is much more evenness in the cycle. I go a little bit below the line and then I go a little bit above the line." For Antonio this was a vast improvement.

Because Antonio was busy at work, and more stable, we began to meet twice a month. His Bipolar symptoms were similar to the diagram he described above, some swings above the midline and some below, but the swings did not move very far in either direction. The leveling-off pattern had been consistent for about three months. He said, "My Bipolar today is fed by anxiety. There is another childhood trauma that affects it." We used the PTSD protocol to target Antonio's childhood trauma, which ended in relief. At the end of the session, as a result of our work, he spontaneously said, "I exist. I'm wanted. I'm important."

True to his pattern, Antonio called the day after the session in a low mood. "I don't know the point of living," he said on my voicemail. When I returned his call, he said, "I know this is just the angst I get a day after our session. I've learned to wait it out for a day and then I'll be better." He was logical about the despair, and recognized it as a common occurrence after we accessed neural networks related to trauma.

Within a few weeks, Antonio's mood had swung below midline into a more depressive state, but he worked with his physician to change his medication. The focus of our work had begun to shift also. By the end of our eighth month working together we seldom targeted his childhood needs. Instead, he asked to target issues related to his creativity and work performance. Antonio was a writer, teacher, speaker, and a manager of many people. He had been accepted into a graduate program and was setting a course for another advanced degree. His concerns focused primarily on accessing his gifts for writing and creativity, as well as the challenges of working while going to school. These concerns are quite a bit higher on Maslow's hierarchy of needs than the despair and loneliness of his internal child-self. Together we targeted the misconceptions Antonio held about himself and integrated artistic aspects into the greater whole.

As family challenges arose throughout the months, Antonio was able to face the struggles as a father and spouse—not as a child who needed to be loved. He said, "A few years ago my wife had a car accident and I made it all about me. Something happened with one of our kids this week, and I was able to be the dad in it."

Antonio started his graduate program and received wonderful feedback about his writing and creativity. The leadership program was stimulating and Antonio thrived in the community. He had also received a promotion and was managing a larger business group, traveling, and meeting the commitment of his graduate program. I only saw Antonio occasionally during these months.

In the fall, Antonio came to therapy again. He said, "I'm loving school. At school my mind expands and my contributions are really appreciated." Work however, was not going as well. He said he was cycling rapidly in his Bipolar Disorder and was feeling the grief of losing his first wife again. I asked him what was happening at work. "I don't like my new boss," he replied.

Antonio's new boss was a woman. She expected extremely large amounts of data via email, and did not interface directly with her subordinates as often as Antonio needed. He said, "The relationship with my former boss Tim was incredible. We were synced up. He'd give me an assignment and let me do it. Sometimes we brainstormed together and he loved my ideas. He trusted me to get the job done. I could go into his office, tell him what we needed to do, and he said, 'Go for it.' I always brought back the results he needed." With his new boss, Antonio felt like an outsider. His new vice president supervised an elite group. Eight out of the ten group members had been in their positions for several years. Antonio and another man were newcomers to their circle. The new working relationships were quite different than the ones Antonio had left. Since Antonio had been emotionally more consistent over the last few months, I suspected that something specific about his work situation was bothering him, rather than his distress being due to the cycling of his Bipolar Disorder. I guessed it was related to his belief "another woman doesn't love me," but I've learned to trust the client's body—not my insight—for direction.

"Where in your body is the feeling you get at work with your boss?" I asked.

Antonio pointed to his heart area. "Right here," he said. Using Standard Protocol LI, I asked him to focus on the feelings in his heart and let his mind be blank. After a few seconds he opened his eyes to tell me a scene he was remembering. Antonio said, "My parents sent me to boarding school when I was nine years old. They were missionaries and all the missionary kids were sent away to boarding school. I was at a big school all by myself. It was pure survival. The nine-year-old wants to be recognized for not crying when he left his mother." I asked Antonio to join his child-self in the memory and assure him that it was over. He opened his eyes and said, "The little boy can read people's hearts. He has so much fear, anxiety, loneliness, and no direction." I ached for the child myself.

Throughout the session, Antonio imagined that the little boy showed him the models he had built at school. The little boy also said, "I want to be a poet because I can read people's hearts." By the end of the session, the little boy Antonio was beginning to understand that he lived with the adult. At the end of the last timeline, Antonio said, "I'm holding him really tightly into myself and loving him."

The next day I received the regular call from him. Antonio said he cried on the way home "The little boy felt invisible," he said, "No one even knew I was there. At the boarding school I had to develop perfect behavior. It was hard to find anyone who cared for me. I felt no love." Referring to his plan in the present, Antonio added, "I'm going to write poetry." I sensed again the integration of Antonio's child-self who was tender and poetic with the adult who felt motivated by the child's need.

The next week we targeted the needs of the abandoned child again. Antonio said, "My parents have left me. I'm being orphaned. It is not okay. I needed my father. The little boy needed guidance." I coached him again to take his adult-self to the nine-year-old Antonio and be the adult presence the little boy needed. At the end of the session, the man before me said, "This was all for a purpose. I feel really strong."

Antonio's work schedule was very intense so we met approximately once a month over the next few months, using LI in each session. Fifteen months after our first session Antonio told me, "The manic stuff has completely died down from where it was. I used to shop compulsively online, but that's completely gone." I pressed him for more details to make sure I was hearing his story accurately. He reassured me, "That's completely gone. I used to get into buying binges which I couldn't stop, but that hasn't happened for months. And it doesn't feel like it will happen again."

"What about the Bipolar pain?" I asked.

"That's gone, too. I'm not having any Bipolar pain. It's been months since I've had it," Antonio answered. He described his emotional life as neutral. He continued to take his lithium and other mood stabilizers, but he was doing well at work and in his graduate program. The relationship with his wife was stable, but not as romantically charged as Antonio would have liked.

One month later when we met Antonio was still in a neutral place and it bothered him. He said, "I don't feel depressed and I don't feel high." As we explored his feelings further he remarked, "I've always wanted to have a wonderful relationship with a wife." I sensed that Antonio was discouraged about his marriage, like most people who couldn't get vital needs met within their intimate relationships. Before targeting Antonio's distress, I asked him about other aspects of the Bipolar Disorder. He reported that he had not had any of the physical Bipolar pain over the last few months, nor did he notice obvious high and low swings of Bipolar.

"And work?" I asked.

"Oh, it's fine. I'm getting along with my new boss now. She thinks I'm great. We had a meeting and I asked her outright if she liked what I was contributing. She said, 'Definitely! I'm afraid I'm going to lose you to another division.' She asked me to make a five year commitment to work for her," Antonio said.

I guessed that Antonio was feeling more of a situational depression than a Bipolar episode, although I could not be certain. A Bipolar episode would call for continued Birth-to-Present protocol. Instead, I opted for Standard Protocol again and asked Antonio to point to the place in his body where he felt his feelings. He pointed to his chest again and said, "I feel sadness right here." Using the affect bridge, Antonio remembered being a young child in his parent's home. "There is absolutely no affection here! There is no touching," he stated with anger. Although the friendship with his wife was stable, Antonio longed for an intimate connection with her. The present feelings in his body took him back to a childhood with no touching or closeness. I asked Antonio to visualize the youngest child-self he could imagine who longed for touch. He imagined himself as a baby again. I coached Antonio to soothe and comfort the baby, followed by timelines. By the end of the session, Antonio was holding his baby-self in the present. The child in his imagination was sleeping peacefully and Antonio felt close to him.

We met the next week and targeted the lack of intimacy in Antonio's marriage again. During the session he said, "I was very closed off to my mother and I've been very closed off to my wife." We used Standard Protocol. At the end of the session, he said, "Mom genuinely cared. She wrote letters to me at boarding school every week. I've taken a very harsh view of her." He concluded our session by saying, "I feel much more softened toward my wife."

I did not see Antonio for six months. In our final two sessions, two years after therapy began, he said, "I've been loving and caring toward my wife. We have a friendly, easy-going relationship between us. It's a get-along mode. I don't want her to hurt and have pain. It's more about protecting her than it is about my needs."

"What about the spending?" I asked.

Antonio replied, "I don't have any inkling to do that at all."

"And the Bipolar?" I inquired.

"When I go down, I don't go down nearly as far as I used to. The Bipolar pain is completely gone. I feel myself swing a bit, but I'm not spending. I've lost weight and I'm not 'white-knuckling' it. I haven't even tried to lose weight, but I lost quite a few pounds." I asked Antonio what he wanted to target in our session. He said, "I still feel some loneliness from the little boy inside." We used Standard Protocol again and Antonio emerged from the process speaking of himself as a leader.

We agreed that Antonio would call me for appointments on an as-needed basis. I have not heard from Antonio in several years and I trust that he is maintaining the same level of stability I witnessed in the last year of our work. Antonio's story is typical for clients with Bipolar Disorder. They seem to be intelligent, creative individuals who lack an internal connectivity between self-states. Resolving Bipolar clients' trauma, integrating their lives from birth to the present, and guiding them to nurture their young-selves appears to create a more stable platform from which to live their adult lives. Clients diagnosed with Bipolar Disorder seem to respond positively to LI and report lasting results from the process.

11. Parts Model

In Lifespan Integration, the Parts Model is used only after the client is well integrated, grounded, and evidences a solid core self; reflected in the ability to manage affect. It is not a primary method for treating therapeutic targets, but is an adjunct method used for specific troubling behaviors such as anorexia. The Parts Model is rarely used because highly dissociated clients do not need the reinforcement of separate internal states. Repeated sessions of the Birth-toPresent protocol resolve much of the distress held in the client's separated neural networks, and is the preferred method for increasing integration. Pace teaches the Parts Model at the Advanced Level LI Workshop. I have included a discussion about the Parts Model here with the caveat that the parts method is only employed in a limited-use capacity with clients who clearly exhibit a solid core self.

Parts Method

On a good day, if we're lucky, we go into the garage, put the key into the ignition and our car starts. Without thinking too much about this "miracle," we back out of the driveway and begin our day. On another day, we may have the same expectation when turning the key only to find that the car battery has died and needs to be recharged. This leaves one sitting in a car that has great potential, but is going nowhere because a single part has failed to do its job. This analogy portrays the essence of the Parts Model of Lifespan Integration: when one part malfunctions, the system's overall effectiveness is hindered.

Integration—the key to mental health—depends on each individual part's working capacity in the system. A perfectly working automobile can be derailed by the ineffective performance of its battery—a common, relatively inexpensive part. We, too, often derail when a 'part' of us performs its job in a way that is counter to our system's overall best interests. It may sound peculiar to think of people in terms of 'parts,' but our common experience confirms that this is our nature. As mentioned previously, we naturally talk about the "part of us that feels strong and confident," as well as "a part of us that isn't so sure."

So what kind of parts do we mean? Parts are as varied as the clients we see, but have some common characteristics. Parts generally specialize in some behavior or viewpoint, such as the anorexic part. The principle behind the Parts Model of LI is based on the assumption that somewhere in time a part or aspect of the personality developed a perspective or behavior that was intended to help the client with his or her life. Invariably, the part had a protective role. Strategies develop in childhood and reflect the best thinking of the younger-self at that moment in time. However, when applied to adult situations, these created roles are usually ineffective and often detrimental to the health of the overall system. In every case without exception, the part developed to provide a positive solution for some aspect of the client's life. This cannot be overstressed because parts can appear to have very negative qualities until fully understood in the context of how they arose to their defined role. To a fault, parts are trying to be helpful.

Because parts perceive their role as positive and important, it is essential to approach them with an open, inquiring style. They are dedicated to their jobs and know that they play an integral function for the self-system. Berating or chastising parts will not engender cooperation. They are already tirelessly serving in their roles and will continue to do so until they understand that a greater good can be accomplished through change. Understanding these parts in context and showing them the timeline are the only methods that will encourage a healthier adaptation for parts.

Since one part of the internal system is dedicated to its job, other parts are free to do their jobs. This could be likened to the human eye, which specifically performs many functions but is not primarily concerned with the workings of the hand. Parts generally feel that they are the only one in the system dedicated to their function, and in many cases this is true. For example, if one part is designated to hold a traumatic memory out of consciousness, the rest of the self may continue to grow. Problems occur when events trigger the unconscious memory, leaving the part too overwhelmed and too isolated to handle the interruption. This is why integration works miracles. Integrating a part and giving it current, up-to-date knowledge helps the part do its job more effectively. Parts are eager to update their functions when they perceive it is safe to do so.

The three most important aspects of the LI Parts Model can be summarized as follows:

1) A part will not change until the client understands the positive reason why the part is doing its job.

2) The part will only integrate once it understands that it can be an important part of the system with a new job—often a task in the same area as its current specialty.

3) Change always occurs with timeline repetitions. Even hidden or resistant parts will be changed by every repetition of the timeline.

Parts are usually found by going into an imaginary basement. The therapist guides a client to close his or her eyes and imagine going down nine steps while the therapist counts from nine to one. At the bottom of the stairs, the client enters the basement or conference room, and asks to see the part in charge of a certain behavior or belief system.

In the imaginary basement, parts present in many forms. It is safest to ask to speak to the "younger-self" who is in charge of a specific behavior rather than "the part" in charge of the behavior. We prefer to find a younger image of the client, because parts can appear as anything visually imaginable. Distorted, unrealistic parts are a clue that the client is dissociated and needs more repetitions of Birth-to-Present protocol rather than a specific focus on a certain part of the self.

All parts and aspects of the self have a benign purpose and must be understood and integrated. No part is to ever be exorcised; it is made up of the self and cannot be severed. When any part, negative or childlike, is shown enough repetitions of the timeline, it will transform into something positive.

Parts do not always show up right away when sought out in the basement. To address this, the client speaks into the empty or dark basement, even though he or she cannot see or identify the part. Trusting that the appropriate part is listening although not seen, the client says into the empty basement, "What was happening when you started doing your job is not what is happening now." Generally, after two or three introductions like this followed by timelines, the part will be seen or felt. With enough repetitions, all parts eventually appear to the client. Many more repetitions of the timeline plus dialogue will then be needed to convince the part it belongs inside a bigger, more resourced system.

A kind and inquiring approach, along with many repetitions of the timeline, will draw out parts and their functions. Clients often have to be guided by the therapist to be compassionate to parts. Parts can be holding unacceptable qualities of the self, which lead clients to be intolerant or impatient with the very part that is trying to help them. The therapist must monitor the client's interaction with the part until a positive alliance has formed.

I cannot stress enough that most conditions clients present can be resolved with Standard Protocol, Birth-to-Present protocol, and other protocols of Lifespan Integration. The parts method is only intended for occasional use when a specific, troubling behavior such as anorexia needs to be addressed. Conditions such as self-harm through cutting, binge eating, and self-induced vomiting are best treated through the Birth-to-Present protocol because of its ability to increase affect regulation.

Multiple Personality Disorder is now included in the diagnosis of Dissociative Identity Disorder (DID),which is the condition in which aspects of a person have developed separate and non-integrated states. The most successful way to treat DID clients using Lifespan Integration is through many, many sessions of Birth-to-Present protocol. Even though clients with DID exhibit a fragmented self, it is best to use the Birth-to-Present protocol in treatment because it strengthens the client's core self which is missing in highly dissociated clients. The Parts Model is not to be used with DID clients because it will reinforce, rather than integrate, their separated states. Yet there are appropriate times to use the Parts Model in Lifespan Integration.

Rachel

On a single occasion I used the parts method with Rachel who was completing her divorce after 23 years of marriage. Up to that point, my therapy with Rachel consisted of multiple sessions of BP, Standard Protocol, and the Relationship Pattern protocol of LI. As we were nearing completion of our work together, Rachel said, "I still don't understand how I got into an affair. I don't believe in affairs! My value system tells me that it is wrong to have an affair and yet I had one. I kept trying to end it, but I couldn't get out of it and now I have contempt for myself."

"Would you like to find out why you had an affair?" I asked.

"Yes," she replied.

I guided Rachel to picture herself going down a set of stairs into an imaginary basement. When she was at the bottom of the stairs I coached her to say into the empty basement, "I am your adult-self and I want to talk to the younger Rachel who is in charge of having an affair." Rachel told me that she could not see anyone in the basement, but she could sense the presence of an aspect of herself. "Tell her that things have changed and you have grown since she started having the affair with Kent." I paused while Rachel repeated this phrase to the younger presence in the basement. "Ask her to watch these pictures because this is the proof that things really have changed and you are making different choices," I coached. After Rachel had a moment to speak this phrase into the basement I lead her through the first timeline. Rachel's affair began three years before she came to therapy, so I started her timeline at the start of her affair and used three cues per year, in order, to prove to her younger-self that she had developed new ways of coping with her situation and much had changed since she got involved with Kent. At the end of the timeline, I asked Rachel to picture herself in the basement again and speak to the younger aspect of herself that was in charge of getting her into an affair.

Rachel replied, "It's definitely a part of me, but I can't understand why it happened. I don't think of myself as someone who would have an affair."

"Let's show her the pictures again," I guided. "Tell her that you know she had a good reason for it and she wasn't trying to hurt you."

"But it's bad," Rachel interrupted, opening her eyes and looking at me in disbelief.

"I'm not saying affairs are good," I defended, "But, I'm confident her motive was positive. She did not set out to hurt you, even though affairs cause pain for people." Rather than argue with Rachel, I guided her through two timelines from the beginning of the affair to the present. When she entered the basement again, Rachel saw a younger version of herself who was sad and lonely. Rachel's response to her younger-self softened.

"She just wants love," Rachel said with compassion. "She is really lonely and has no one to turn to. My husband Paul is traveling all the time, playing sports, or working on the computer. I can't reach him. We were married, but I was alone."

"Tell her that you know she was trying to help you by getting you into an affair, but things have changed and now you can take care of her," I said.

"I want to put my arms around her," Rachel spontaneously offered.

"Please do," I answered with kindness. "Take her someplace where she and you can be together. "What would make her feel less lonely?" I asked.

"She wants to talk and tell me how she feels. She tries to be good, but no matter how good she is, my husband still ignores her," Rachel explained. In her imagination, Rachel took her younger-self to a coffee shop and ordered each of them a latte.

"Let her talk," I suggested, "And validate what she's telling you. Tell her that you know how lonely she was back then and that it seemed impossible to get Paul to respond to you. Tell her that you are going to respond to everything she needs and that you have the resources to do so. You are not ever going to leave her at home while you travel or use the computer. She will always be with you." After Rachel repeated these phrases to her younger-self I guided her through the timeline.

We repeated this exact sequence again with some additional appreciation for the younger-self. At the end of the fifth timeline I asked Rachel to show her younger-self what was happening in the present and the hurt that was eventually caused by the affair. "She only wanted love," Rachel said in a subdued, but understanding tone.

"And she got you love," I affirmed. "This part of yourself

found a loving relationship even though it didn't fit your values. She knew you were emotionally starved and she handled the problem for you."

"I think there are better ways to solve that problem," Rachel offered.

"Yes," I countered, "But, you were having trouble finding those solutions at the time so a part of you took matters into its own hands." We repeated the timeline sequence two more times until the younger-self was well integrated into the more mature Rachel who had confronted her relationship with Paul and took steps to end the marriage. At the end of the seventh timeline Rachel was peaceful.

"I guess that explains it," she said.

"Essentially, it does," I concurred. I validated that Rachel did not set out to have an affair, but she could not ignore her relationship needs indefinitely. Therefore, an unconscious aspect of herself acted on Rachel's behalf without the full benefit of Rachel's values and beliefs.

"I'm guessing that you ignored your own needs, too," I said kindly.

Rachel was pensive "Yes, that's true," she answered. I thought if I could be the perfect wife and support Paul then he would love me. I see it didn't work that way."

During our several months of therapy, Rachel addressed loneliness from her years as an only child and her penchant for people-pleasing. We healed specific, traumatic memories with Standard Protocol and I held her baby-self— symbolized by the infant doll in my arms—as I communicated worth to the newborn Rachel followed by timelines. Loneliness had plagued Rachel throughout her life. After the earlier occurrences of loneliness and separation were healed, we briefly entered into the Parts Model of LI to help Rachel understand and integrate the part of her that led her into an affair while she was married.

Having an affair violated Rachel's values, but after one session of finding the younger-self in charge of getting her into an affair, Rachel had compassion and understanding for her own behavior. The overall integration accomplished for Rachel through Lifespan Integration increased her self-awareness and her capacity to accept undesirable aspects of herself. It is important to remember that we used the Parts Model briefly only after Rachel exhibited coherence and strength of self. It was not the central component of her therapy. The strength of the Parts Model is its ability to address a specific troubling behavior for coherent individuals.

I've been following a girl for two years since she was 12 years old and suicidal. I helped her process the suicide attempt with LI, and through the timelines she reduced her reactivity and made connections about why she went that far. Doing the timelines was such a relief to her.

Sheila Mohn, LI therapist

12. Children

Children respond extremely well to Lifespan Integration. Their internal world is still being formed and their brains are very pliable. As a result, new data and reparative experiences seem to easily take hold in their young brains. Surprisingly, children are also easily exhausted by repetitions of the time-line. It is common for a school-age child to be fatigued at the end of two timelines and barely able to make it through a third timeline in a one hour session. Nevertheless, the outcomes from using LI with children are profound.

My clinical experience with children is generally based around those who have anxiety, trauma, adoption issues, and loss. I know many parents are looking for solutions for children who have Attention Deficit Disorder (ADD) or Attention Deficit/ Hyperactivity Disorder (ADHD). Though I personally do not have much experience working directly with ADD or ADHD, colleagues of mine report levels of success helping children with these problems using LI. I have observed that some behaviors which appear to be symptoms of ADD or ADHD actually turn out to be symptoms of trauma, and trauma symptoms can be significantly reduced or eliminated through Lifespan Integration. Amen (2001) proposed that there are six types of ADD. Pace postulated that some types of ADD are a client's attempt to regulate emotion. As a collective group of LI therapists, we have seen positive outcomes using LI with children diagnosed with ADD depending on the type of ADD, the child's capacity to regulate emotion, and the contributing aspect of trauma.

Treating a child's trauma with Lifespan Integration is almost miraculous. Within a few sessions, most trauma symptoms completely disappear when targeted with LI. Unlike other therapies, with LI, children do not have to share very much about their trauma in order to heal it. They are remarkably capable of finding younger states within themselves that need healing, and integrating those states through the timeline. In my clinical practice I have treated children with birth trauma, early surgeries, sexual abuse, auto accidents, and other concerns. In most cases, according to the child's and parents' reports, trauma completely resolves within a few sessions.

The Timeline

With young children, it is useful to have a cue sheet containing two memories for each year, generally six months a part. It is not necessary for the child to help construct the timeline, it is only important for the child to actually remember the events on the cue sheet. When I ask parents to write a timeline for their child, I suggest they begin with birthdays for each year and then think of something approximately six months later. Most kids remember their birthdays and easily distinguish one birthday experience from another.

Photographs are not a useful substitute for the written timeline. When a child recalls a memory, neural networks are activated and have the opportunity to expand. Using photographs instead of remembered events seems to diminish the spontaneous firing which we observe through repetitions of the written timeline of memories. In my experience, photographs seem to produce less of the memory expansion and may not be tied to something the child actually remembers. We want clients to directly remember the events on their cue sheets because doing so will trigger other associated aspects of the memory. As previously mentioned, a client's timeline experience will be influenced by the emotion present at the beginning of the timeline and will change with each repetition. We want to enable children and adults to have the richest and most connective experience possible through Lifespan Integration which requires recalling real memories.

Trauma

Trauma treatment, for an adult or child, consists of two phases. The first phase is treating the trauma memory itself. Repetitions of the LI timeline prove to a child that the bad thing that happened to them is over. It is common for a child to say that his or her younger-self did not know that the trauma was over. Generally, more than one session will be required for the child to fully resolve the body memory and associated emotions connected to the trauma. Since trauma appears to be stored and resolved in layers, it is normal to target different aspects of the trauma in follow-up sessions. After children have been abused, frightened, or experienced a seriously threatening event, they are still braced to defend themselves against the injury until they discover, on a mind-body level, that the trauma has ended.

The second component of trauma treatment involves the strategy a child develops for coping with the trauma. When children experience trauma, they develop coping mechanisms to survive in life after the trauma. Children and adults must find ways to carry on after their painful experiences. Unfortunately, children have few resources for handling trauma and no power to stop the bad things they experience. Children's emotional systems get clogged with anxiety and distress after trauma. Unless someone helps them offload their negative experience, children direct energy and resources toward holding the episode, leaving them with divided attention and reduced emotional resources. After trauma, it is common for children to withdraw from people and activities they love. Their childlike level of trust is usually lost and they find themselves closed off from love, or over-pursuing love, through attention-seeking behavior. Children may develop ways to dissociate from the trauma, become highly sensitive, or have increased anxiety. Not understanding the child's experience, adults tend to find fault with them for being anxious or distracted, and a cycle of self-blame, distress, and poor self-image is set in motion.

Children's coping methods often resolve concurrently with the LI trauma treatment. If they don't resolve, the strategies a child developed to endure the trauma will need to be directly targeted. The coping methods children develop may have become so intertwined in their lives that it is not possible to see the need for resolving them until the initial trauma symptoms are cleared. Jasmine was one such client whose challenging behavior was a follow-up strategy from abuse, not defiance. Jasmine's mother complained that her daughter's name had to be called several times before she would lift her head out of the book she was reading. Her mother believed Jasmine was being defiant, but the child protested that she really did not hear her mother calling. Through the course of therapy, it became apparent that Jasmine had been sexually molested by a close family friend more than once and had learned to dissociate to cope with the abuse. She lost herself so completely in stories that she was not attentive to the outside world. Jasmine's dissociation was a coping mechanism for something she was powerless to stop. Although useful at the time of the trauma, dissociating had become problematic in Jasmine's life. Her treatment with me was not complete until we eliminated the symptoms of trauma and the subsequent dissociation it created. In treating trauma, it is important to resolve the trauma as phase one, and the subsequent coping methods concurrently or as phase two.

Adoption

Adoption is one of my favorite issues to address for children. Lifespan Integration helps them resolve confusion, any related trauma, and mixed loyalties of being adopted. With children and adults I use a toy set of nesting cups to describe the principles we will be working with in therapy. Nesting cups are a child's play toy comprised of plastic cups in different sizes and colors that fit inside one another. The first cup is about an inch in diameter and the largest of ten cups is approximately three inches wide. If stacked correctly, they form a colorful and compact group of cups that perfectly fit together inside one another. To describe the principles of treatment, I separate the cups and hold the smallest one between my fingers.

"This is your baby-self," I say to the child and his or her parents. "When you were just this big you were a little baby inside your birth mother. Then you were born and within a day or two you went to live in a foster home," or I mention the correct information for the child's adoption. Still holding the smallest cup, I continue, "When you were this big you had thoughts and feelings. You were probably confused, wondering, 'Where is the person whose voice I've been hearing and whose body I've been sharing for nine months?' Lots of things are going on for this little baby," I say kindly.

Picking up the next larger cup I continue, "When you were in foster care people took care of you and your little body was recording the thoughts, feelings, and sensations of living with those people."

The human self is recording memory all through life, including in utero. This form of memory is called implicit memory because it stores in the body without cognitive awareness and precedes the picture-like concrete memory which emerges around two years of age. Some adopted children were not in safe or healthy foster homes after their births. I have worked with several families whose adopted children were found abandoned in a train station or were left on the street in a paper bag. These children experienced hours and days of neglect, and possibly abuse, before they were abandoned. Their implicit memory includes fear, distress, neglect, abuse, and legitimate concerns about their survival. Even though these children have been adopted and currently live in safe homes, the implicit memory of their early experience is still present in their bodies' cells. In order to help these children stabilize, we need to reach back into the younger state and prove to their bodies that the bad thing that happened to them is over. We can do this through LI without explaining the facts of their abandonment. Most parents whose children were left on the street have not shared these facts with their children. Yet the implicit memory of the frightening situations they faced will activate in their current bodies and cause out-of-proportion distress. We truly are a living collection of all of our life experiences—known and unknown.

For my demonstration, I tuck the first cup into the second cup and continue. Holding up the third cup in the set I say, "This little cup represents when you were one year old and got adopted by Mom and Dad." I briefly tell the facts of adoption in a positive way, but include, "And that might have been a bit confusing to your younger-self, because your little baby-self was used to living in foster care and all of sudden you ended up with your mom and dad." When any child accesses memory, he or she draws upon all of their implicit memory. For adopted children, and those with trauma, their implicit memory contains confusion, heightened fight or flight responses, and abandonment. This is why parents of adopted children often struggle with their child's lack of trust in them. Adoptive parents generally work hard to give their children love and care, but often receive anger and mistrust in return. Because the brain uses the past to predict the future, injured and abandoned children unconsciously use the past information stored in their minds and bodies to defend against the very people who are trying hard to love them in the present. With Lifespan Integration we can heal the earlier 'rings,' or 'little cups of information,' held within the child's body. The child can then generate new ways of responding based on his or her current experience instead of the past.

To finish my explanation, I move through the rest of the nesting cups. Holding up the fourth cup I say, "This is your two-year-old self who learned to run and jump." I continue through the cups until we reach the child's present age.

At the appropriate age, I mention, "And here is where you got adopted and started living with your mom and dad." At the end of my description, I put all the cups together and turn them over so that the child can only see the largest cup. "This is you, right now at age ten." Turning the set of cups over I continue, "You can see that your ten-year-old self is made up of all these cups. When you turned ten, you became a ten-year-old with a one-, two-, three-, four-, five-...year-old inside you." Children usually nod in understanding.

Intuitively, young clients resonate with the feeling states inside themselves when I mention their ages through the cup demonstration. I explain that we will be inviting them to go back to earlier younger-selves and explain what happened through the adoption. I promise that their baby-self will feel lots better when he or she understands what happened and how things turned out.

Generally, with children under age 12, we do not have them take their oldest-self back in time for LI as we would with an adult in Standard Protocol. When we are targeting a single incident with a child, we prove the trauma is over using the PTSD protocol or we imagine a trusted adult rescues the younger child-self from the bad situation. Children need the help of empowered adults to help solve their problems in real life and in imaginative scenes. Adoption is the one exception I make to this practice when working with children.

Since children have the best access to their internal younger-self states, I ask the child in my office to go back inside him or herself and explain to the baby what happened. I tell them, "You are the only one who can get right to that precious baby on the inside." Children always agree to this task. Later, when the confusion, fear, and disorientation from the adoption have cleared inside the earliest ego states of the child, we can have their adoptive parents create imaginary interventions for their younger selves. Neurons fire and load into a neural network during imagined exercises. Timelines integrate the imaginary experience so it appears to become part of a child's inner world.

There are three critical components to consider when using Lifespan Integration with adoption: 1) All adopted children are dissociated, 2) They need to understand the 'bad stuff' is over, and 3) The 'good stuff' needs to be put in where it was missing. Treating a child's adoption is complex because their defense of dissociation impacts the work, we have to skillfully handle the details of their adoption and prove it is over, they have organic, natural loyalties to their idealized birth parents, and we have to create positive, retrofitted experiences of attachment repair to include the adoptive parents.

Dissociation

With all children, their only defense against difficult experiences is dissociation. Children do not have the power to solve or prevent most of the situations that bring them to therapy. The only recourse children have to adoption, surgery, molestation, violence, etc., is to dissociate. Because they cannot solve the problems which create their distress, their only solution for responding to it is dissociation.

Children cannot stop the adults in their lives from requiring that they babysit young children when they themselves are quite young, they do not have the option to turn down a directive to shoplift for the family, they cannot choose to live somewhere else if mother or father are drug-addicted, they cannot decline a surgery, and they cannot prevent the sexual advances of adults in their lives who frighten, abuse, and violate them. What else can they do to exist in difficult circumstances besides internally separate themselves from their experience? Hence, children can only respond to adult-generated difficulties with confusion, genuine powerlessness, and dissociation.

It is tremendously helpful to explain to children that the difficult thing that happened to them is a grown-up problem that only grown-ups can solve. When they believe this truth, their bodies relax and their mindsets begins to shift. It is a relief for them to know that they were genuinely powerless to solve the impossible circumstances they were in. Because they were powerless, children dissociate to cope with their situations, and this dissociation is a factor in helping them endure their distress. Children with many difficult circumstances can be quite dissociated which means the Lifespan Integration work will require many, many repetitions of their timelines.

I have noticed that adopted children ignore subjects raised in a counseling session focused on their adoptions. They do not remember aspects of their story that they were old enough to remember, and they often pretend events did not occur as they did occur. When resolving their distress and associated complexities of adoption, they need more sessions and more repetitions of their timelines than children who have secure attachments. This does not make the work any less successful; it only requires that counselors understand the level of dissociation adopted children carry and consider this in their work. A non-adopted child might resolve a trauma in a handful of sessions, whereas an adopted child will need many LI sessions focused on a single trauma due to the dissociation. As clinicians work with adoptees to take the 'bad stuff out,' they need to understand that it may not be as straightforward as is common with other children.

Taking the 'Bad Stuff' Out

We believe we change the neural networks in children's little bodies by proving to their tiniest-self through the timeline that they have grown up to their current age. We can guide the child in the office to inform his or her baby-self on the inside about the confusion or trauma around the birth circumstances, and prove that time is over through repetitions of the timeline.

When implementing Lifespan Integration with an adopted child, we begin with the child telling his or her baby-self the overall truth about the adoption, appropriately framed, and that the situation surrounding the adoption is over. We keep reminding the child that what happened was not his or her fault and there was nothing he or she could have done about it. We remind them that it is okay to keep loving their birth mom and dad because all children have love for their parents in their hearts. Moms and dads whose children are adopted were not in a position to take good care of children and keep them safe, but it is okay to still love them. We ask boys and girls to tell their baby-selves that the baby did not do anything wrong that caused the adoption. Yes, grown-ups stepped in to make things right for the baby because the baby is so precious and wonderful, and he or she needed to be kept safe and loved in just the right way. We keep returning them to the baby-self, followed by timelines, until the child reports that the baby understands he or she has grown up to be the child in my office. It is typical for strong and tender emotions to arise during this process. Babies are always confused about what is happening in their worlds when separated from their mothers through events like adoption, medical interventions, or time in the incubator. I know this because children tell me it is true. When the internal infant finally releases the distress he or she has been holding, the child often cries, looks, and feels like a baby in my office. It is a tender and sweet healing.

Adults adopted as infants demonstrate the same crying and deep exhale when the mystery of their adoption is understood on a neural level in their baby-selves. Shannon was a nurse who was convinced that she had no unresolved distress about her adoption. She insisted that she fully understood the reasons for her adoption and she loved and appreciated her adoptive family. Shannon reported that her adoptive family had been wonderful to her.

When I invited Shannon to speak to her baby-self just in case there was some confusion for the baby, the nurse in front of me cried like an infant when she accessed her youngest-self. Shannon's sobs were heart-wrenching. When our session of LI was complete, the adult very peacefully reported that the baby was calm and grateful, and well integrated into her adult-self. Up to that point in her life, Shannon had no interest in seeking out her birth mother and had refused her adoptive mom's help to do so.

A few weeks before the LI session with Shannon, her adoptive mother read a newspaper article with a photograph, which she suspected was about Shannon's biological mother. She saved the article and contact information in case Shannon wished to meet her birth mother someday.

After one LI session in which the confusion and distress were resolved for her baby-self, Shannon made contact with her birth mom. They had a positive meeting, and Shannon said she was glad to meet her birth mom, but her real family was her adoptive family and would always be so. Shannon reported a peaceful resolution about this part of her life, which she previously had no idea held so much distress for her.

Putting the 'Good Stuff' In

We 'put the good stuff in' for adopted children by creating positive feeling states for the past by guiding the child to imagine the adoptive parents were wonderful, loving caregivers for the baby-self from the beginning. These imaginary, positive experiences will not harm or confuse children. Instead, they retrofit the feeling of safety and security into the place where it may have been missing.

One of the ways I do this is by asking the child to imagine that his or her adopted mother and father were in the birth room when he or she was born. I give the baby doll in my office to a parent, and describe a beautiful meeting with the adopted mom and dad. I say, "You just came out of your birth mom and everyone is happy about you. Your mommy here is holding you and crying because she's so happy about you. Your daddy is crying too, because here is the baby they have been hoping for." Usually at this point, the child looks to his or her adoptive mother and father to see if this is likely, and they support the notion that they are filled with joy and happiness about the birth of their child. We follow this initial intervention with positive, imaginary incidences of care and attention from the adoptive parents, followed by the timeline.

After I have created a template for the imaginary repair of birth and babyhood with the adoptive parents, I encourage them to repeat this process at home with their children at bedtime, story times, or cuddle times. Children love to hear their favorite stories over and over. They delight in hearing made-up stories about themselves from the past which include their present family. Parents can accelerate a child's healing through LI by inputting the good stuff at home followed by timelines, while I work to resolve the painful body memories in therapy. Since both are required, parents can help the healing by making up positive stories about their early, loving experiences with the child. To reiterate, we are not changing events that actually happened in the past with birth parents and we do not create interventions that imply birth parents acted differently than they acted. Rather, we believe we are enhancing attachment repair by helping children formulate neural networks of early developmental needs being met through imagination. Children do not get confused about the truth. This process helps them change their view of themselves in the past, and sets them up to create better relationships in the future.

Three Mommies

I was working with a young family who adopted Nicholas from Romania. They already had their four-year-old daughter, Anna, when three-year-old Nicholas arrived. The family prepared by traveling to Romania frequently before Nicholas' adoption, and provided his foster family with food, shoes, and dental care while they met and loved their new son. Overall, the family was having a better-than-average transition.

I had brief appointments on occasion with Nicholas in the context of family therapy, but his attention span was short and there were no obvious red flags about his adjustment to America. Nicholas was outgoing and personable, and was noticeably attaching well to his new mom.

A year after Nicholas came to America his seemingly smooth and openhearted transition came to a halt. Getting out at a gas station to fill the car, Nicholas' mom accidentally locked the doors with the keys and the children inside the car. The two children were safely buckled into their car seats and Nicholas became very frightened. With her mom's coaching from the outside, Anna was able to wiggle out of her car seat and unlock the door. She did not seem troubled by the incident, but Nicholas was changed.

After the gas station incident, Nicholas' mom reported that he was now clinging to her constantly, crying if she went downstairs to do the laundry, and whining by her side if she talked on the phone. When left at home with his dad and sister Nicholas was almost inconsolable. Pulling into a gas station made him cry and beg his mom not to leave him.

For two sessions I focused directly on the gas station mishap using a different therapy modality, but nothing was significantly shifting in Nicholas' behavior. I guessed that the root of his distress might be a series of mother-child separations. By the time he was four, Nicholas had known three mommies and three grandmas. Though he appeared to be handling his adoption well, I wondered if Nicholas had reached his limit for trust when the separation from his mom at the gas station occurred.

Nicholas' adoptive mother had experienced Lifespan Integration and agreed for me to try it with him. If long-standing separation anxiety was the issue, my goal was to use the timeline to integrate and inform each ego state, from in utero to the present, that Nicholas was safe now and in a permanent home. Nicholas was the first child I treated using Lifespan Integration. I asked Nicholas to crawl into his mother's lap and I sat in front of the mother–child couple on the floor.

I asked Nicholas to imagine that once he was a very little boy who was this big (I held my hands about ten inches apart) and he lived inside his mommy. She was his birth mommy and he lived right inside her. Her body made his body grow, and she made sure he was strong, healthy, and safe. Nicholas nodded that he could imagine the baby. I asked him to tell his baby-self on the inside that one day the baby got so big it was time for him to come out of the birth mommy so they went to the hospital where the baby was born. The baby was a wonderful boy who was good and lovable. Nothing was wrong with him. That was his first mommy. The family knew nothing about the birth mother or why she could not keep her baby. I continued that the doctors delivered the baby and took him to an orphanage where some nice ladies put him in a crib and took care of him. They smiled at him and thought, *He is a really good baby; we are really glad he's here. We really like this baby.*

After my description of the orphanage, I asked Nicholas to show the baby pictures in his mind of how the baby grew up to be four years old. We began by showing the baby how the ladies in the orphanage took care of him for a few days by giving him bottles and keeping him warm, and smiling at him while they held him. It does not matter if things actually happened this way. The purpose of this intervention is to create the sense of being securely loved and cared for as the baby and the four-year-old self. It is of primary importance to have attachment to one's self and to others for healthy functioning.

I then asked Nicholas to imagine that his foster family was coming to get him and to show this to the baby. Nicholas' mom filled in a few brief details about the foster family for the baby to know. I said, "That was your second mommy. Her name was Angelina and your grandma was Meemaw. They loved the little boy and took care of him." Then I asked Nicholas to imagine the baby was big enough to turn over by himself and this made Angelina and Meemaw happy. Then I asked Nicholas to imagine what it was like when he learned to sit up (pausing while Nicholas imagined this)…then crawl…take steps…say words, etc. I continued with his timeline by saying:

- Show the baby his first birthday and how his new mom, dad, and Anna came to visit him and brought him toys. They loved him, too, and wanted to be with him whenever they could.

- They took baby Nicholas to the school yard to play with balls because he was big enough to run and play outside.

- Then his American family went home and got a room ready for the little boy with his own toys and little bed. They were thinking about him and loving him all the way over in America.

- Imagine how the little boy turned two in Romania.

- Then the day came for him to go to his new home in America with his next mommy. This was his last and forever mommy.

At this point, Nicholas was beginning to remember actual events from life in Romania and the transition to America. I prompted him to remember more cues from his life:

- His first house.

- Playing with his sister.

- The time his foster parents and Meemaw flew over to see him.

- Their second house.

- Turning four and his birthday party.

- Dance class.

- Preschool.

I then asked him to remember the gas station and how Anna was able to get out of her car seat and open the doors. I concluded by saying, "Bring the little Nicholas baby from the orphanage into your house and show him his third and final Mommy who loves him very much. Imagine that Daddy and Anna are kissing and hugging the baby too. They are so happy to have him in the family. Show him your toys and your room. Let him see that even though all those other people loved and took care of him, this is his forever home. His American mommy, daddy, and sister will always love him and take care of him."

I could tell Nicholas was showing these images to the baby inside. When he was done, Nicholas turned and clung to his mom like a little Koala bear. She snuggled and smooched him.

After a short break and more snuggling, I suggested we show the pictures again to the baby who grew up to be four-year-old Nicholas. He settled into his mom's lap and we began with the same imagining of the little baby inside Nicholas' birth mom's uterus and continued with the cues up to the present.

We repeated Nicholas' timeline a third time. In each repetition of his timeline I noticed significant state changes in Nicholas. In the beginning he was like a little baby, with tender baby sounds and gestures. When I looked at him for confirmation that he was listening and getting the pictures, he was vulnerable-looking and non-verbal. As we progressed through the story his body language changed. When I asked him to remember the part about his foster family, Nicholas wrapped his arms around his mother's neck, nuzzled into her shoulder, and mournfully said, "I miss Meemaw." At that moment Nicholas looked as if he was two years old. When we got to the part of the timeline he actually remembered, Nicholas appeared interested in his flight to America and the foster family's visit. During the second timeline, he interacted with his mother and named important aspects of each event. When we arrived at his present age in the memory timeline, Nicholas looked and acted like his four-year-old self again. We concluded our session.

Nicholas' mother reported some change the following week but nothing equal to his positive behavior before the gas station event. At the beginning of our next session we played a bit, and then I asked him to show the pictures to the baby again about how he grew up. We wanted to make sure that the baby knew he had three mommies and his American mommy was the last one who would love him forever. Nicholas was happy to participate in the story about himself and climbed into his mother's lap.

Once again, I repeated the timeline for Nicholas to imagine and remember, beginning in the uterus of his birth mother. With mom's help we added a few more memories. I mentioned Nicholas' first mommy, second mommy, and reinforced that his American mommy was his third and final mommy. In that session we completed the timeline twice. Each time Nicholas looked and acted like the age I was describing. In this session however, he was still shy but was a bit more animated through our reading of the timeline. At the end of the second timeline Nicholas was still sitting in his mother's lap but was an active, wiggly boy who wanted to move onto the next activity.

When Nicholas and Anna came to the family appointment the following week, Nicholas said, "I don't need a turn this time. Sissy can have all the play time with Cathy." Nicholas' mom reported that his clinging behavior had dropped off significantly. She felt a very important shift had taken place and credited the timeline for the change. She reported that he was still a little reluctant to be left in the car at the gas station, but overall, things were much better. For the next few months when I saw the family Nicholas said he did not need a turn with me and his mother confirmed he was doing fine.

I have since used Lifespan Integration with many children after first using it with Nicholas. I try to use it with all adopted clients, adults and children. After one or two timelines, clients can report the feelings of their baby-selves, which include confusion and loss, even if intellectually they know their adoption was for the best. The adopted client is the only one who can fully reach and explain to the infant-self what occurred during and after their birth. When the infant-self truly understands what happened, which would have been impossible for a baby to understand at the time, clients change their view of themselves, consequently changing their world.

Anxiety

Anxiety is a common reason parents seek out therapy for their children. Lifespan Integration is a highly effective modality for treating anxiety. All the children I have seen for anxiety have had their symptoms of anxiety significantly diminish or completely disappear. Common concerns for children include the fear of monsters in the closet, scary creatures under the bed, bad guys coming into the house at night, Mom and Dad being away, vomiting while sleeping or at school, and many more realistic and imaginary problems. Although adults might find these fears trifling and often annoying, they can be debilitating for children. Families can be significantly impacted by a child with a heightened fear which cannot be soothed. Telling a child that his or her fear is unrealistic and explaining the facts will not eliminate the distress. Opening the doors and proving that no monsters are in the closet also will not eliminate the fear. As soon as a caregiver leaves, the impending danger resurfaces and the child becomes frightened and anxious.

I have a working hypothesis that anxiety is triggered by the feeling of powerlessness. When children have a debilitating fear that requires therapy, they are usually accessing an earlier memory, sometimes unconsciously, of a time when they were truly powerless and had a problem they could not solve. I am not advocating for permissive parenting to avoid this feeling. Instead, I am referring to an experience the child had which may have occurred before his or her brain began storing concrete memory—a process that begins around age two. Anxiety may also result from a child being in a double-bind situation where he or she was powerless to resolve the situation.

Whatever its derivative, anxiety is always an unprocessed set of feelings which are being held in the gut. Accessing and processing these feelings provides a 'cure' for anxiety. In my opinion, anxiety is not an organic, basic feeling such as mad, sad, glad, and afraid. Instead, anxiety is one of the afore-mentioned feelings which have not been allowed into consciousness. Children and adults with anxiety have lived in family systems where some feelings are generally unacceptable. Anxiety is eliminated by learning to access and experience feelings. The work of Lifespan Integration for anxiety is the simple procedure of identifying the place in a client's body where anxiety is held, activating the neural networks holding unprocessed feelings, and leading clients through their timelines.

Zack

Zack was a 12-year-old boy who was had too much anxiety to sleep alone in his room. He had been adopted by a protective and loving family. After two years in their family he was still too frightened to sleep alone in his bedroom at night. He desired the autonomy of an adolescent boy, but no coaching, bribing, or reassurance from his parents made Zack feel secure enough to sleep alone. He lived in a safe home and safe neighborhood, yet the thought of sleeping in his own bedroom created too much anxiety for him.

The underlying, unprocessed feelings which drove Zack's anxiety came from the pre-adoption years. At six years old Zack was frequently left at home with two younger siblings while his biological parents stayed out all night working or partying. Zack and his brothers slept huddled in one small bed. His parents also required that he shoplift for them at the grocery store. When we addressed his 12-year-old fear of being alone in his bedroom, the memories and associated body sensations of the earlier powerless memories surfaced. When we proved to his younger-self that he was no longer a young boy who had to steal food and protect his brothers alone at night, Zack's 12-year-old self began to consistently sleep comfortably in his own bed. His body got the message through LI timelines that he was no longer in the situation in which he was genuinely powerless and afraid. Was Zack truly powerless in the earlier situations? Yes, because he could not have kept his brothers and himself safe at night if he faced a serious problem, nor would his parents have tolerated Zack refusing to shoplift. His parents told him that little boys would not go to jail if they got caught, but grown-ups would go to jail, so he had to carry out the shoplifting every week. Zack faced the double-bind problem of following his parent's instructions—which frightened him until he shook—or possibly losing his parents to jail when they did the shoplifting.

Without help, parents often do not see the connecting powerless feelings under their child's anxiety. Yet in my experience, the powerless feeling, and other unprocessed emotions, are always present in an anxious child or adult.

Eddie

Eddie's parents brought him to therapy because his anxiety was so high he could not sleep without the light on, go into bathrooms alone, or ride in elevators. He was afraid of lightning and thunder and all these fears were getting in the way of his social development. By the age of ten, he was not able to attend birthday parties or go to movies with friends. Eddie was adopted and the theme of powerlessness ran deeply in his history.

When I met Eddie he had seen two previous counselors for many sessions. He was reluctant to see me because, as he told his father, "Nothing will work. Nothing has worked before, and I don't think anything will ever work for me." Eddie's anxiety symptoms had not resolved through the earlier counseling and he was discouraged. Eddie's father, Dave, knew a co-worker who had experienced Lifespan Integration. Dave persuaded Eddie to try one more counselor based on the recommendation of his friend. Eddie reluctantly agreed to see me, but only for one session, unless he de-cided to come back.

With his parents input, Eddie and I compiled a list of all the things that made him anxious. As he reported the items, I placed them on a rectangular graph according to his direction. Eddie sorted the anxious situations by high, middle, or low anxiety. In my experience, all children are able to accurately report how distressing their problems are when asked to position them into simple categories. Eddie's chart of anxiety-producing situations is as follows:

EDDIE'S CHART OF SCARY THINGS

High	Sleeping in my room alone.
	When it's dark at night I'm afraid something will pop up.
Medium	Going inside elevators .
	Afraid someone will snatch me.
Low	Going into a bathroom, someone might hurt me.
	Thunder and lightning.

After we had completed the chart, I asked Eddie which one he wanted to fix first. "Being scared at night," he quickly answered. I was not surprised about his answer since it was at the top of his chart. I find it worthwhile to engage all my clients in prioritizing the most important issues they want to address in therapy. It is a simple way to directly hit the mark for the client's greatest need.

To begin reducing his anxiety around being scared in his room at night, I asked Eddie to remember a time recently when he felt scared. He described the scenario to me and added, "I'm especially afraid if it's windy and rainy outside. I'm afraid the power will go out and I won't be able to get my dad."

"Point to where you feel that in your body," I directed.

"Right here in my heart," Eddie answered while pointing at his chest.

"Can you really feel it?" I asked.

"Oh, yes," he answered, "I feel shaky inside."

We did not use an affect bridge to float the body-based feeling to an earlier time because that method would not take us into the realm of zero to two years old. Given Eddie's history of adoption at age three, it was highly likely that the unprocessed feelings underlying his nighttime anxiety preceded age two, the approximate age where concrete memory begins. Because Eddie had a definite body sensation, I knew that the related neurons were firing in his brain. I did not have to know the exact circumstance underlying his distress because the body tells no lies. Repetitions of the timeline based on Eddie's body feelings would resolve the contributing factors of his distress no matter when they occurred. To make sure we covered every possible contributing situation, I started his timeline at birth. I guided Eddie to imagine the day he was born and followed with developmental cues until we reached the first age on his written timeline. Our first session consisted of making Eddie's chart of scary things, focusing on the feeling in his body linked to being scared and alone in his room at night, followed by five repetitions of the timeline from his birth to the present.

Because Eddie was adopted, I knew that it would be important at some point to have him go back in time and explain the adoption to his baby-self. He had spent several years in an orphanage. The facts about his birth and the months before the orphanage were unknown. Eddie's baby-self needed to have the trauma and confusion about his abandonment clarified as much as possible so that Eddie could know for certain—on a neural level— that those years were over. I chose not to begin with this target because Eddie had agreed to only one session and I wanted him to get relief from the concern that troubled him most. I knew that by starting the timeline at birth with his body-based fears about nighttime we could create change. I trusted that if Eddie's fears were related to birth or abandonment, they would be integrated as we used the timeline from the day he was born. At the end of our first session, Eddie agreed to come back a few more times.

When Eddie returned for his second session he said, "I was still scared at night for about two days, and then it was a lot better. I still wanted to have the light on, but I fell asleep after a few minutes and slept all night. I told my dad that this counseling is helping me."

The target for our second session was the same as the first. Eddie was still worried about being in his room in the dark, especially if the power were to go out at night. He said, "I can't handle it if the power goes out when it's windy and everybody is asleep. I'm afraid a phantom will appear in my room." I asked him to point to the place in his body where he felt distress about his nighttime fears. Again he pointed to his heart. "It's not so great in my heart," Eddie said.

We began our work together. Throughout the session Eddie's anxiety reduced and he made comments like, "I could close my eyes and wait it out until morning. I could think about what I did during the day and then I would fall back asleep." And near the end of the session Eddie said, "I think I can handle it. If the power went out during the night I could take a flashlight and find my dad." I validated his great insights and problem-solving methods. At the end of our session Eddie felt quite confident that he could safely sleep in his room and manage himself if the power were to go out during a storm.

At our third session, Eddie reported no distress about being in his room alone at night. Remarkably, his distress about riding in elevators had almost completely dissipated as well, even though we had not specifically targeted that fear. "My dad works in a tall building downtown," he said, "and I rode in his elevator twice. It didn't scare me at all." In this third session Eddie decided to focus on going into bathrooms alone. He was reluctant to go into any restroom without his dad. "I'm afraid someone in there might hurt me," he said. Specifically, Eddie wanted to target going into a school bathroom where he was afraid the school bully might be waiting to hurt him.

Eddie's parents told me that he had been abandoned as a baby. A passenger found him in a bus station restroom when he was approximately three months old. The passerby contacted officials who placed Eddie in an orphanage while they sought to locate his birth parents. After a year in the orphanage, Eddie was available for adoption. His adoptive parents began the work of bringing him into their home, but the process took more than a year. When Eddie finally moved in with his new family he was nearly three years old. By age ten, Eddie's parents had yet to tell him about the abandonment in the bus station. Eddie knew that he was adopted and had lived in an orphanage, but he did not know the details of his separation from his birth mother. I understood why they did not think Eddie needed that information during his young childhood, but I suspected that it might be playing into his fears about being alone in restrooms. Since Eddie would have cellular memory of the separation, I wanted to be sure we integrated it through our timeline work. With Lifespan Integration we had the power to heal the painful memory without even speaking about it.

To heal Eddie's fear, I asked him to focus on the place in his body where he felt distress when he thought about going into the school restroom where he might find the bully. He pointed to his stomach and heart. I began timelines starting with Eddie's birth and mentioned all the developmental stages until we could use the memories from his cue sheet. I deliberately mentioned the developmental tasks of two weeks old, six weeks old, three months old, etc., in order to activate and integrate the implicit, body-based memory from Eddie's abandonment. I refrained from having Eddie's ten-year-old-self explain to his baby-self the truth about his adoption until we had cleared the body memory component of his trauma. Our goal for the session was to heal his fear about being in bathrooms. I trusted that we would have another opportunity for Eddie's older-self to clear up the confusion about adoption for his baby-self. We were able to complete six repetitions of the timeline from his birth to the present during our session. As per usual, Eddie was tired at the end of our work, but told me he thought he would be okay going into restrooms alone.

When Eddie's parents brought him to the fourth session, which was two months after our first meeting, his dad queried, "You went into the restaurant bathroom alone this week, didn't you?" Eddie responded affirmatively. "I think that was first time Eddie has ever done that," his dad continued. I suggested that even though it was the first time Eddie had the confidence to use a public restroom alone, neither one of them noticed the milestone because it was a normal thing for a ten-year-old boy. "That's right," his dad said, "It seemed so normal we didn't pay any attention to it."

"How about going into the school bathroom?" I asked Eddie.

"That part is fine, too," he replied. "When I go to the bathroom the bully is in another class. I just look to see if anybody else is in there and then I'm okay."

At our fourth session, in addition to this new behavior of going into bathrooms alone, Eddie was still sleeping through the night alone in his room. He preferred to go to sleep with the bedside light on, but that is normal for many children. Eddie had begun to enjoy riding in elevators and sought out opportunities to ride in them when possible.

To pick the topic for our current session, we looked at Eddie's initial chart of scary things. Eddie selected the subject, "afraid someone will snatch me," which he had placed in the medium fear category. When asked to explain, he said, "I'm afraid construction workers will steal stuff like me." Eddie carried a definite fear on the inside that someone would separate him against his will from those he loved. Other adopted children have mentioned variations on this fear of being snatched, and I've personally noticed they tend to have fears associated with sudden breaks with their family that are beyond their control.

We used body-focused timelines starting at birth to lower Eddie's distress about being taken away against his will. I was refraining from having Eddie speak to his brand new infant-self and show him the pictures of his life. I delayed my agenda so we could target another specific item on Eddie's anxiety list since it was his primary reason for coming to therapy. I trusted that we could go back and explain all the confusing, frightening aspects of his life and adoption to his baby-self in a follow-up session. At the end of session four, Eddie was relaxed and tired. He said, "I'm not worried about hoboes or construction workers stealing me now. There are a lot of kids in my neighborhood who play outside in the front. I like to play with them in our cul-de-sac. If somebody wanted to steal me, I could kick, run, and yell for my parents. Plus, the other kids would see it, too, and they would help me." His response displayed self-empowerment and age-appropriate thinking. This felt different from the helplessness of the infant-self Eddie's body was most likely accessing when the fear of being taken arose.

"Let's meet again," I suggested at the end of the session. Eddie and his dad looked at each other.

"What do you think?" his dad asked Eddie. They had apparently discussed this topic before our session.

"I don't think I need to come back," Eddie answered. "I'm not afraid of that stuff anymore."

"Okay." I replied with enthusiasm, once again holding back my wish that we could use a session for Eddie's ten-year-old-self to explain things to his baby-self. Since Eddie had agreed to only one session with me from the beginning, I wanted to honor his desire to guide the number of sessions we had together. Eddie was nearing his eleventh birthday, an age burgeoning with autonomy and self-authority.

"How about if you call me if something else comes up?" I asked. "We could have a session or two and probably make it better if something still bothers you." Eddie and his dad agreed to my request. We parted company talking about Eddie's plans for the summer and his upcoming baseball season.

If I had felt a genuine concern that my therapy with Eddie was not complete, I would have shared my perspective with his parents. I did not force the issue for two reasons: 1) Since things had worked so well in spite of Eddie's initial misgivings, I believed his family would call me if he continued to be troubled by anxiety, and 2) I guessed that all the timelines we completed from Eddie's birth to the present had resolved the infant-self's distress even though we had not made the baby's distress explicit. By targeting the distress in Eddie's body, we probably resolved the confusion, loneliness, and anger that adopted children commonly share.

The Wonder of Healing Birth Trauma

Eight-year-old Ben tipped me off to his creativity on the intake form. He indicated his occupation as "Cartoonist." He began our first session by showing me the scary monster he was drawing for his current comic book. His reason for coming to therapy was common—difficulty with sleeping. Ben required that his mother stay by his bedside for an hour or more at bedtime and usually called out to have her return in the middle of the night. Ben was afraid of scary monsters coming out of his closet to eat him and he was also afraid to be alone on one floor in the house while his parents were on a different floor.

As reported by Ben's mother, his birth was difficult—20 hours of labor after which Ben was suctioned out. Ben's mom said, "He was just stuck, so the doctor vacuumed him out of there." Ben, who was delightful and funny, made a joke about being born with a vacuum cleaner. I focused on his birth as the first LI target because I suspected that the powerlessness underlying his anxiety was possibly related to being stuck in the birth canal. It is common for clients to have some form of birth trauma when their presenting issue is anxiety. Ben and his mother helped me compose a timeline of his birthdays, plus one more remembered event per year, up to his current age of eight-years old.

After we had his cue sheet completed, I asked Ben to prove to his baby-self that he was all right. He chose to sit in front of his mother on the floor while he imagined himself being born. I coached Ben to tell the baby how good and lovable he was, and to imagine how the doctor got him unstuck with a vacuum. When we proceeded through the timeline, I asked Ben to imagine showing the baby pictures in his mind of how he grew up to be eight-year-old Ben. I read Ben two memories for each year from the cue sheet one at a time. For the early years in which Ben had no concrete memory, I asked him to imagine the different normal developmental stages, cueing them one at a time in chronological order. After I mentioned each cue Ben was quiet and thoughtful for a moment, then he nodded and said, "I've got it." We repeated the entire protocol one more time, finishing when Ben brought his baby-self into the present and showed him around his room.

The baby liked it in the present and Ben reported that in his room the baby was carefree and sleepy. Reflecting on his birth, Ben told me, "I'm coming out strong." I asked Ben if he would like to show the pictures to the baby one more time and he declined because it made him tired, which was an indication that a lot of integration was occurring.

The family was using a behavioral reward system for going to bed. During the following week Ben was able to fall asleep five nights on his own. I attribute some of Ben's ability to relax and fall asleep to the work he did integrating his sleepy, carefree baby-self through the timeline work.

Another issue impacting Ben was the death of his grandfather a year earlier. Ben had been close to his grandpa who lived only a few blocks away. When asked about this, Ben said the hardest part when remembering his grandpa was, "Mom coming home and telling me he was dead. I'll never have another grandpa again." As he was telling this, Ben crawled into his mother's lap like a baby, noticeably sad. I asked him to focus on these things concerning Grandpa. Astutely, Ben told me the feelings were in his brain, heart, and in Mom. I asked Ben to focus on the feelings in his heart, brain, and Mom and once again I started a timeline at his birth.

"Imagine you're coming out strong with the vacuum," I said. Ben acknowledged earnestly. "Now you can smile at people and look into their eyes."

"Got it," he answered.

"Now you're lying on the floor and you can scoot around and put things in your mouth," I guided.

"Yum. Markers taste so good," Ben replied. We continued through the developmental stages until I could use Ben's written cue sheet. When we entered the year of his timeline in which his grandpa got sick and died I included extra cues to help him integrate the experience. At the end of three repetitions Ben said, "I've solved the problem in my mind. I am going to have a grandpa when I go to heaven. And his dog Scout is up there, too!"

During the two weeks that followed this second session Ben's sleeping patterns were generally the same: going to sleep on his own about five nights during the week, but waking up several nights. In our third session, I searched again to find the source of Ben's anxiety which was keeping him up at night. I asked him to check on his baby-self who had been stuck. "He's out of there and doing fine," Ben enthusiastically reported. Ben's mother could not identify any trauma that might be influencing Ben, nor could she think of any other contributing factor to his anxiety. With children it sometimes helps to get creative in finding the source of their distress. Artistic and creative children like Ben seem to have more problems going to sleep than others. Their bright, creative minds work hard in the evening hours and through their sleep.

Because Ben demonstrated a solid sense of self and secure attachment to his parents, I decided to use the Parts Model to find the source of his nighttime distress. Using the Parts Model would be contraindicated for an insecure, fragmented client. I told Ben we were going to find the part of him that was in charge of keeping him up at night. I guided Ben him to imagine walking down steps into an imaginary basement. At the bottom of the steps I asked him to look around for the part who was keeping him up at night. I told him, based on my experience with other young clients, that it might be his imagination.

"I can see it. It's on the right side of my brain and it looks like a hut," Ben said.

"Is there someone inside?" I asked.

"No, it's just a hut," Ben answered.

"Tell the Hut you are his big, eight-year-old self, and you're going to show him that he's an important part of you." I guided him through a timeline from his birth to the present, using the written cue sheet of his birthdays. The purpose of the timeline was to integrate the part into the bigger Ben-system. At the end of the timeline we returned to the basement. I invited Ben to ask the Hut, "Why do you give me scary things to think about?"

The answer from Ben came, "He's just trying to help me think of things for my comic books."

"Does he know it scares you and keeps you up at night?" I inquired.

"No, he doesn't know that," Ben said.

"Please tell him that you love the many things he can think of, but the scary monsters at night are a real problem," I suggested.

Ben described the problem to the Hut, closing with the remark, "I told him to quit it, Bub." After this interchange, I took him through another repetition of the written timeline. After three of these interactions in which Ben explained to the Hut that it wasn't helpful to have him think of scary monsters at nighttime, the Hut agreed to do something else at night. We assured the Hut that it was still important for him to think of these monster ideas during the day because Ben loved drawing them for his comic books.

"What else would he like to do?" I asked.

Ben replied, "Think about a true, funny story from first grade."

I was not convinced this would be enough to dissuade the Hut from doing the job he had been doing for such a long time. I asked, "Would it be possible for the Hut to help with some other project also?"

"He has made two friends," Ben said. "My imaginary friend who can make himself turn into a giant spider who likes to eat pigs, and a grizzly bear from the central part of my brain. They are going to jump off diving boards."

I encouraged Ben to see these three characters doing what he described. He told me, "They're jumping off diving boards in my brain, on Skull Island, and in me. Instead of thinking of scary things, they're happy to go to places inside me." In this internal world, Ben took them into his bedroom and the kitchen where he gave them something to eat. After they finished, I asked Ben to show them a timeline, starting with his birth, proving that they were all a part of the big, eight-year-old Ben. After the timeline, Ben said, "They would all like to have a stuffed animal bear." He gave them each an imaginary bear, and explained again how important it was for them to play together at night rather than wake him up with scary ideas of monsters. They agreed and we finished with another timeline.

Two weeks later, Ben's mother called and reported that everything was 99 percent better. Ben was going to sleep virtually every night on his own. He was falling asleep easily and most nights slept through the night. The times Ben did call out to his mother in the night, she was able to encourage him from her bedroom without getting up. Ben was also able to go into the basement while his mother was upstairs or he could work on the computer in one room while his parents were elsewhere in the house. Ben's mother was quite pleased with the noticeable changes in Ben after only three appointments. She scheduled one more appointment to see if we could help Ben sleep through the entire night without waking.

In the final appointment, Ben asked to draw a picture. He knew the topic of our session was about sleeping through the night and I suspected his drawing reflected it. Ben drew a small green character which slightly resembled a tomato with legs. He called this a "Thing." The expression on the Thing looked worried and baby-like. Next to the green Thing Ben drew an identical, but larger, blue Thing who looked like a mother. The mother Thing was smiling toward the green Thing with compassionate eyes. Three flowers dotted the landscape around them and the sun shone brightly in the picture. When Ben was finished with his picture, I asked him to travel down again into his imaginary basement. Again, this technique was only used because Ben had internal and external stability and secure attachment with his family. I told him to look around the basement to find "the part of him in charge of waking him up at night." No one appeared. I assured Ben that soon the part would show up. We proceeded with a timeline starting at birth. After the first few cues, Ben interrupted and said, "The part just showed up."

"Okay. Tell him to watch these pictures," I replied.

We continued with the timeline. Without much dialogue we repeated the timeline a second time. When we entered the basement a third time, I asked Ben to tell me what he found.

"It's the nervous system," he said. "The sense of touch—the part that feels. It knows I'm more comfortable when my mom is touching me."

I encouraged Ben to validate the part and show it how he grew up to be Ben, the big eight-year-old boy. When we went back to the basement, I asked Ben if, by any chance, the part was a baby part.

"Yes, it is," he answered.

I asked Ben to tell the part, "It's really important that you were able to wake me up at night when I was a baby and get my mom to come in to feed and hold me. But I'm not a baby anymore. I'm a big boy and I can sleep through the night now. I don't need my mom and dad to feed or hold me during the night. I need to sleep all night so I can get up and do the big-boy things I like to do, like work on the computer." Ben's parents rewarded him with computer time when he slept through the night. He was quite motivated to get more computer time. We showed the part another timeline from babyhood to the present to prove that Ben's needs really had changed through the years.

Back in the imaginary basement, Ben said the part would be quite willing to do a new job. He fully understood that Ben was not a baby anymore and did not need what babies need during the night. I assured Ben that the part could do something like it had been doing before—something in the area of touch.

"What job would he like now?" I asked. "Help me type on the computer," Ben excitedly burst out.

"Let's also hook him up with a friend during the night," I suggested. Since integration is the key to transformation, I encouraged Ben to associate this aspect of himself with other parts rather than be isolated.

"He's going to be friends with Imagination," Ben replied. Ben informed me that he thought our work was done and asked to draw another picture. With his eyes closed and pencil in hand, he drew a big boy with something like sparks or fireworks coming out of his head. It was an energetic-looking picture and quite unlike the baby-that-needs-comfort picture of the two Things he drew in the beginning of our session. It was noteworthy that Ben drew the picture with his eyes closed since the focus of our work was about sleeping.

As his mother and I talked, Ben drew another picture which was a replica of something he had drawn earlier in the week. It was a very big flower. F-14 fighter planes were coming out of the flower to bomb the feelings of "sad," "angry," "bad," and "worked up." The word "joy" was written in large letters in the center of the flower. Ben's illustration suggested to me that he was resolving sad, angry, bad, and worked up feelings and was becoming more aware of joy. I felt confident that Ben's mom would probably notice a very significant change in Ben's waking during the night within a few days.

Two months after we completed our therapy, Ben's mom called and said, "Thank you so much for helping Ben. Things are going really, really well. He's sleeping through the night most nights and if he does call out during the night I say, 'Night, night, Sweetheart' and he goes right back to sleep with no problem. We're also seeing a world of difference on all kinds of fronts. Ben finally learned to ride a bike. Before, he hadn't been able to get himself to do it. He also went off the high dive at a friend's swimming party and was able to go on a play date which he hadn't been willing to do for a couple of years. Overall, he's making wonderful progress. Thank you."

These results are typical when using Lifespan Integration with children. Thanks to Ben, I learned that monsters, who appear to live in closets or under the bed, actually reside in children's imaginations. Sometimes, these can be warning signs that other distressing factors are occurring in the child's life. By using Lifespan Integration, clinicians can explore a child's inner world to find and integrate the aspects of self that are generating frightening ideas. I hypothesize that creative, artistic children are more likely to have trouble with imaginative creatures than children with other temperaments. I also suspect that other emotional problems can present as a heightened need for comfort in the guise of nighttime fears. This should be considered when targeting the problem of monsters and childhood fears.

Posttraumatic Stress Disorder
Protocol for Children

Lifespan Integration resolves trauma because LI appears to fire and rewire neural networks that hold implicit and concrete memories held throughout the mind-body system. Success with LI depends on activation of the right neural networks for healing a client's distress and the coherence of the therapist. With children, sometimes creativity is required to activate the neural networks holding certain memories. In Ben's case, because of his pre-existing level of integration, I was able to access neural networks related to his sleeping problems through the Parts Method of LI. This is an exception to the rule. Generally, we ask children to remember directly the bad things that happened to them or we activate the neural patterns through projective play and storytelling. Any method that activates the body and emotions related to a problem will create an opportunity for healing the child's distress with the repetitions of timelines.

To engage five-year-old Latisha's month of trauma with her father, I chose to enact the events with various dolls and stuffed animals in my office. When Cheryl, Latisha's mother, dropped Latisha off at her father's home, she was a verbal, active kindergartner who was eager to spend time with her daddy. When Cheryl came to retrieve Latisha a month later, the father refused to give Latisha back to her mother. The initial attempt to take Latisha home failed so Cheryl commandeered a rescue attempt with a friend in which she grabbed Latisha from the front yard and sped away in a waiting vehicle.

Latisha ate four sandwiches and drank six bottles of water in the car. She appeared to have been denied food and water while in her father's care. After an eight-hour drive to her mother's home, Cheryl asked Latisha to get ready for bed. Latisha hesitated. When Latisha was changing into her pajamas, Cheryl noticed fresh welts and severe bruising across Latisha's back and bottom.

The next day Cheryl took Latisha to the doctor who called Child Protective Services. Photographs were taken of Latisha's injuries and eventually the Child Protective Service instigated permanent suspension of the father's visiting rights with Latisha.

In the weeks after she returned to her mother's home, Latisha was fearful about being away from her mother. She anxiously clung to Cheryl in situations where she would have previously been happy to play or explore. Latisha would no longer go to the homes of neighboring children with whom she had previously played with, and she cried when her mother left her in daycare.

Over the next few months, Latisha revealed some of the incidents which occurred during the month with her father. These items are listed on her cue sheet which includes:

- Eating a piece of chocolate without permission and being beaten with a belt.

- Daddy holding her over water and threatening to drown her.

- Taking her to the zoo and holding her over the lion exhibit. Latisha was told she would be fed to the lions.

- Denying birthday cake when other children were allowed to eat birthday cake.

- Forcing her to lie on her bed with arms and leg extended into the air for an hour. If she put her arms or legs down Daddy beat her with a belt.

- Hiding in the closet in fear that her dad would find her.

A few months after the visit with Dad, Latisha started first grade and the teacher found her difficult to have in the classroom. At the fall parent conference, Latisha's teacher said that Latisha was inattentive, hyper-active, and was having trouble learning to read. She displayed reactivity in social situations which alienated her from other children. Cheryl said these traits were not present before Latisha spent a month with her dad. Previously, Latisha had been active but generally cooperative. The kindergarten teacher did not have the same challenges with Latisha that the first grade teacher mentioned.

Before my first session with Latisha, I interviewed Cheryl and compiled a chronological cue sheet of Latisha's experience from the day Cheryl dropped her off at her father's house to the present. When Latisha came to meet with me I introduced the concept of "telling the story about what happened at Dad's and how it is over." Fortunately, we do not have to have children tell their horrific stories in order to heal the PTSD they carry in their bodies. Instead, I asked Latisha to select a doll or stuffed animal in my office to represent herself, Dad, Dad's girlfriend, Mom, and Mom's friend who drove them away in the get-away car. I asked Latisha to snuggle into Mom's lap while I told the story.

Beginning with the moment right before Cheryl took Latisha

into her dad's house, I read the cues as Cheryl had described them to me. I briefly enacted the scenes with the dolls and stuffed animals Latisha had chosen. The first scene on her cue sheet was, "Going to Dad's house. Mom and Dad argued." I briefly enacted an argument between the mom with the dad figures in my hand, and then turned to Latisha for her acknowledgment that she remembered the scene. Latisha shyly acknowledged that she remembered, and I moved onto the next cue on her sheet. I did not re-enact every cue on her sheet, but read all of them, after which I asked Latisha to acknowledge that she remembered the items I was mentioning. As we progressed through repetitions of her timeline, Latisha added information as we came to various memories in her timeline. During the session Latisha was subdued. At the end of our first session she was tired and quiet.

When I met with Latisha for a second session, two months after our first session, Cheryl remarked that Latisha was not as dependent as she had been before. Cheryl commented that Latisha was more willing to play with neighborhood children and was doing better in school. For the second session, I asked Latisha to select characters again to be herself, Dad, Mom, Dad's girlfriend, and the friend who drove them away. After selecting the characters to re-enact the story, I asked Latisha to climb into her mother's lap again while I told the story of her month with Dad.

As mentioned, Standard Protocol Lifespan Integration often involves four phases: 1) Proving the trauma is over with repetitions of the timeline, 2) An empowered adult expressing anger on the child's behalf, 3) The younger-self expressing anger to the offender, and 4) Creating a positive, imaginary repair to heal the injury for the child-self. Session one with Latisha was dedicated to proving her month of trauma with Dad was over. In session two, I moved into the aspect of LI where an empowered adult expresses anger on behalf of the child. I interjected the role of a policeman to rescue Latisha from her father's abuse and inflict the same type of injury on her father that Latisha had experienced. Each time we came to a violent memory on her cue sheet, I brought forward a blue stuffed animal to serve as a police officer who beat the father figure in our story, held him over a lion exhibit (as was done to Latisha), threatened to drown him at the pier, and eventually threw the Dad figure in jail. At appropriate times, the blue-stuffed-animal-police-officer beat Dad with an imaginary belt. At the end of the month of cues, I enacted the police officer throwing Dad in jail. As we progressed through the remainder of Latisha's cue sheet to the present, she occasionally interjected that Dad escaped from jail, at which point I had the police officer punish him again and return him to jail.

During session two we repeated Latisha's timeline five times. She was quite engaged in the re-enactment of Dad being hurt the same way she had been hurt. When our session was over, and I was debriefing with Mom, I noticed Latisha pulling Dad out of jail and punishing him again with the police officer figure. I noticed that she was hitting him repeatedly with the blue stuffed animal. Eventually she threw him back into jail under a table and joined her mother to leave my office.

These re-enactment measures might seem extreme or unnecessary, but the human brain naturally wants to resolve injury by inflicting injury in return. When we are pushed, our organic response is to push back. When we are hit, our natural response is to hit back. We do not encourage clients to actually return evil for evil, but a great deal of mind-body release is accomplished by allowing clients to envision a natural, physical return of the injury they have received. Latisha had loaded severe trauma into her body and the re-enactment of injury to her father quickened her healing.

A month after our second session, Cheryl called and said Latisha was more like the child she knew before her trauma at her dad's house. Her first grade teacher was astounded at the changes she witnessed in Latisha. She had improved her reading exponentially and was playing well with other children. Latisha did not strike at other children like she had previously done, and she was able to listen attentively when the teacher was speaking. Here again, we see the parallel symptoms of trauma and ADD for children. Latisha might have been identified as a learning-challenged student if we had not cleared her trauma with the timelines of Lifespan Integration. Her symptoms which appeared after a traumatic month with Dad manifested in similar ways to the markers for ADD and ADHD. As mentioned, Latisha's first grade teacher found her difficult to have in the classroom. After our PTSD work with LI, Latisha was able to play cooperatively with other children and was no longer sent to the principal's office for bad behavior.

By using stuffed animals to recreate their trauma stories, I believe we activate the neural networks holding children's traumas, which become integrated by repetitions of their trauma timeline. In addition, children appear to release their unexpressed anger vicariously when a figure that represents their abuser is punished, hit, and given the same mistreatment they received. In many sessions with children in which we have enacted the abuser being hurt, I find them repeating the punishment with the same characters after the session has ended. When I am talking with their parents at the end of a session, children are often pulling the abuser-representative out of the corner where we had banished him, and are hitting him directly or with the figure that most represents the empowered adult from our storytelling session.

Using Lifespan Integration to heal trauma works with children. With children we can be creative in activating their neural networks and using repetitions of their timelines to prove their traumas are over. Whether birth trauma, physical abuse, sexual molestation, or adoption, we can prove to children that their losses and sorrows are over, and help them heal.

A child's identity invariably shifts toward a negative sense of self when he or she has been abused and traumatized. All children assume their mistreatment is a reflection of an inherent negative quality about themselves. When bad things happen to children, they believe they are bad. Unless an adult helps them heal these misconceptions, they will move through life with cellular memory convincing them that they are inferior to other people and deserve less than the best in life. Why let these children believe a lie when we can heal them with Lifespan Integration?

We live in a society that notoriously oversells and under-delivers, so I'd be lying if I said I wasn't skeptical when first hearing about LI. Then I started using LI with clients and I was sold. Daily, I am still amazed at the power—and gentleness—of LI.

Joelle North, LI therapist

13. Conclusion

Client Stories Revisited

Becky, whose 9/11 story opened this book, came for a third round of Lifespan Integration sessions because she was having anxiety at work. Her employment covered six sessions of counseling and Becky chose to use them for LI. Becky had been quite satisfied in her work environment after we resolved her PTSD from 9/11, but after five years she was assigned a new supervisor who was disrespectful and controlling. After six sessions of LI, Becky left with a completely changed approach to her supervisor saying, "It's amazing how different things are at work now and all I did was change myself. This therapy is amazing!" She went onto another job position in her company after the short round in therapy. Reflecting on the anxiety-producing situation she had, Becky commented, "My boss really is a difficult person. No one can get along with him. Together he and I created the perfect storm. After you and I had these sessions I began relating to him differently and then I left." A simple solution evolved for Becky when she untied the knot within herself that kept her attached to a bad situation.

Antonio, whose story is in the Bipolar Disorder chapter (Chapter Ten) spoke with me two years after we completed his Lifespan Integration therapy. He said, "My PTSD is completely gone. It will always be a part of my memory, but I have no night-mares, no conflict in my head, no anger or bitterness, and the nega-tive stuff that goes with PTSD is gone."

Regarding the Bipolar Disorder, Antonio said, "The biggest thing in my life is that I feel stable. Stability is the main thing. I take my medication religiously—exactly as prescribed—everyday. I am much more stable in all factors of my life. I am in a comfort zone in my marriage and I'm having a really good time at work."

"What about the Bipolar pain?" I asked.

"I never have Bipolar pain," he said. "It has gone completely out of my life. That was the suicidal part. Bipolar people can't do anything about the pain, so you think the only solution is to kill yourself. I have not had Bipolar pain since I saw you." Antonio came to therapy to heal his marriage and through Lifespan Integration gained complete freedom from his PTSD, stability with his Bipolar disorder, and moved into the most satisfying job of his career.

One client for whom I used the Birth-to-Present protocol said after three years of therapy, "I can't believe how differently I am functioning. There is a lot of stress at work and I am handling it really well. What used to make me anxious is not bothering me at all and I have no thoughts of self-harm any more. I used to think about suicide every day. Now I don't even think of it." The col-league who referred this patient confirmed the same remarkable changes the client reported.

Kaeli, whose story is mentioned is Chapter Two, is doing well. Her mother said, "After three LI sessions, Kaeli is better at making new friends and is expanding her friendship network. She has a higher ability to focus. Now I can direct her like a typical child." She continued, "I am a great rule-follower and I tried to follow parent-ing books. The professionals told me Kaeli's challenges were about me as a parent, but I knew her stress was coming from within her nervous system. When we targeted her birth trauma, Kaeli stopped wetting the bed and calmed down." Kaeli's mother concluded, "The most significant thing for me personally is that this work validated my mothering instinct."

The clients mentioned here have experienced the basic protocols of Lifespan Integration. Other LI outcomes also deserve mention before concluding this book.

Eating Disorders

Lifespan Integration is producing remarkable results with eating disorders, specifically anorexia and bulimia. Surprisingly, anorexia and bulimia disorders have been easy and quick to treat with LI. I personally have limited treatment of anorexia, and no experience with bulimia, but my colleagues report consistent results treating these conditions with Lifespan Integration.

When Pace developed LI in 2002 she was working in a college community. When a physician referred four anorexic students to her, they were all symptom-free within two LI sessions, but received a third LI session as a follow-up. These students were college-age adults who developed the disorder in their early teens. Using the methods of LI, Pace proved to their younger selves that the circumstances around the development of anorexia were over and showed them repeated timelines of their lives. Each of the four clients stopped their anorexic behavior. Pace later moved her office to another community and no longer received referrals for college students. Pace has not treated anorexic patients since, but LI therapists around the world report equally positive results in the cases of anorexia which they treat.

The one client I treated for anorexia was a high school student who developed the diagnosis at the end of junior high school. Ingrid was diagnosed by a physician and treated with traditional approaches for anorexia. She was under the traditional regime of food monitoring by a parent and was pending inpatient treatment when Ingrid's mother brought her to me for LI. In our first session, we proved to the young eighth-grader inside Ingrid that she had grown up to be a high school sophomore. We also discovered the root cause of her restricted eating. Anorexia was her way to deal with some stressful situations which were occurring in her life at the time. By sophomore year, those stressors had somewhat resolved and we showed Ingrid's younger-self what had occurred in the intervening months between eighth grade and mid-high school. In three sessions, we treated the issues of restricted eating and over-exercise. In our final and third session, when I asked the beautiful sophomore girl in front of me if her eighth-grade self would let the sophomore Ingrid be in charge of eating, she replied, "Yes, she's fine with it. I've always known how to eat and she's really immature."

During the three weeks of treatment Ingrid appropriately increased her weight, stopped restrictive eating, and resumed a normal pattern of exercise. I have seen Ingrid several times since those sessions and she continues to maintain a healthy, appropriate weight. Her parents reported that her eating and exercise behavior is holding at a normal level—one similar to the years that preceded the anorexia diagnosis.

Other clinicians report success with LI and anorexia, but they are not my own case studies so I do not know the specific details from their clients. Generally speaking, LI appears to be a promising treatment for anorexia, and eating disorders in general.

Regarding bulimia, our Lifespan Integration community reports virtually complete success with the cessation of emotionally-based vomiting. Carol Lindlow, the Clinical Director at Hope Place, told me she has seen women in their treatment program free from bulimic vomiting in just a few LI sessions. One woman in their program stopped self-induced vomiting after two sessions of LI, but had a relapse when she was in jail for two weeks. When the woman returned to the treatment program, Lindlow led her through another LI session. The woman's bulimia had not recurred within the fifteen months that followed her two weeks in jail. We can anticipate that it will not return.

Concerning obesity and compulsive overeating, Pace hypothesizes that these are conditions based on an inability to regulate emotions. She believes these conditions can be helped with sessions of Birth-to-Present protocol to increase the client's emotional stability and strength of self. As our experience with LI broadens, we will continue to gather data on the hypothesis that increasing emotional regulation equips obese people and compulsive eaters to better self-soothe and change their patterns.

Future Inroads

Given our initial success with eating disorders, my personal hope is to see LI incorporated into clinical eating disorder programs, including inpatient treatment. We have a remarkable tool in our hands that appears to do what no treatment option has done before in resolving, rather than managing, anorexia and bulimia. I hope that as LI spreads, it will find its way into these clinical arenas.

Another area where I long to see Lifespan Integration applied is in the treatment of veterans with Posttraumatic Stress Disorder (PTSD). Other therapies have been applied to the treatment of trauma, but I believe we can increase the number of successful cases of veteran's PTSD resolved through LI. Once again, our collective experience informs us that Lifespan Integration does not re-traumatize the patient during treatment. One therapist recently remarked that she noticed there is no secondary trauma for the therapist either. Some PTSD treatment modalities leave the therapist with residual trauma from hearing the gruesome details of the client's experience. With LI, we focus on proving to the mind and body that the trauma is over with repetitions of the PTSD timeline. It appears that the client and counselor exit the process with resolution and no lingering residue from the violence of the trauma.

LI therapists have worked with individual soldiers to heal their war trauma. With permission I share the following story from a colleague:

I had an LI session with a military person who spends six months of his year in Afghanistan and on his last tour was involved in his first true combat situation. He exhibited classic military-level PTSD. He was quite triggered and had a hard time finding any safe feelings at all, except in his house, alone at night. He was reticent to leave his house except under certain conditions such as being alone, at night. He responded incredibly well to our PTSD session this morning. He left with zero triggering by the end of our session and had a noticeable ease and "smoothness" to him. He was smiling and connecting like he hadn't previously.

Two weeks after the first session the therapist said, "The military man I mentioned earlier reports that he's able now to walk through crowds. He notices when he's scanning for danger and he's more able to tell himself it's not needed. He's more comfortable than before—but he still scans."

After another few LI sessions, the soldier's scanning will most likely be eliminated as will other aspects of his PTSD. I believe that LI is a cure for PTSD. I'm eager for the time when our continued research substantiates our clinical experience that Lifespan Integration is unparalleled in the treatment of PTSD and can therefore be incorporated into broader practice.

Another colleague worked with a Vietnam veteran who is now completely symptom free from his PTSD. He describes himself as "emerging from a coma that lasted many decades." Now he is looking for true intimacy and finds joy and meaning in his life for the first time.

Addictions

Lifespan Integration is an important contribution to the treatment of addiction. Feelings of powerlessness, trauma, the need for self-soothing, and poor attachment to others contribute to the symptoms of addiction. Generally speaking, when clients have established several months of sobriety from their addiction and are in regular support groups, LI will aid in resolving the trauma and emotional distress that contributed to their addictive behavior. Mate (2010) writes about recovery from addiction:

> Healing, then, must take into account the internal psychological climate—the beliefs, memories, mindstates, and emotions that feed addictive impulses and behaviors—as well as the external milieu. In an ecological framework, recovery from addiction does not mean a 'cure' for a disease but the creation of new resources, internal and external, that can support different, healthy ways of satisfying one's genuine needs. It also involves developing new brain circuits that can facilitate more adaptive responses and behaviors (p. 360).

Three scenarios are possible for LI concurrent with addiction recovery:

*1) **Sobriety** automatically follows emotional healing.* These clients resolve long-term emotional stressors and find a more positive sense of self through LI, after which the need for addictive practices subsides. When I first began using Lifespan Integration, a man returned to my office after six or eight sessions and said, "I've decided to stop drinking. I used to have a few beers every night after work and I looked forward to those beers. I feel so much better now that I don't need the crutch of alcohol." A year later, this man's new pattern of living without alcohol was holding. It was my first experience in therapeutic practice where a patient spontaneously shifted one area of his life after targeting a seemingly unrelated issue.

*2) **Lifespan Integration** increases clients' emotional regulation and self-awareness, which causes them to accurately see their compulsive behavior and seek out recovery.* Addictive behaviors and responses which seemed normal before LI appear as dysfunctional coping methods after clients increase connection to themselves and their adult resources. The empowered choice to pursue 12-step and other recovery programs often appropriately follows increased self-awareness.

3) **Dissociated individuals** *need several months of sobriety and support before beginning their trauma treatment through LI.* Lifespan Integration can *temporarily* be dysregulating for some clients, therefore it is crucial for addicts who are also highly dissociated individuals to achieve sobriety before entering into LI work. For these patients, the challenge of working with addiction and LI is pacing the work so that the client can maintain sobriety from the addiction while simultaneously facing unresolved emotional aspects of their lives.

Meredith

A specialist in the field of addiction counseling recently referred Meredith to me saying, "I think her trauma diagnosis is more severe than her addiction diagnosis. She has spent many months at an inpatient treatment facility where they taught her skills for overcoming her addiction, but didn't address her trauma at all." In our first LI session, Meredith asked to target a rape from adolescence. She reported no rape distress at the end of the session. "I actually feel better," she remarked with surprise. Other types of counseling had not left her feeling as changed as her first LI session did.

At the next LI session, Meredith reported continuing to feel no distress when remembering the high school rape. During the second session we targeted Meredith's pattern of childhood molestation that occurred over many years of her life. Because there were many incidences of abuse, we were not able to bring this entire subject into resolution within one session. Meredith left the session with some dysregulation. The day following our session Meredith called in distress. "I really feel like using drugs," she said.

"How is the little girl from the memory we focused on yesterday?" I asked.

"Not good," she replied. "I'm remembering more about the abuse and other times it happened." For Meredith, we had activated the neural networks that held the molestation memories but we could not fully integrate them within one session. We scheduled a follow up session as soon as possible, and Meredith said she had to "white-knuckle it" through her sobriety until she saw me again. At the end of the second session, a day or so later, she felt much more resolved. This is an example of the temporary dysregulation which occurs for many clients—something that can be too challenging for clients struggling with new sobriety from an addiction.

Shari

Shari, another client with severe early trauma and neglect, came to therapy several years after she had recovered from drug and alcohol addiction. Shari was quite dissociated. When I used the Birth-to-Present protocol with her, she often reported an urge to drink or use drugs during the first two days following an LI session, but the length of her sobriety enabled her to notice the craving and not give into it due to the tools she had learned through many years of recovery. As we progressed through therapy, the urge to drink or use drugs after LI completely subsided for Shari.

Shari's story is representative of those who are quite fragmented and have had severe early trauma. With these clients, we only use the Birth-to-Present protocol for proving to the clients' bodies that their traumas are over and that they have grown up. In so doing, repressed memories or body-based, non-concrete memory will be integrated through LI. Integrating these unconscious memories can be destabilizing for a time. If clients have been successful at overcoming an addiction for only a short time before beginning LI, they might lose sobriety unless they have good support for their recovery.

Even though some disorganization may follow LI for dissociated clients, their systems will always reorganize to a higher, more functional level. The client's level of stability determines how quickly he or she can benefit from LI concurrently with addiction treatment. In some cases, Pace recommends that clients have at least six months of sobriety and ongoing support before they start the healing work of Lifespan Integration.

Staci Sprout is an LI therapist and Sex Addiction Specialist who uses LI effectively in sex addiction treatment. She commented, "Lifespan Integration gets at the core wounding that fuels addiction. It could be called Life *Force* Integration because it breaks down compulsive behavior in a gentle and effective way so that one has access to the whole self—a client's whole life force. It's the most powerful trauma healing tool I've ever worked with or experienced in my own life."

Change Always Occurs

With a well-grounded therapist, people change every time they experience a Lifespan Integration session. Pace and I observe that clients always come to follow-up sessions with a shift in their lives. Some changes are quite noticeable to the client and other changes are present, but may not be within the client's awareness.

For example, a patient named Stephanie told this story after five LI sessions.

She said, "Last week, my teenage sons and I flew to Tennessee to visit my mom. My mom and I fight every time we are together."

"How did things go?" I asked.

"Just fine," Stephanie replied. Then she paused and looked at me with shock. "We didn't fight one time on the trip! I don't think that has ever happened before."

Stephanie cited an example. She told me that her mother said to her, "Roll down your window, Stephanie. I think you'll like it better rolled down."

Stephanie replied, "No thanks, Mom, I don't want my window rolled down."

"Yes, I think you do," her mother countered.

Rather than responding in her typical, combative way, Stephanie replied with humor and said, "Mom, I think *you* want my window rolled down." The boys in the backseat joined Stephanie and her mom in laughing about the exchange. Stephanie did not roll her window down and a fight did not develop in the ordinary way it would have before Stephanie experienced LI. In our Lifespan Integration sessions, Stephanie and I had focused on her growing up years under her mother's extreme control. After several LI sessions, Stephanie inadvertently side-stepped her mother's attempt to control her without even noticing that she had done so. Her new adult response was so natural to Stephanie that she did not notice that for the first time in her life she had spent an entire weekend with her mother and did not have conflict.

This type of outcome is typical for clients after Lifespan Integration. Clients feel better about themselves and respond to life differently after LI, but their change seems so natural they may not attribute the change to Lifespan Integration.

LI: The Gift That Goes on Giving

A remarkable outcome from Lifespan Integration is that clients continue to get better after LI even if the therapist does not continue to see them. The integrating and reorganizing component of LI continues working even after clients have completed their sessions in therapy. The brain appears to move toward better organization and health on its own after LI.

Lori had an early life filled with neglect and trauma and I saw her every week for two years before she moved away. At our closure session, I assured Lori that she would continue to gain clarity and resolution on things from her childhood even after our work. One year later Lori called and said she wanted to return for more LI therapy even though it meant a three hour roundtrip drive. She said, "The lights just keep going on. I haven't seen you for a year, but things about my life continue to get clearer and clearer. It's unbelievable. I didn't know how dissociated I was, but now I am seeing things for what they were. My whole life was a trauma."

In the beginning work with Lori she could barely tolerate three repetitions of Birth-to-Present protocol in a session. During the third repetition of her timeline Lori would often become disoriented and say, "What? What was the memory you just said?" I could feel the depth of her fog in those sessions.

After the one year break in which things continued to get clearer, Lori was able to process through her LI timeline quite cogently. After two repetitions of her timeline in a session, rather than becoming dissociated, Lori often responded with insight such as, "My life was worse than I thought it was. I can't believe how I made it through those years." Given the level of her childhood trauma, it is a marvel that Lori functioned as well as she did. During the year-long break, as clarity increased, Lori took impressive action steps to resolve difficulties from her past. Lori's life continued to get better after LI treatment ended. This is just one testament to the observation that Lifespan Integration is a gift that keeps on giving after treatment has ended; not only do clients live their lives in healthier ways, but their mental health usually continues improving without further LI sessions.

Training and Support

Pace initially began training clinicians in Lifespan Integration on the west coast of North America and in Western Europe. As therapists learned the method and passed their success stories onto others, the need for trainings increased. Lifespan Integration is continuing to expand and trainings can be found in other parts of the world as well. I personally hope we will offer trainings in lesser developed countries, inpatient clinics, and agencies that treat veterans. In order to meet the demand for training, Pace has a team of Approved Consultants and trainers who teach the beginning LI course and provide follow-up consultation and supervision.

Two levels of training for LI are currently offered. The

Beginning Level LI workshop teaches practitioners with advanced degrees the basic steps of Standard Protocol, Birth-to-Present protocol, and the scientific theory behind the method. Attendees bring their own completed timelines to the training and experience LI as the client, therapist, and observer over the two-day course. The Beginning Level workshop includes video clips from Pace's clinical practice in order to demonstrate the methods of Lifespan Integration.

The Advanced Level LI workshop is the second level of training. It is best taken several months after the Beginning Level workshop to give therapists time to develop their own working knowledge of LI. The advanced course is focused on trauma, early neglect, clients with a high level of dissociation, and brief review of basic LI concepts. Video clips in the advanced course show the progression of a Dissociative Identity Disorder (DID) client who heals early childhood neglect and preverbal trauma over two years of LI therapy. The client's remarkable change is evident. There is no experiential opportunity for practitioners in the advanced course, but teaching and video are used to expand on advanced LI applications, such as Attachment Repair, and applications of LI with highly dissociated clients.

Outside the required two trainings, approved consultants offer workshops on other aspects of LI applications. In addition to teaching the Beginning Level workshop, I teach workshops in the United States and abroad focused on LI with children and adolescents, depression, marriage counseling, and other topics.

Therapists newly trained in Lifespan Integration often ask, "How can I get my clients to agree to LI?" The answer is based primarily on the clinician's confidence that Lifespan Integration is the most effective modality that can be offered to the client at that time. Experienced talk therapists may have trouble believing that LI can produce insight, emotional release, and behavioral change in a shorter time than the traditional path of talk therapy alone. In my experience, the reluctance to use LI is generally rooted in the therapist and not the patient. A medical doctor usually does not try to convince a patient about the need to order an X-ray. Similarly, a therapist who has observed exponential outcomes from LI will propose it as a course of therapeutic treatment when he or she has personally experienced its benefits and seen it successfully applied to clients. Pace often remarks that one of the best ways to learn LI is to experience LI.

There is a good reason why LI training is only available to professionals with clinical experience. Due to the possible temporary dysregulation aspect, LI is a professional method which needs the expertise of trained therapists for its application.

In America, television commercials depict crazy stunts with the phrase written on the bottom of the screen, "Do not try this at home." In that light, it is important to note that this book is not a training manual. The case stories presented here are intended to introduce the reader to Lifespan Integration and offer support for therapists, but *this text does not equip the reader to practice LI.* Lifespan Integration may appear simple to use, but the modality is not simplistic and people are complex. Lifespan Integration is a very powerful method for achieving therapeutic results. The timeline component appears to access the deepest constructs of a person's thinking and naturally update that thinking to the most current, positive perspective available in the person's life. The client stories shared here are an endorsement to the LI process, not a set of directions for untrained helpers.

Summary

Lifespan Integration is an emerging therapy which is proving to be helpful with anxiety, phobias, relationship issues, eating disorders, trauma, and other concerns clients bring to therapy. Historically, clients and therapists talked about these concerns, hoping that understanding an issue would bring resolution to it. Many clients have said, "I've talked about this issue so much. Why is it still bothering me?"

Talking and thinking about a problem activates the neo-cortex of the brain, but these approaches do not necessarily reach into the part of the brain and body holding a difficult memory in a way that resolves it. In contrast, Lifespan Integration is built around neuroscience and incorporates factors critical to neural integration. Pace hypothesizes that neural integration occurs throughout the mind-body system as a result of repetitions of the memories and images in the LI timeline. The lasting outcomes from Lifespan Integration serve as an endorsement of her theory. One client summarized this process by saying, "The back part of my brain can talk to me but I haven't been able to figure out a way to talk back. LI has finally done this for me." Talking is still an important component of good therapy and many therapeutic approaches are built around it, but Lifespan Integration is filling a unique niche by resolving issues by holistically integrating them.

As more clinicians continue to use LI with their clients, we will build a collective reservoir of experience which validates the truth that, "Integration is mental health." The case studies in this book are a sampling of this reality and are typical of the outcomes achieved from LI. People change when they experience LI. I deeply appreciate the gift Peggy Pace has given us through this therapy and I feel privileged to participate in telling others about it.

Catherine Thorpe, MA

 Cathy Thorpe received her MA in Systems Counseling from Bastyr University in 2000 and has a private practice in Bellevue, WA (USA). She specializes in relationship issues, anxiety, and trauma for children and adults. Cathy is a Licensed Mental Health Counselor and Lifespan Integration Consultant and Trainer. In 2002, Cathy began using LI and assisting Peggy Pace with workshops. She currently teaches Lifespan Integration in the United States and abroad. She also provides individual supervision and adjunct workshops for LI trained clinicians.

Before clinical practice, Cathy counseled through an Inner Healing Prayer ministry. Cathy conducts a workshop for Christian pastors and lay counselors titled, "The Healing Timeline" which is a simplified version of timeline therapy as developed by Peggy Pace. *The Healing Timeline: God's Shalom for the Past, Present, and Future* describes the lay person's method and is available at her website www.healingtimeline.com (US only) or www.amazon.com.

For workshop and other information, contact Cathy Thorpe at:

PO Box 53473
Bellevue, WA 98015 (USA)
425-454-7447
cathythorpeLI@gmail.com
www.CathyThorpe.com

Peggy Pace, MA

 Peggy Pace is a licensed mental health counselor and marriage and family therapist in Washington State, USA. Peggy Pace received a Bachelor of Science degree in Chemistry from the University of Washington in 1969, and a Master of Arts degree in Counseling Psychology from Antioch University in 1985. For the past twenty years, Pace has specialized in working with adults who were traumatized as children.

In 2002, Peggy Pace developed the Lifespan Integration technique while working with clients in her private practice. In 2003 she self-published the first edition of her book, *Lifespan Integration: Connecting Ego States through Time*. Since 2004 Pace has been dividing her time between her private practice in Washington State, and traveling and teaching Lifespan Integration throughout the United States and Europe. Pace has presented Lifespan Integration at the EMDR International Association conference (2003), EMDR Association of Canada (2006), and at The Association for Comprehensive Energy Psychology Conference (ACEP) (2006).

Peggy can be contacted by e-mail at:
ppace@LifespanIntegration.com

Finding an LI Therapist

To find a therapist trained in Lifespan Integration, access the therapist directory at www.lifespanintegration.com.

Trainings

Peggy Pace regularly conducts LI workshops in the United States and international locations. For current workshop information or to plan a workshop, visit: www.lifespanintegration.com.

References

Amen, D. (2001). *Healing ADD: The breakthrough program that allows you to see and heal the six types of ADD.* New York: Berkley Publishing Group.

Badenoch, B. (2008). *Being a brain-wise therapist: A practical guide to interpersonal neurobiology.* New York: W. W. Norton & Company, Inc.

Balkus, B. (2012). *Lifespan Integration effectiveness in traumatized women.* (Unpublished doctoral dissertation). Northwest University, Washington.

Begley, S. (2007). *Train your mind, change your brain: How a new science reveals our extraordinary potential to transform ourselves.* New York: Random House, Inc.

Brett, R. (2010). *God never blinks: 50 lessons for life's little detours.* New York: Grand Central Publishing.

Cooper, R. (2001). *Other 90%: How to unlock your vast untapped potential for leadership and life.* New York: Three Rivers Press.

Clements, T. (2011). Improving success in substance abuse treatment. *Christian Counseling Connection: A Publication of AACC. 17,* 4.

Dispenza, J. (2007). *Evolve your brain: The science of changing your mind.* Deerfield Beach, FL: Health Communications, Inc.

Doidge, N. (2007). *The brain that changes itself: Stories of personal triumph from the frontiers of brain science.* New York: Penguin Books.

Gerhardt, S. (2004). *Why love matters: How affection shapes a baby's brain.* New York: Routledge Taylor & Francis Group.

Horowitz, M. (2011). *Assessment-Based Treatment of Post-Traumatic Stress Disorders.* Sausaliso, CA: Greyhawk Publishing.

How to read a mind. (2007, January 29). *Time Magazine. 169,* 74.

Jung, C. (1950a). Uber mandalasymbolik [Concerning mandala symbolism]. *Gestaltungen des Unbewussten.* Zurich.

Jung, C. (1950b). Zur empirie des individuationsprozesses [A study in the process of individuation]. *Gestaltungen des Unbewussten.* Zurich.

Mandala. (2009). *Collins English Dictionary - Complete & Unabridged 10th Edition.* Retrieved from: http://dictionary.reference.com/browse/mandala.

Mate, G. (2010). *In the realm of hungry ghosts: Close encounters with addiction.* Berkely, CA: North Atlantic Books.

Medina, J. (2008). *Brain rules: 12 principles for surviving and thriving at work, home, and school.* Seattle, WA: Pear Press.

Neuroplasticity. (2012). In *Encyclopedia Britannica.* Retrieved from http://www.britannica.com/EBchecked/topic/410552/neuroplasticity.

Nicholson, C. (2011, January 22). Meditation correlated with structural changes in the brain. *Scientific American.* Retrieved from http://www.scientificamerican.com/podcast/episode.cfm?id=mediation-correlated-with-structura-11-01-22.

Pace, P. (2012). *Lifespan integration: Connecting ego states through time.* Roslyn, WA: Self-published.

Schore, A. (2003). *Affect regulation and the repair of the self.* New York: WW Norton & Company.

Siegel, D. (2003, February). Healing trauma: Attachment, mind, body, and brain. *R. Cassidy Seminars.* Lecture conducted from Meydenbauer Convention Center, Bellevue, WA.

Siegel, D. (2010). *Mindsight: The new science of personal transformation.* New York: Random House Publishing Group.

Washington University School of Medicine (2000, December 8). New therapy helps stroke victims recover arm movements. *Science Daily.* Retrieved from http://www.sciencedaily.com/releases/2000/12/001208074028.htm

CPSIA information can be obtained at www.ICGtesting.com
Printed in the USA
BVOW071445300912

301655BV00004B/3/P